Mary and Margaret

—

Whence Comes Freedom

Clark Thomas Riley

DEDICATION

My mother, Margaret Crim Riley, made sure I did my homework, and she regularly met with teachers at school in parent-teacher conferences. My father, Thomas Leslie Riley, pushed me to pursue the best education possible. To all my family for inspiring my love of adventure. My wife, Debbie, put up with so much while this work underwent its long incubation. My children, David and Sean, inspired me with their unending enthusiasm and bright curiosity. My Novel Workshop Group made sure that this work was worth reading.

CONTENTS

ACKNOWLEDGMENTS

Our novel workshop group is perhaps the main reason my works have seen print. Our regular meetings foster a commitment to writing, an irresistible deadline. The camaraderie of the group instills a desire to please our fellow readers. Our leader, Lucy Hoopes, contributed her critical grammarian mind. Her keen eye and grammatical thought process have been crucial for smoothing the paper-to-brain pathway. Lauren Goodsmith is one of the finest writers I have had the pleasure of knowing. Her insistence on honest relationships and proper cause and effect has relieved you, dear reader, of arduous suspensions of disbelief. She also speaks wonderful French. Alex Duvan has urged passionate relationships between the characters and is ever properly impatient with storyline cul-de-sacs or tangents. Judy Tanner insisted on familial authenticity in the story. Judy Rousuck is a master of the theater and blessed this work with her knowledge of story and play. Karol Edlund is an Austen scholar of the first order, warning me of the audacity of approaching Jane Austen's works. Her wise insight has saved me countless embarrassments. Special thanks to Izzy Rodriguez for her talents on display on the front cover. She is a woman of extraordinary talents and rich portfolio of skills

Thank you all!

Chapter One
Kerfuffle at Pemberley

Elizabeth Darcy, mistress of Pemberley, dedicated her life to the public service befitting a person of privilege, honor, and noble position. If one were to listen to the private conversations of Pemberley's staff, one would never hear any disparagement. To a person, all agreed that Master Darcy had chosen a mate every bit his equal. And it was not only in her personal dealings that she comported herself with distinction. Elizabeth, it turned out, had quite the head for business. She executed these estimable qualities with consistent humility and calm.

However, today was not a calm day.

For the third time in as many years, Mary Bennet had been … requested to leave … one of her schools. This, of course, was a polite phrasing. Her dismissal from St. John's School for Girls, as had been the others, resulted from one too many outbursts regarding the social status of women and their inequality to men. Elizabeth Darcy was hard put to disagree with the logic of her young sister, but Elizabeth had found ways to assert her equality without attracting the ire of those who might disagree with the sentiment.

Elizabeth had the good fortune on this occasion to have the sympathetic ear of Charlotte Collins. After all these many years, Elizabeth and Charlotte could still be of one mind, often finishing one another's sentences. Charlotte had permitted her best friend to understand, without ever saying so, that Elizabeth had been accurate in her assessment of Mr. Collins as a ridiculous man: pompous and arrogant. Elizabeth permitted Charlotte to understand, without ever saying so, that Charlotte had indeed achieved admirable financial security for herself and the Lucas family, her original, practical objective.

The marriage of Charlotte Lucas and William Collins was the very model of a pragmatic loveless union. Charlotte accepted this reality. Mr. Collins occupied most of his time with study and with writing his weekly sermons. The burden of listening to his finished sermons fell to the unfortunate inhabitants of the parish, trapped as they were by convention and geography. Outside their parish, though, his writings came to the favorable attention of academics — even as high as Oxford and Cambridge. Charlotte, who had listened to his embryonic sermons and had read them on occasion, noted this

attention of scholars early on and parlayed the quiet publication of his
collected sermons into a tidy stream of income, a stream that covered
— and then some — the occasional gaps in the income generated
by his inheritance. Elizabeth assisted Charlotte in the mechanics of
investment so as to protect the family income both from bankers
and from Mr. Collins. Both women were of the firm opinion that
he would disapprove entrusting these responsibilities to the wives,
despite their obvious skills.

Charlotte remained childless but doted on her godchildren,
Elizabeth's son and daughter.

The marriage of Elizabeth and Fitzwilliam Darcy was the
very model of an engaged and loving union. On the few occasions
when Mr. Darcy's older, gruffer self emerged, Elizabeth was quick
to remedy without aggravation, sparing the world that discomfort.
The Darcys worked quietly with Charlotte to secure control of
Longbourn, ensuring that Mr. and Mrs. Bennet and Kitty would
live there without interruption. Mr. Darcy's agreement to this arose
from his simple desire to please Elizabeth. But, it pleased him in turn
to discover Mr. Bennet's talent for estate management and detailed
matters of accounting, subjects that had never held Mr. Darcy's
interest. Mr. Bennet now contributed his skills to Pemberley as well.

Thus their network of relationships and skills promoted a stable
and prosperous situation for all its members.

Elizabeth early sought to rectify some of the slight long visited
on her sister, Mary, inviting Mary to reside with them at Pemberley.
Mary was a peculiar child, quite unlike Lydia or Kitty. Not given to
vanity or silliness, Mary had begun reading by age five, had grown
fond of philosophy and politics by ten, and was now quite able to
hold her own in principled debate. Without doubt, had her gender
been male, she would have been university bound. Being female, her
best prospect was to wed a gentleman who treasured — or at least
tolerated — her talents and temperament. Elizabeth often reflected
on her own good fortune in achieving just such a union herself.

The mid-afternoon autumn sun cast warm yellow beams into
the sitting room. "What about John Chamberlain, Lord Edward's
son?" Charlotte inquired. She continued with the needlework in
her hands, a clerical stole nearing completion. Charlotte found the
rhythmic motion of her needle and the delicate art of the fabric
accessory very restful. Although she knew there was murmuring

within the congregation about the fact that she and her husband remained childless after years of marriage, some of the women from the parish had confided in her that they did not sense in Mr. Collins the makings of a good father. They praised her for her unwavering support of poor and infirm members of the parish whom her husband seldom noticed, so concerned was he with matters of liturgy and protocol.

Elizabeth shook her head. "As with her other suitors, she did meet with him at the dance a fortnight ago. To be accurate, I should say they had an encounter. I know that you are aware that Lord Edward's fortune is very much tied to the sugar trade in the Caribbean. As such, it means that his fortune is very much tied to slavery, and that is one institution that Mary will never abide."

"So Mary will not be seeing Mr. Chamberlain again?" Charlotte looked up from her handiwork.

"Not if Mr. Chamberlain can avoid it. Their argument sounded through half the village. When it became clear that John was not going to change his mind at the risk of his fortune, she stormed out of the hall and stomped her way here in the dark."

Charlotte chuckled. "I admire her spirit. Mr. Collins also believes that slavery is evil."

"Seriously? I have not heard him mention that in his homily."

"Nor are you likely to, my dear." Charlotte shook her head. "Three of the five wealthiest parishioners are quite intolerant of any abolitionist sentiment. It was on this topic that Mr. Collins's predecessor, the Reverend Mr. Satherthwaite, ran afoul and was forced to leave."

"I did not know that." Elizabeth raised her eyebrows.

"Few do. The Reverend Mr. Satherthwaite threatened to preach a sermon that would shake the parish with convulsions. He had the talent to do so, but the three offered him such a sum — a severance — that he could not responsibly turn it down. He has acquitted himself with honor since by writing on the subject."

This evoked the faintest trace of a smile from Elizabeth. "I must avail myself of his writing at some point."

The sound of determined footsteps in the marble hall cut short their discussion. Twice they heard "Good afternoon, Miss Mary," followed in turn by "Good afternoon, Julie" and "Good afternoon, Thomas." Mary was always courteous to their staff.

Mary Bennet entered the library at a stomp, her face stormy with a scowl. In the years since leaving Longbourn, Mary had transformed from an ungainly young teen of fourteen into a tall, dark-haired beauty at nineteen. She disdained embellishments, allowing her natural complexion to glow and dominate. An avid rider, she acquired a trace of bronze tan — at once both scandalous and enchanting. Her riding strengthened her arms and legs, a quality more than one over-amorous suitor had come to regret.

Mary tried to appear serious as she bowed to Charlotte. "Mrs. Collins."

Charlotte laughed as Mary and Elizabeth joined in. Charlotte had rid them of Mr. Collins's immediate presence while still serving as a bridge to their cousin. Charlotte even managed the challenging feat of maintaining a proper relationship with Mr. Darcy's aunt, Lady Catherine de Bourgh. While neither the Bennets nor the Darcys wished contact of any length with her ladyship, it was prudent to know what was afoot in the de Bourgh household. She had early on threatened to disinherit Mr. Darcy as a result of his marriage to Elizabeth, but given that he was her sole male heir and she was resolutely opposed to her estate's falling to the Crown, she retained a consistent cold but proper relationship.

Elizabeth stared down at the hem of Mary's uniform. "You walked here from St. John's. Why did you not ride Narnia?"

Mary looked down at the burs clinging to her skirt and the mud on her shoes. "Narnia is in the stable here, and it would have taken the school half an hour to get a carriage ready. I walked here in less time than that."

Charlotte set down her needlework. "Half an hour? My word, you must have been galloping yourself."

Mary shrugged. "Something akin to that. I had no desire to argue further with Mrs. Mason. It was clear that neither of us was about to change our fundamental principles."

"And so you are now expelled from the third of the only three schools in the area." Elizabeth tilted her head.

"How would you know that?"

Elizabeth handed Mary a note. She took a seat and frowned as she read it.

"How could you have received this before I even arrived home?"

Elizabeth shook her head. "Thomas was returning from Meryton and passed St. John's not ten minutes after you stormed off. Mrs. Mason had already written your dismissal, and had Thomas deliver it forthwith."

Mary put the note down in her lap and gazed out the window at the fall colors surrounding the fountain in the lake. "I would say that I am sorry, but I am not. St. John's was a dreadful place and I was not getting an education of consequence."

"Perhaps," Charlotte offered, "but now you have exhausted all the schools in the area. It would seem your education is at an end."

Mary continued to stare out the windows. "Then, London. Or Oxford." She turned to Charlotte. "You have connections at Oxford through Mr. Collins's writings. Perhaps you could recommend me."

Elizabeth and Charlotte exchanged knowing glances. "I think not," Elizabeth said. "Those are men's worlds. Women may hold their interest, but not for their minds. And with your hot temper, I cannot see you staying there any longer than at our Hertfordshire schools."

Mary rose from her seat and walked to the window. "Then I must make my own name, my own education. I can write. You both know I can." She turned to face Elizabeth and Charlotte. "I can write as well as or better than any man. You both have read my work." Were she not Mary, she would be on the verge of tears, but stubborn resolve forbade such a capitulation.

Elizabeth and Charlotte stared at her, nodding in agreement.

Charlotte looked thoughtful. "I may have a plan. Mary, you are aware of Mr. Collin's collected sermons, are you not?"

She nodded. "Of course. I have read them all — all seven volumes."

"All seven? But the seventh entered publication only eight days ago."

"Yes. You left your copy with Elizabeth overnight."

"And you read it in that time?" Charlotte exclaimed.

"Indeed. I could not put it down. Whatever else we may say of our cousin, his insights into the nuances of redemption are profound." Mary raised her eyebrows.

"Ah." Charlotte glanced at Elizabeth. "I must read his works with more care next time."

Elizabeth laughed.

"Well, but my point, Mary, is that, as 'profound' as his scholarship may be, his original drafts are abominable. Alas, he is neither a reliable speller nor legible writer. Before publishing the tomes, an editor at Oxford cleans them up. I am told by scholars there that the editor has been quite faithful to the spirit of Mr. Collins's philosophical intent."

Mary returned to her seat. "I see. Good for the editor. Is that the plan? Sounds a bit thin."

"It *was* the plan, my dear. But the editor is leaving for America, and will not be able to work on the next volume, which is approaching completion in rough draft. I was set to musing just now whether you would like to have a go at editing. You listen to his sermons with more attention than anyone I know and you both read the same authors."

Mary appeared stunned. "My mind is reeling. You must know, you surely must, how I would relish such an opportunity. But what would he think of that?"

Charlotte sat back in contemplation. "He is not aware that his sermons have been edited and published. I dare say he has never actually read the collections and does not know of their wide publication, for he seldom communes with outsiders." She looked at Elizabeth and nodded. "There are some things we women keep to ourselves … for everyone's benefit."

While Elizabeth and Charlotte nodded, Mary grew quite serious. "It would be an honor. What do I need to do? How shall we proceed?"

"I have not fleshed out my scheme. I can spirit a couple of sermons to you here. I know that you have a place to write. And I presume you have access to paper. We do not have a great excess of paper."

Mary nodded and looked to her sister, who nodded in return.

"Now please understand, this is a trial. You would need to provide the editing in a timely fashion and the work must proceed in complete anonymity — *complete* anonymity. Is that acceptable?"

"Yes. Absolutely yes."

Charlotte turned to Elizabeth. "Does this seem like a good scheme or madness?"

"I would call it a great, mad scheme. I have always been an avid reader, but I have never been much of a writer beyond personal letters. Mary is both. I would have been wary of her youth, except having observed her lo, these nineteen years; I have faith in her stubborn determination. This scheme should be a brilliant success."

Charlotte seemed satisfied. "Then I shall send over two sermons tomorrow. Try it, and we will see what comes of it."

Having settled on the skeletal details of their plan, conversation turned to Mary's dismissal from St. John's, her disdain for John Chamberlain and the source of his family's fortune. Their conversation was a lively blend of scolding and laughter.

As the sun moved lower to the horizon, Charlotte bade goodbye and boarded her carriage to arrive at Hunsford Rectory before sunset. She wrapped her cloak against the autumn chill and smiled all the way home at her good fortune in solving two problems at once, one hers, one her good friend's.

* * *

Charlotte approached the door to her husband's study. "I am returned."

Mr. Collins looked up from his writing, a blank look on his face. "Where was it again that you went?"

"I was visiting your cousins, Mary and Elizabeth."

"Ah yes. Now I recall. Must have been a lot of silly girl talk."

"Of course."

"And how are things at Longbourn?"

"Pemberley."

Chapter 2

Kerfuffle at Barton Cottage

"No, young lady, I do not believe your story. You still have not explained why you were in the carriage house with him."

"I told you, Elinor, we were merely talking."

Elinor Ferrars crossed her arms, glaring at her youngest sister. "People 'merely talking' do not get sent home with instructions to please not return."

Margaret Dashwood, face stern, turned away from Elinor. "He pushed himself on me. He was not acting as a gentleman. So I put a stop to his advances."

Elinor sat down at the table and put her face in her hands. "Margaret, this is by no means the first time we have had this discussion. I will not excuse any man taking advantage of a young woman. But once again, you were with a young man — alone — under circumstances that invite inappropriate intimacies. And I believe, once again, that you were encouraging the very situation in which you find yourself."

Margaret faced Elinor again. "How can you say such a thing with no evidence?"

Elinor leaned back in her chair and pointed to the floor beneath Margaret's dress. Pieces of hay had fallen from her skirt. "And when you turned from me, I could see that your blouse had been re-buttoned askew. I am quite certain I would have noticed that as you left home this morning."

Margaret's cheeks colored bright red, their brilliance enhanced by her tangle of golden hair. Even in her bare feet, she stood a good six inches taller than Elinor. At nineteen, she was still wont to climb trees or run dancing through the meadows above the cottage. Her athleticism gave her the strength to put an end to overzealous suitors she encountered.

Margaret's natural beauty and free spirit engendered the envy and scorn of the young women of the parish. Her reputation had long ago reached abysmal depths. But these opinions did not seem to bother her.

Elinor wished Margaret had a role model who could talk sense into her. Edward was more than supportive of Elinor and had spoken many times with Margaret with the same earnest combination of sternness and logic, but to little avail. She had long given up on help from Mrs. Jennings, who was more interested in the intrigue and gossip she could wheedle out of Margaret, as the young woman managed to attract and then frustrate the sons of some of the most prominent families in the area. Colonel Brandon and Marianne enjoyed some sway in Margaret's upbringing, but his tales of adventure in the Caribbean implanted in Margaret a wanderlust both inspiring and frightening.

Still, Elinor smiled recalling the evening she came to Margaret's room to find her pouring over a map of the New World given to her by the colonel. Margaret gazed up from her map, a far-away look in her eyes, and said, "I must go."

Mary and Elizabeth watched in silence as Charlotte flipped through arbitrary pages in the stack of papers. After skimming eight to ten pages, she looked up amused to see Mary's nervous attention. "Your penmanship is quite good."

Mary put her face into her hands and shook her head.

Elizabeth and Charlotte exchanged glances.

Charlotte grinned with mischief. After a few more pages, she set the papers down. "Mary, you have exceeded even my most optimistic expectations. Well done. Your work is better than that of the editor I commissioned from Oxford. And you completed the work so quickly!"

Mary beamed and bowed to Charlotte. "Thank you. It was a happy task, though you were quite right about his spelling and grammar. Given his elevated thoughts, I would have expected better."

Charlotte nodded. "In Mr. Collins's defense, he shuffled among many relatives as a child. He did not have one full year in the same school. Perhaps that is why he cannot be more attached to his parishioners."

Mary raised her eyebrows and countered, "He has always been more than civil to me."

"True," Charlotte acknowledged, "but then you are family, however distant. And I dare say that you are one of the few in the congregation who actually listen to his sermons and comments on their points."

"Then the others are missing a great education."

"Still, be on guard that you do not reveal your present efforts to him. I doubt he would react well knowing that a woman was correcting his work."

The three sat in silence a while. Then Charlotte spoke to Mary. "I saw that you altered some of the Latin text. I did not realize that you knew Latin."

"Yes. I did enjoy that part of my studies."

"And the Greek?"

"Alas, no. I transcribed it only as he had written it. I checked Mr. Darcy's library, but it has none of the cited works. The library did have a basic Greek grammar, so I can at least recognize the proper characters."

"Mary, we have not mentioned how I might compensate you for your work. When your sister and I were first pondering this endeavor, I guess we did not have enough confidence in your abilities."

Elizabeth chimed in, "You have done well, little sister. You should enjoy some fruits from your labor."

Mary frowned. "The work was its own reward. When first we discussed this enterprise, it was to promote my education and standing. I should like to have a go at schooling again, perhaps in London. I understand there are some new schools more open-minded there. If I complete the current volumes, would you be my patron?"

Charlotte and Elizabeth looked at each other in surprise. Elizabeth was the first to speak. "True, it was to promote your education, and we were quick to point out the very great difficulty entering that world of men."

"You did. I know it will be difficult, but still, I want to try. Will you sponsor me?"

The other two considered the question for some time. Finally, Charlotte spoke. "If your sister agrees, I will make inquiries."

Charlotte turned to Elizabeth. After a bit, Elizabeth nodded.

Mary stood up. "Splendid. If you will provide me with more sermons, I shall get back to work. By my notes, there should be twenty-four sermons in need of editing."

Charlotte smiled. "Right."

* * *

Sunday routine continued its clockwork predictability. Mr. Collins greeted his parishioners as they filed out of the church after an hour and a half, more dazed than inspired. As was their habit, Charlotte and Elizabeth left for lunch together, this week to Pemberley. Mary, as was her habit, lingered until the church was empty before greeting Mr. Collins.

"Masterful interpretation of the material," she offered.

He looked her straight in the eyes. "You are too generous, Miss Mary. I saw that you, at least, had your eyes open, which I cannot say of many others."

"Perhaps the others were savoring your study in prayerful contemplation."

He smiled. "Perhaps. Still, you must know that I do appreciate your attention — to the sermons, that is."

She returned his smile.

"But again you have missed returning home with your sister and Mrs. Collins."

"Quite right, for I have exciting news to tell you. I have undertaken to learn Greek."

"Learn Greek? Whatever for?"

She frowned. "Whatever for? How can you ask that? Not a week goes by that you do not cite that language as a source in your homily. The value is obvious, is it not?"

He mused on her answer. "True. But it is rare that a woman would choose to study the language."

"And it is also rare in this parish that a man chooses to study the language."

He chuckled. "You are right, of course. I do not think there are any others."

"And yet you still include Greek in most of your sermons. Now you will have one congregant who understands what you are talking about."

"I see. And how may I be of assistance?"

"I need books. Mr. Darcy's library has but one Greek grammar and two classics — *The Odyssey* and *Aeschylus* —but that is all. And given their pristine condition, I doubt anyone other than myself has taken down any of the three. Judging from your citations in your sermons, you have a dozen and more."

"I would not wish to chill your ambition, but it is not a simple matter to learn Greek or any other language. The learning occupies many years. One does not just pick up a book and start reading."

"I am aware of that. I have been diligent in my Latin studies for nine years. I expect I will do likewise with Greek. Do not underestimate me."

He stared at her as they left the church and strolled down the lane. "No, I will not. I would never do that. I am resolved to assist you. Have your man Thomas come to Hunsford on the morrow, and I will send you some volumes."

"I do not think that will be necessary," she offered "Since you and I are passing right by your cottage on the way to Pemberley, I can pick up a book or two now and get started."

Mr. Collins pursed his lips, frowning as he stared straight ahead. "I do not think that wise."

"Whyever not?"

"Appearances. I should think that a pastor, especially a married pastor accompanying a young woman to his home, would raise questions."

"Questions? I cannot imagine," Mary said, turning away.

He kept his eyes straight ahead. "Yes, you can. I know you can. In this small community, tongues wag for the least hint of scandal."

"Then we must be discreet. As I leave, I shall stay close to the hedgerow until I take leave of the property."

He turned back to Mary. "I would say you have planned this out rather thoroughly."

She smiled.

At the entrance to the walk leading to the Collins's cottage adjoining Rosings, they paused and scanned their surroundings.

"It appears that Sunday dinner is the order of the day for the whole countryside, and even Lady Catherine cannot peer through the hedge." She pointed in the direction of Rosings.

He looked about again as he unlocked the cottage door and opened it for her.

Mary loosened her coat and draped it over the sofa in their parlor and placed her reticule beside it. "How lovely. Charlotte has done a fine job furnishing this home. Her tastes are exquisite."

"Yes. That is her mission. I suppose I once regarded decorating as frivolity, but I am happy that it pleases our guests. Lady Catherine has been most supportive. She has taken quite a liking to Charlotte."

He stopped talking, but continued to stare at Mary. As the church lacked heating, congregants attended with their coats on. Beneath her coat, Mary had worn a pretty gown, flowing ivory with pearls sewn into the design. A wide satin ribbon accentuated her trim waist, and the gown's short sleeves presented her strong arms to good effect.

She watched his eyes darting up and down her figure. She gave a sweet smile. "Books?"

He shook his head as from a trance. "Yes, books. Wait right here and I shall retrieve them."

He made his way toward the library, Mary following just behind. He turned to her. "The library is not so tidy as the rest of the house. Mrs. Collins has little interest in books, and, to be honest, I have my own way of ordering matters."

"Of course," she replied. "Libraries are for reading, not entertaining."

He opened the door, and she followed him in. Standing in the center of the room, she turned around, gazing at the shelves. "Magnificent!" All around the room shelves rose from floor to ceiling. On many shelves, the books reached the width of the wood, with more books in horizontal piles atop. She approached one wall and caressed the bindings, taking a deep draft of the aroma of old books. "Our library at Pemberley is larger in area, but does not have so many books by half." She looked back at him as he continued gazing at her. She smiled at him and turned back to her survey. "If I have judged you correctly, the Greek texts should be together close to your writing desk." She approached the shelves closest to the desk and spied two rows of books with bindings that included Greek characters. She turned back to him. "And so I have."

"Were you seeking anything in particular, Mary?"

"If you will not be using them for the next two weeks, I would like to borrow Daikon's *History of Early Asia Minor* and Edward Smith's *Eschatology and Patmos*."

Mr. Collins looked surprised. "How on earth would you know about those?"

She lowered her head, still eyeing him. "Who do you suppose cleans up after services on Sunday? It does not happen by itself, you know. Some attend to the flowers, some to the candles. I tidy the altar area. I see the side notes on your reading copy and I make sure they are in order and ready to return."

"Your interest and attention is inspiring. No, I will not soon be needing those volumes," he confirmed.

Mary eased the two books from their shelf. As she did so, she glanced at his desk. Besides the open books and partially-written pages, she took notice of a small stack of notes in the upper right hand corner of his desk. They were notes she had written, complimenting him on particular points in his sermons. Each was signed simply "Mary." Judging by the size of the stack, she considered it likely the complete set of her letters. She looked at the notes awhile, and then turned to see him following her gaze. He was biting his lip.

He looked up at last and motioned for the door. They returned to the parlor where she covered the two books in her shawl and he helped her with her coat.

"Thank you for the loan. I shall take good care of them, of course."

He extended his hand to take hers. She instead pressed close to him, wrapped her arms around him and kissed him.

Collins did not resist at first, but placed his hands on her shoulders and nudged her away. "This is not a good idea. This is what I feared."

She smiled, opened the door, and stepped out, turning but a moment. "Then we must be discreet."

Still smiling, she dashed along the inner hedge until she reached the corner of the property. Peeking between the bushes, she saw that the path was empty and resumed her walk home. The chill wind brought a rosy glow to her cheeks.

Arriving at Pemberley, she found Charlotte and Elizabeth engaged in conversation in the sitting room.

Elizabeth looked at the clock. "Where have you been? Service was over two hours ago."

"I have been reveling in the glories of nature's autumn — the sun and the sky and the rainbow of leaves."

Charlotte laughed. "Well, best get some hot nourishment. There is beef and tea still on the sideboard. Jenny can bring you anything you like. Please ring for her. Your sister and I have been discussing your future. Join us when you are settled."

Mary smiled and pulled the cord by the fireplace.

Chapter Four
Voyager

"And how long shall I be held prisoner here?" Margaret asked.

"You are not held prisoner here," Edward replied. "We are merely seeking some assurance that you will not bring catastrophe on you or your family."

She picked at her food. "And has a month not been enough to convince you that I have reformed, mended my ways, and set myself on a course for high society?" She sat up ramrod straight and gave her hair a regal shake.

Elinor laughed. "Perhaps you have earned a chance to, as you said, 'set yourself on a course for high society.'" She looked to Edward. "Shall I tell her, or would you like to do the honors?"

Edward nodded. "Colonel Brandon is hosting a dinner for an old friend the night after tomorrow, and he has invited us. Marianne suggested you should come along if you have mended your attitude."

Margaret rolled her eyes. "A dinner party with old friends. How exciting."

"Actually," said Edward, "in this case you may indeed be excited. Captain Robert Johnson and his son have just returned from the Caribbean for a short visit. They are merchant ship officers, engaged in trade throughout the region."

Margaret narrowed her eyes. "Trade? Molasses? Slaves? Rum?"

Edward laughed. "The colonel said that would be your first question. You two are kindred spirits. No, neither molasses nor rum. They trade in spices — ginger and peppers, I recall — and tobacco. In fact, they both are strong opponents of slavery and are here to voice their support for Parliament's abolition of slavery — for that and for the pirates."

"Pirates?"

"So I am sensing excitement. The Caribbean is still thick with pirates. Some months, up to a fifth of the trade is lost to piracy. Captain Johnson is seeking a bigger naval presence in the area. Do you still feel the dinner will be too boring?"

Margaret's appetite had returned, and she finished her meal. "I shall be the very model of decorum."

Elinor laughed.

* * *

Margaret was true to her word, and arrived at the Brandon's in her best gown. She took an immediate interest in Captain Johnson and his son, Robert. Both took an instant liking to Margaret as well, impressed by her knowledge of the Caribbean region and more than willing to ply her with tales of storms and skullduggery. Father and son operated two ships; and they hauled allspice, ginger, hot peppers, and tobacco from farms on a dozen islands to Great Britain on a regular basis. British tastes had not yet embraced hot peppers, preferring the milder Asian black pepper, but the Caribbean varieties were gaining admirers.

She particularly charmed the younger Robert, and they took leave of the others to stroll Delaford's interior, the weather outside having turned dreary and cold.

"How does one get to the Caribbean? I should like to go there."

Robert grimaced. "It is quite challenging. If you were a man, you could sign on to almost any ship as a seaman. But it is not a pleasant life. Aside from the colonials, very few visit there, despite the warmth and incredible beauty."

"Why ever not?"

"It is dangerous. Beside the obvious hazards of travel and piracy, the local populations do not take kindly to our colonial rule, even though their lives are better — in our British view, at least."

"Still, I will go there," she persisted. "There must be a way."

Robert pondered her plea. "Hmm. I do not suppose you know French."

"*Mais bien sûr, monsieur. J'ai étudié le français avec diligence pendant sept ans,*" she replied immediately.

Robert stopped, first stunned, but breaking into a smile. "I do not pretend to understand what you said, but you may have found your passage. We have been trying to establish more business on Martinique and Saint Martin, but no one in the company speaks French. One of my tasks while on this visit home was to enlist the services of a reliable translator and interpreter. Let me speak with my father and with your family. You know, of course, they will worry for your safety."

She smiled. "*Merci, Monsieur.*"

Margaret and Robert continued their stroll of the first floor, the circuit consuming half an hour including stops to admire one art treasure or another. She found that he was fond of alabaster statuary, admiring in particular a small statue of a maiden preparing for her bath. He found, not to his surprise, that she was fond of maps and travel journals. They finished their circuit as dinner preparations were complete. Colonel Brandon took his place at the head of the table, Marianne to his right.

Following their seating and serving, Captain Johnson made inquiry. "And what sort of mischief have you two youngsters found to occupy your evening?"

Robert looked to Margaret, who nodded. "Miss Margaret Dashwood has professed a great desire to see the Caribbean, and proposes to sail there with our company."

Elinor and Edward, Colonel Brandon and Marianne all laughed.

Robert paused and waited until it seemed proper to continue. "In all seriousness, she presents a compelling case. Her knowledge of the area's history and geography rivals my own and, subject to verification, her French skills would make her a most valued member of our company. Of course, I would not wish to interfere with the family's customs and plans, but such an opportunity is seldom presented in any lifetime. With respect, I would ask that you consider such an arrangement."

Elinor was the first to break the ensuing silence. "The proposal sounds on first hearing ridiculous." Her face stern, Elinor looked at Margaret. "She is but nineteen, yet her drive and ambition quite outpace her maturity. To put it bluntly, the idea of a young woman on a ship of men on a long voyage seems a perfect recipe for disaster."

Margaret's face clouded, her cheeks flushed, and she folded her arms.

Robert nodded and smiled. "Your concerns are quite valid and well placed …"

Margaret turned to Robert, her disappointment obvious.

He continued, "… *if* ours were a military or traditional commercial vessel. But ours is not. Our crew is comprised, primarily, of several families. Of course, the idea of women aboard sailing ships is an outlandish idea to many, but we believe that we are the vanguard of a new age of sailing, a more civil and egalitarian company of seafarers. Single crewmembers berth in separate sections of the ship. The boundaries are delineated and enforced. We set ourselves apart from other vessels with our civility and propriety, men and women working at the same tasks, with the same expectations. That arrangement has worked quite well for us. In truth, I think it is the future of the sea trade."

Colonel Brandon turned to his old friend. "Captain?"

Captain Johnson stroked his white beard. "My son is quite the deal maker. The entrepreneur in me is eager for such an associate. Few British companies have the services of loyal interpreters. In my younger days; I would have jumped at the chance for such an adventure knowing what I know now." He looked to Margaret with a kindly smile. "But, knowing what I know now, the parent in me fears for all the dangers and mishaps in that same adventure. These old eyes have seen enough battles, storms, and pestilence to keep me awake many a night." He folded his hands before him on the table. "And yet, I continue. I cannot imagine life on land, life in a single place, devoid of the warm sun and the sapphire sea. A great risk? Yes, indeed. Worth the risk? Absolutely. My son is telling the truth that our ships are our family and that our reputation as upright citizens is unimpeachable. But I think, Robert, that the family will want to discuss this opportunity among themselves." He looked between Edward and Elinor for their reaction. "Regardless, It would change your precious sister forever."

The remainder of the dinner was occupied with polite small talk. The Colonel and the Captain related some of their history together. Captain Johnson's commands had been as commanding officer of supply and support ships, skills that served him well in his current occupation. Colonel Brandon led security forces protecting colonists and property of the Crown. Though he had upon occasion used force, his reputation for fairness and respect for the local citizenry was well known throughout the Lesser Antilles.

Brandon and Johnson grew passionate in their descriptions of the beauty of the islands, and Margaret's face acquired a dreamy quality.

After sweets at the end of dinner, their conversations continued for a short time. Elinor and Edward promised to give Robert's proposal appropriate consideration, but were careful not to set expectations high, and Robert let them know that his ship, *Lady Bridget*, would set sail three months hence, giving them his address in Plymouth.

The return ride to the parish house featured two separate conversations of opposing ends — Margaret expounding on the preparation she must make for the voyage and Elinor listing the dangers and pitfalls of leaving home. Edward was neither asked, nor did he offer, his opinion on the matter.

Chapter Five
Winter Gray

As Mary tidied the sermon notes, she observed how, even with
only a few weeks of Greek, she recognized specific Greek words in his
text. She recognized them despite William's cramped handwriting.
As she continued editing his works, she concluded that most errors
in earlier editions of his sermons derived from misreading his
handwriting rather than outright sloppiness. She mentioned that to
Charlotte, who seemed not a bit surprised.

The church was empty as she gathered his papers and proceeded
to the large doors at the back of the worship space, the church's
entrance. She wrapped herself in a long cape against a more severe
cold than customary for early November. Late autumn's chill
wind denuded the trees, and low gray clouds propagated a gloomy
atmosphere.

Mr. Collins waited for her at the door.

She handed him his sermon. "Every page accounted for,
William."

His face registered amusement at her address. "Miss Bennett, I
hardly think appropriate to call me by my given name."

"And would you stop me? I sign my correspondence with
'Mary,' for that is the address I prefer." She looked about their ancient
church. "Unless these stones sprout ears and grow mouths, there are
none to gossip about our gentle familiarity."

"Such familiarity breeds carelessness. Matters could get out of
sorts. Oh, Mary, why do you torment me so?"

She moved close to him. "Do I torment you?" She reached out
with her hands and clasped his neck.

Mr. Collins winced. "What are you doing?"

"Warming my hands, obviously." She closed her eyes, savoring
the warmth.

When she opened her eyes, she peered into his and they gazed at
each other.

Mary removed her hands from his neck. "Thank you, sir. Much
better." She donned her gloves.

"Were you not wearing them all this time?"

"As I was able, sir. Alas, I must take them off while curating your
notes. You use a thin paper and I find it difficult to separate your

pages while wearing gloves."

They began walking toward Hunsford. Collins seemed initially distracted. Finally, he said, "'curating …' an interesting choice of word."

"I think 'curating' an apt description. Taking care that valuable objects are preserved for the future."

He sighed. "I wish that Mrs. Collins regarded them so."

Mary chuckled. "You underestimate her regard, sir. I know that she is well aware of their value. I have heard her say as much. Theological discourse is not her primary interest, her heart's pursuit."

He regarded her as they strolled. "You are a keen observer, Mary. I have come to value your insight. Theology and philosophy do seem to be *your* heart's pursuit. Am I wrong?"

"Indeed, they are, William," she replied, her head held high.

He shook his head hearing again 'William,' smiling nonetheless. "And what did you think of the sermon?"

"I thought it masterful that you turned the story about. Usually, we portray our beggar at the gate as a sympathetic character. On the other hand, you were correct to point out that he betrayed the gift given him — a most ungrateful and treacherous betrayal. Those around me who were not asleep seemed to take notice. You should try the same passage, portraying him this time with sympathy."

"And you do not think it wrong to toy with scripture like that?"

"The Greek is ambiguous, sir. You were careful to point that out."

"I see. And are you already reading Greek?"

"I can recognize some individual words. Given time, perhaps. I noticed several pages you neglected to share with the congregation."

"About slavery?"

"Yes, sir. Σκλαβιά — slavery. You had two pages near the end. You know that some day you will need to step forward — to take a stand. Winds of change are growing ever stronger. You have the moral authority to do so and intellectual rigor to take that stand."

"As soon as I do, my life as I have known it is over."

They continued on in silence for a while. "You know, there may be a way …," she murmured.

"Pray, tell."

"You could present your thoughts without attribution. Someday, when the tide has turned, you would emerge in safety and honor."

He chuckled. "Why do I suspect that you wish to be a part of such a charade?"

"You are a keen observer as well, sir."

Hunsford came into view. "This week your sister and Charlotte meet at our cottage for their after-service gossip. I would invite you to come in, but …"

"That would generate questions and evince a pattern we do not wish to explain?" She completed his sentence.

"It sounds deceitful, but yes. These meetings of our minds work best with only the two of us."

Before the path divided, they approached a last large shrubbery — an ancient boxwood. Mary put forth her hand to stop him. As one, they surveyed their surroundings. "Winter is upon us, I fear. The season is good for reading, though gray brings on a powerful melancholy. You will be in my thoughts until Sunday next," she said.

"And you in mine. 'Til next we meet." In the sheltering shrubs and landscape devoid of onlookers, they embraced and kissed. When finally they broke their embrace, he bowed to her. "Such sweet torment. I am in agony."

Collins watched Mary until she rounded the bend of the path to Pemberley before he turned to walk to his cottage. Elizabeth and Charlotte sat in the parlor, Mrs. Darcy with a book, Mrs. Collins with her needlework.

Both looked up at his entrance.

"Good afternoon, ladies. I hope you are having a pleasant afternoon."

"We are," Charlotte said. She looked at the clock. "You are quite late. We have already eaten, but there is some left for you."

He nodded. "Yes, I was discussing today's sermon with some parishioners. What did you think, ladies?"

"Erudite, as always," Elizabeth offered.

"Were you not a bit harsh on that poor beggar man?" Charlotte asked.

He nodded. "Perhaps. I am thinking of a second sermon, with inverted perspective. Do you think anyone would notice?"

The women looked at each other. Charlotte grinned. "One or two, I am sure."

Satisfied, Collins bowed a short bow and retired, first to the kitchen for a plate of food, and then on to his study to begin work on next week's sermon.

In time, he stopped and gazed at Mary's stacked missives. He picked up the top item, her most recent letter, and put it to his nose. Her letter smelled of perfume. He closed his eyes.

"I am in such torment."

* * *

Mary stepped up her pace, looking forward to Pemberley's warmth. The memory of their kiss still dwelt on her lips. This was what she hoped for, dreamed of. Still, the reality of their situation weighed on her. Their relationship possessed little room to grow without ruinous scandal.

She would put disasters out of her mind for the present. She had volumes to edit, critiques to write, and preparations to make for the abolition meeting in Oxford on Tuesday.

Chapter Six
Abolition Meeting

Mary continued editing William's sermons, starting with his most recent first. She separated the unpreached segment on slavery from the rest, giving it a separate title, *The Ecclesiastical Imperative for the Renunciation of Slavery*. William had only begun his ruminations it would appear. Those two pages beyond the end of his preached sermon were thin on detail, but were rich in marginal notes, many of which she linked to reference books already on loan to her.

"Dear William," she murmured, "you tragically underestimate the power of your arguments. It is divine providence that I am one of the few who can decipher your handwriting."

She continued this supplemental work, expanding references and polishing the structure until it matured to seven pages. Mary read the finished epistle several times, and enclosed it in her portfolio, satisfied. Then she resumed editing his preached sermon until satisfied with it as well.

* * *

Margaret managed to compress five or six days of clothing and toiletries into a single large trunk. She was finishing her third — finally successful — attempt to close its latch when Elinor appeared in the doorway of Margaret's room.

Elinor scowled. "And where do you think you are going, young lady?"

Margaret looked up in surprise. "The abolition meeting. You consented to my going — months ago."

Elinor took a seat. "You are quite right, Margaret. I fear that local events crowded it from my mind."

Margaret appeared the picture of serenity. She smirked. "I fancy you thought I was running off on an adventure."

"To be honest, the thought had crossed my mind." Elinor looked at Margaret's single trunk. "Though, this time of year, you would not have traveled far with that alone."

Margaret tried the lock twice and smiled. She looked up. "And can I still not convince you or Edward to attend? It is a cause of epic moral imperative."

"You are quite right, dearest, but we are much engaged here with our flock and their infirmities. You heard, no doubt, that Mrs. Vincy took a turn for worse during the night? Her physician does not feel that she is long for this world. We support the cause of abolition, of course, but must rely for now on your energy to represent us."

Margaret looked down. "I am sad for Mrs. Vincy, but happy that her family is about her at such a time. I shall do my best to represent us all with honor and courage. I sense that big changes are near, Elinor. Freedom is coming to the Empire. I want to be part of that change."

"And you shall. Remind me for I have forgotten; where will you be staying? Who will accompany you?"

Margaret grinned. "You have been much burdened, Elinor. I have been in correspondence with another young woman of Derbyshire, Miss Mary Bennet of Pemberley. We will lodge together at The Swan in Oxford, where some other young women of our movement are staying. Many families of means are keeping their heads down, while allowing their hot-blooded children to take their stands. As you suggested earlier, Jane will go with me. She says someone needs to keep me out of trouble."

Elinor nodded. "Excellent. Jane is both wise and loving. Pemberley? Is that not Mr. Fitzwilliam Darcy's estate?"

"It is. Do you know the Darcys?"

"Oh, I do not know them personally, but Mr. Darcy is a prominent personage. Does not a family of his stature derive a measure of substance from human bondage?"

Margaret raised her finger. "They did — until recently. It was on that point of interest that I came into acquaintance with Mary. She persuaded her family to change their holdings in favor of more noble investments. Her efforts proved a successful model to rebut those whose first concerns are for wealth over humanity."

Elinor shook her head. "I cannot hide from you some fears that my hot-blooded little sister will allow her passion to override her safety. I hear a great deal of rowdiness occurs at some of these gatherings. You will be safe, will you not?"

"Marianne has given me the same stern lecture, Elinor. Colonel Brandon, bless him, has expressed great confidence. Nevertheless, he has given me a letter of introduction to one of his old friends from the regiment, and I promised I would make that contact should I have need for security."

Elinor relaxed. "Well, dearest, you have made admirable

preparation. I look forward to your report. I presume that Thomas will escort you to the coach and will be waiting for you on your return."

"Thank you, Elinor."

* * *

"And the case law rests on …?" Elizabeth continued her drill.

Mary sat with her eyes closed, retrieving her studied facts from memory. "Lord Mansfield's judgment in the Somersett Case, 1772."

Elizabeth put the last page face down. "Very good. Your recall is perfect."

"I must be able to know the history of the movement so I can enter into discussions," Mary said.

"The last practice of your greeting was fine, but do you want to try it once more?"

Mary shook her head. "No. I have been reviewing for many days now and should rest before the trip to Oxford."

"Have you packed for your trip?"

"Oh, yes. It is a light trunk. This is not, after all, a social call."

"Still, you must dress for the weather," Elizabeth said, "The chill this time of year can be dreadful. You know that."

"I have packed appropriately, Elizabeth."

"I still have my concerns. Abolition stirs some violent passions. There are those who would defeat the cause by riot rather than reason."

"Which is why we have chosen Oxford for our meeting. That community is quite supportive, and its constabulary friendly to the movement."

"And you told me that you will be boarding with a Miss Dashwood from Devon."

"Yes. One of her brothers-in-law is in the Church, Reverend Ferrars, and her other brother-in-law is Colonel Brandon, who served in the West Indies. Margaret writes that she plans to travel there soon."

Elizabeth raised her eyebrows. "Oh, my. That sounds frightful to me. You are not thinking of that, are you?"

Mary laughed. "No. It may seem a romantic idea to Miss Dashwood — and I admire her enthusiasm — but I am quite content to fight my battles with my pen right here. In fact, Mr. Collins has given me letters of introduction to several Oxford scholars he respects,

and Charlotte has given me letters of introduction to publishers in
Oxford. I will be carrying some of Mr. Collins's writings opposing
slavery under the pen name we have chosen — Joseph Weatherstone.
Mr. Collins's writings have grown quite strong and passionate — after
a little polishing. In my role as 'Mr. Weatherstone's editor,' we posted
a small sample work to another publisher from London who will
be in attendance at the meeting, and have received an enthusiastic
response."

"Bravo. I must share with you Charlotte's gratitude that you
have been working with Mr. Collins. She tells me that his melancholy
has been much relieved as a result of your collaborations. We believe
that his isolation was the cause, and Charlotte, by her upbringing, has
very little to share with him. She says he is a renewed man and much
better company. You have been good for them."

Mary turned to gaze out of her window. "I am glad to hear that.
I too have been able to grow in my own skills. Our works are very
much a blend of his scholarship and my writing. Charlotte has even
permitted me to write in his name to those publishers in Oxford
and London regarding our edited sermons. Our blended persona has
attracted a good following."

She paused a bit. "In regards the writings on slavery, I have
kept that subject completely separate. I hope to meet some of
Weatherstone's supporters and detractors while I am there. I may be
able to find a publisher willing to accept that treatise."

"Anonymous is the word," Elizabeth said. "This treatise you have
refined would end his position here if his authorship became known.
I fear that Lady Catherine would turn him out forthwith if she got
wind of it."

"You may be right, my sister, though I am by no means certain
of that. That is why I will be the tip of the sword. I am unknown
and have little to lose in this world. Lady Catherine's opinion of you
has no farther to fall, and she has little or no sway over my beloved
brother-in-law. I am the perfect vessel as such."

Elizabeth laughed. "You sound like a martyr!"

Mary laughed in return, but then grew serious. "You must be
aware, Elizabeth, that the charade we have constructed, with my
editing Mr. Collins's work and Charlotte promoting their publication,
cannot long continue. I am quite certain he knows something is
afoot. He and I now spend many hours in serious discussions, and the

volume of correspondence that Charlotte is receiving must raise some suspicions."

"True, true, my dear. You are wise beyond your years. Charlotte has been pondering the same problem. She is searching for a way to introduce him to your collaboration. Perhaps the two of you can come up with a plan on your return, when you have gathered some intelligence on the scope of his influence in both the theological and the abolitionist circles."

Mary turned again to her window, watching a chill wind rocking bare branches against gray sky. "Perhaps," she said.

* * *

With Jane's assistance, Margaret packed for the sojourn in Oxford. Margaret could not recall a time when she had thought of Jane as a servant. Rather, Jane was her surrogate big sister, closer to her than even Elinor or Marianne. Jane was a confidant and, on occasion, a co-conspirator.

For her entire journey from their cottage in Devon to Oxford, thoughts of a voyage from Plymouth to the Caribbean occupied Margaret's mind. Elinor was correct. Her single trunk would not suffice for a journey of that duration. According to journals in Colonel Brandon's library, a ship's voyage would take about thirty to forty-five days, compared to this simple excursion.

One consolation was that she would not require formal wear or other vanities. And, once their ship entered subtropical waters, she would have no need for heavy clothing against winter's cold. She would need writing and drawing supplies, but not a grand amount.

Margaret had already accumulated these calculated quantities over the last several weeks, being careful to keep them out of Jane's sight. But how to escape, if she did not obtain her family's blessing, was still her prime obstacle.

* * *

Mary, accompanied by the beloved family servant Jenny, appreciated an improved ride as they approached Oxford. These roads were less rutted than in Derbyshire, and the carriage ride was tolerable. She arrived early enough that she continued her writings in the Swan's lobby while awaiting Margaret. She wrote at a leisurely pace, pausing to catch discussions and arguments filling the lobby of The Swan. The quality of those conversations made Pemberley seem provincial by comparison.

She had finished but two pages in three hours when she looked up to see a tall young woman with tight curls enter the lobby, accompanied by a modest, but handsome older girl. Mary got up and approached her, recognizing her from the letter she had received. "Margaret Dashwood?"

Margaret broke into a broad smile. "Mary!" They hugged and Mary introduced Margaret to the innkeeper. A servant took Mary's trunk and carried it off to her room. Margaret then introduced Mary to Jane. They tried to induce Jane to join them, but Jane insisted on the propriety of lodging with other servants and departed.

"Are you hungry?" Mary asked.

"Yes. Our station in Berkshire was not serving food." Margaret looked around in fascination. "So many people. I am not used to this at home."

They walked toward the dining room. "Nor I. I have already seen Thomas Clarkson and William Wilberforce."

Margaret began looking about. "Where?"

"They are not here now. But we shall hear them tomorrow."

The young women found an open table and enjoyed a long meal together. The inn's kitchen staff prepared even ordinary sounding entrées with a flair and flavor beyond that to which Mary and Margaret were accustomed. Even the finishing sweet was an Italian delight, part cake and part creamy filling.

Mary inquired about Margaret's plans. "Tell me, when will you be traveling to the West Indies?"

Margaret lowered her voice. "That is a problem. My sister and my brother-in-law do not approve of my going. They say it is much too dangerous."

Mary nodded. "They are likely correct. How, then, are you going to accomplish this?"

"It is as if you know me already," Margaret said.

Mary folded her arms. "One thing I am learning is that we never achieve anything of value with timidity. If you see a goal as worthy, then you must pursue it. I realize every day that if I were to stop and consider the cost of a quest, I should never start. My question would be what do you expect to achieve there?"

"I would write about life on plantations. And I have a good hand at drawing, if I do say so myself. The press today needs input from the scene. I am not sure how I would get my observations published, but hope that I can learn how here."

Mary became excited. "Well, you have come to the right place. I have seen my own writings circulated quite widely. Not under my own name, of course. They still will not even look at a woman's writings — if they know."

Margaret cocked her head. "Do you then write under a man's name?"

"Have you ever read Joseph Weatherstone?"

Margaret's eyes grew wide. She leaned forward and spoke in a whisper, "You are Joseph Weatherstone?"

Mary nodded. She then put her finger to her lips. "Not a word. Some day he will be revealed, but not yet. Mind you, I am only half of Joseph Weatherstone. I collaborate with a very real learned and gentle man. 'Joseph' is a confluence of the two of us. It amazed me to witness the impact made here by this imaginary man in such a very brief time."

Margaret extended her hand, grinning. "Honored to meet you, sir. I have already read your clarion call. You are one of the reasons I am here."

"The speed with which ideas can propagate here caught me by surprise," Mary said. "Even in the brief time I have been here, I have heard these scholars arguing over Joseph's writings. I simply sat and listened at first. After a bit, I could not resist arguing with a chap who had not actually read our writings. In a refreshing change from rural Derbyshire, they actually listen here. By the time we parted, he said that I was well informed on Weatherstone's writings and that he looked forward to discussing my thoughts at the meeting. It was all I could do to hold back my laughter."

"That is something I have often wished for: that I could be someone else for a time."

Mary opened her hands. "Then do it. What is holding you back?"

Margaret mused over her question for a while. "Devon is a small world. I cannot imagine holding a secret for long."

"You are not in Devon. Here, *you* do not matter — only *your ideas*. Some may find that depressing, but I find it most liberating. In Derbyshire, secrecy is too often needed to protect one's happiness ..." Her voice trailed off.

Margaret raised her eyebrows in query.

"We will discuss my quandary another time. Social convention can be a powerful force for good, but can be a tight binding as well. It is peculiar how scripture is used on the one hand to support a dark institution like slavery — which it certainly can — and then be completely ignored in support of conjugal relations not sanctioned by present society. Happiness rests on such a thin veneer of assumptions and expectations."

Margaret watched Mary's wistful gaze. "Sounds complicated. A love interest? I will not press you for I would not wish to pry inappropriately."

Mary nodded. "It is complicated. Love is but an element of my dilemma. I must resolve my challenges with serious reflection. That is enough for now."

* * *

Tuesday dawned crisp and cold. Mary and Margaret walked from The Swan to the grand auditorium on Oxford University's ancient campus. On arrival, they found Clarkson and Wilberforce already deep in argument in one of the passageways.

Mary turned to Margaret. "That young man approaching us is the very chap I told you about last night."

He bowed to Mary. "I do apologize. In my immersion in conversation yesterday, I did not properly introduce myself. I am Thomas Fowell Buxton."

She bowed in return. "Ah. It is an honor, sir. I am Mary Bennet of Pemberley in Derbyshire." She turned to Margaret. "Sir Thomas Fowell Buxton is a member of the House of Commons and is a tireless champion of freedom. It will likely be by efforts of him and those of like-minded members of Parliament that we will see the end of slavery throughout the Empire."

Buxton turned to Margaret. "Welcome, Miss …?"

"Margaret Dashwood, sir. Of Devon."

Mary said, "Miss Dashwood is contemplating a sojourn in the West Indies to document conditions there."

Buxton grew excited. "Excellent. We need authentic narratives. Do you know how you will get your reports published?"

"No, sir, not yet," Margaret replied.

"Well, you will benefit from associating with Miss Bennet. She appears to know Joseph Weatherstone quite well. Perhaps he can see that your work receives its due attention. I find it most regrettable that women writers have not had wide access to publication. We are all the poorer for that disrespect."

Margaret eyed Mary and then turned back to Buxton. "Thank you for your kind counsel, sir. I hope that you might make his acquaintance."

"Yes. I would have expected him here today. He is a most passionate advocate for our cause. I have not met him myself."

Mary continued, "You may come closer than you think, sir, for Mr. Weatherstone entrusted me with a missive for this very gathering. Health and weather prevented his travel, alas."

Buxton's face lit up. "Splendid! Would you be willing to present his message to the gathering?"

"I have no experience speaking in public," Mary said, "but I am willing to give it a try."

"Then I shall let our moderator know. I will return to you to let you know when you will have an opportunity to present Weatherstone's greeting." An argument escalating on the side of the auditorium drew his attention. "I must go. Best wishes for your endeavors. Thank you for your contributions to the advancement of freedom."

Mary and Margaret watched him go. They turned to each other, suppressing mirth, as they took brief leave from the auditorium.

"Pity Mr. Weatherstone could not be here. I am sure that the respect he has found here would please him," Margaret said.

"Well, you see what we can do. When you go to the West Indies, members of the abolitionist movement will find a way to have your reports published. I may be able to help, as well. Are you ready to travel?"

"You are a bad influence, you know," Margaret said.

Mary laughed but then turned serious. "Yes, I probably am. Someday my disregard for boundaries will turn out badly." She reflected a moment, and then turned to Margaret. "When does your ship leave?"

"One month hence, from Plymouth. But Elinor is quite set against my going."

Mary puckered her lips. "Then perhaps it is not to be for now. But you will go someday. Of that, I am certain."

* * *

Mary's missive was inserted into the day's program at eleven in the morning. She spoke with a strong voice. "Friends, I am humbled to bring you greetings from Joseph Weatherstone, who unfortunately is unable to attend this august gathering. I am honored to present some of his thoughts:

'Greetings, my dear brothers and sisters engaged in the great struggle upon us to bring liberty to all men. I regret that infirmities of age do not permit me to travel to greet you in person and I pray every day that your efforts will bear the desired fruit while I still dwell on this Earth. I will soon submit for publication my treatise on the divine imperative for the abolition of slavery, that most vile of blasphemies.

'For too long, sacred scriptures of Hebrews and Christians alike have been offered as support of the institution of slavery. But, as I have found by deep study these many years, there is no affirmative support, but merely acknowledgment of an existing system. Every book, every section of our sacred texts cries out for freedom, reaching upward and onward to a time when there is, as Paul preaches, no Greek or Jew, no master or slave.

'Why, one may ask, was there no overt call for abolition? My studies find that throughout the ancient world, such calls were common. But they were embers only; small sparks in a vast world acquiescing to human bondage. Their voices were unable to coalesce, unable to speak loud and clear in a world of darkness and ignorance.

'But now, my friends, now we are no longer solitary embers. We are many. We live in a world in which our words can travel in print, words that endure and reach the multitudes. We are no longer isolated, no longer capable of being cast aside and ignored. Our time has come. Our cause is just, our movement is founded on enduring principles, and our victory is inevitable.

'I look to Isaiah for my strength, 'It will come about after this that I will pour out My Spirit on all mankind; And your sons and daughters will prophesy, Your old men will dream dreams, Your young men will see visions.' My friends, you are those sons and daughters. You are those old men and young men. March forward and conquer in the name of humanity and the Lord.

Your devoted servant,
Joseph Weatherstone'"

Mary returned her papers to her portfolio as the room responded with applause. She took her seat next to Margaret, who reached over and embraced her.

"Well done, my friend. Joseph will be pleased."

* * *

By the time the meetings ended, Mary and Margaret were well known to most leaders of the abolition movement. Mary was sought for her connection to Joseph Weatherstone and she promised to pass their requests to him when next they met. Sir Thomas Buxton acquired a copy of Joseph Weatherstone's greetings and a copy of his treatise, which Buxton promised to publish.

The attendees pressed Margaret to provide reports on conditions throughout the Caribbean, particularly on Trinidad and Jamaica.

On Thursday morning, Mary walked with Margaret and Jane to their coach. "My dear, I am thankful that we met. I have a kindred spirit, a complement to my likes and preferences. When we confront strictures of this male world, we can look to each other for inspiration."

Margaret said, "We will. But did you notice that no one objected to a woman speaking prominently at yesterday's gathering? In fact, you were exceedingly well received."

"Ah, but I was presenting for Joseph Weatherstone."

"True," Margaret continued, "but soon enough, the world will know who *she* is."

They hugged and Margaret climbed into her coach, turned and leaned out the window. "Give my best to Mr. Weatherstone. And great good fortune with your complicated involvement."

Mary gave a small smile. "I will be seeing Joseph tomorrow night. I will pass on your greetings. As to that other matter, I promise you a full accounting only on your return from the Caribbean. Do keep in touch. The General Post Office services are becoming available throughout the Empire."

They clasped hands through the open window, breaking finally as Margaret and Jane's carriage pulled away.

* * *

Mary's coach departed three hours later. Her mind swirled with ideas for Joseph Weatherstone. She had recorded the names of all the scholars with whom she had spoken in order that Joseph could address their thoughts and concerns by name.

She found herself trembling at thoughts of her newfound reach and influence. She longed to return to William, to talk with him for hours, to resume their walks, to have him in her presence and her in his.

She thought of Margaret wrestling with the choice between her family and her freedom. Mary knew that she had supported dangerous ideas in Margaret's mind and realized that she would bear some responsibility should tragedy ensue.

* * *

While Jane dozed, Margaret sat quiet in deep thought through the return trip to Barton Park. They spent the night with Sir John and Lady Middleton, soliciting their feelings regarding her desires to travel. Returning to Barton Cottage in the morning, Margaret did not mention the voyage again, but talked of her encounters at the abolition meeting and of an invitation for a long visit to Pemberley assisting Miss Bennet with her publications for the movement.

These developments pleased Elinor.

As Margaret lay in her bed, unable to sleep, three words kept repeating through the night. "Three weeks hence."

Chapter Seven
Taking Wing

"Mr. Collins, you appear vexed," Charlotte said as she entered his library to announce the noon meal.

He took a deep breath. "It is a small concern. Some months the income of the parish is painfully close to our expenses, and this appears to be such a month. Do not fret, my love. Matters always seem to resolve themselves."

Charlotte pulled up the second chair, the chair added as Mary and Mr. Collins occupied more and more time collaborating in the room. "I do not fret, William. I am certain that finances will not be an impediment to your mission shepherding our congregants."

He leaned back in his chair with a puzzled smile.

"There is something I must tell you, a secret I have kept from you for fear of your disapproval. Beyond her ladyship's patronage and the offerings of the parish, *you* have contributed a great deal to the finances. I have collected your sermons, had them edited, and they are published — to considerable acclaim I should note."

He took a moment to recover. "My sermons? Published? How is this possible?"

She smiled as she gazed at the towering shelves of books. "I know you believe me indifferent to your passion for all things spiritual, but I have been your first listener throughout our marriage. Though I may not possess a theological education, I recognized your gift of insight and your keen understanding of holy matters. Some years ago, I had a conversation with a visitor traveling to visit his sister. He was a professor at Oxford University and he remarked with favor on your sermon that Sunday. He told me that your sermons would be well received in the academic world of religious studies. We began a correspondence, he made my acquaintance to a reputable publisher, and I have been providing copies of your sermons ever since."

"I am dumfounded. I had not noticed any of my sermons missing … and I do refer to them from time to time."

She nodded. "That is because I transcribed them for the publisher. I do not wish to seem mean spirited, but that was also essential because your penmanship is dismal."

He laughed. "I had never thought of another reading my

sermons."

"Besides, your grammatical constructs were not satisfactory for a proper printed work. I secured the services of an editor, a Mr. Broadman of Oxfordshire."

"Broadman? I scarce can take it in." He swept his arm around the room. "I have many tomes that he has edited. That he would be willing to entertain my work pleases me more than I can express. But I thought he left England for America."

"Works. In all he edited seven volumes before leaving for America. He hewed very closely to your writing."

"Seven? My word! You must know how grateful I am that a publisher would continue after an initial printing. Do you know if they sold many copies?"

Charlotte relaxed as she continued, "The initial printing was fifty copies. The sales were slow at the beginning since you had no name in academic circles. But within a few months, those early readers returned and enquired after more volumes. The second volume printing was two hundred and sold out within a bit more than a month. Each following volume has had a larger run and better sales, the seventh volume comprising at least six hundred copies. The income from those sales is kept in safe accounts and from time to time some has gone to cover expenses in the parish."

He shook his head. "My love, I have underestimated and undervalued your skills most shamefully. I was unaware of your financial acumen."

"Credit for that belongs to our dear friend, Elizabeth. She procured the services of honorable bankers and accountants. She is also responsible in part for your new editor, the one who completed volumes eight and nine. Their receptions have even outpaced the previous seven."

"My joy is boundless. Do I know of him?"

"I believe you do. 'His' name is Mary Bennet."

He began laughing and continued for some time. Finally restored to calm, he said, "This development is wonderful. Everything fits; everything makes sense — all our discussions, her questions, her interest in the languages! From our collaboration as Joseph Weatherstone, I am certain her ministrations on my pages have lifted them to a higher plane."

"Then you are not angry with our secret enterprise? I prepared for your displeasure."

He looked surprised. "Why would I be displeased? The labors that are my passion are now shared with those I respect. And you tell me that the enterprise has brought in a few pounds for the parish."

She shook her head. "We imagined you would take offense that women had so intruded on your realm."

"I would have in times past, wouldn't I?" He frowned. "It is sad, but your concerns originate in our society's attitudes much akin to bondage. I have begun to realize that the female mind is no less capable than the male. Perhaps the winds that are stripping away the legitimacy of slavery will also tear at that injustice."

Charlotte smiled. "It saddens me to end this blissful exchange, but it is time to eat." She reached out her hand and they walked to the dining room. "And, the income has not been a few pounds, but hundreds of pounds."

"It is as if I were in a dream from which I do not wish to awaken," he said, and leaned over and kissed his wife.

* * *

The Sunday after Mary's return, Charlotte and Elizabeth met as customary at Pemberley.

"Has Mr. Collins discovered your publishing successes?" Elizabeth asked.

Charlotte laid her needlework down in her lap. "Funny you mention that. I brought up the subject Wednesday, dreading he would discover it on his own. Though I feared he would react badly, he seemed not the least troubled. As a matter of fact, the only bit of the news that surprised him was the amount his publications have earned. He had worried of late that the parish treasury was getting a bit thin and I revealed to him that some of the income had gone to that upkeep. I dare say he was pleased in the extreme."

"Well, that is a welcome turn of events. And did you inform him that Mary has been part of this conspiracy?"

"I did. He said it made sense in light of her intense interest in the subjects and particularly the languages. He asked me not to let Mary know we have told him. He wishes to enjoy that pleasure."

They both laughed. Elizabeth said, "I hope that she is not making herself a nuisance."

Charlotte shook her head. "Oh, no, having her about provides him an outlet and sounding board for his deepest thoughts. As hard as I try, I am not as engaged in the fine points of theology as she. He seems quite satisfied in his role as a teacher. He is more at ease now, and …" She broke off with a smile, coloring as she did.

"Yes?" Elizabeth leaned forward.

Charlotte bit her lip. "He has become rather romantic. We have even had … relations … for the first time since a few weeks after our wedding. William is a changed man, and I am most happy about that."

Elizabeth smiled. "And I am most happy for you, too."

* * *

Mary finished tidying the pulpit area and met William at the back of the chapel, portfolio tucked beneath her arm. Together they surveyed the interior of the sanctuary, a habit that had become routine after nearly being observed by one of the old maid parishioners, quite prone to gossip, as they embraced a few weeks back. Satisfied that they were alone, they kissed a moment and each smiled.

"Was my sermon to your satisfaction, my love?" he asked.

She flashed him a coy smile and extended her hand in the direction of Hunsford Cottage. "More lively than in the past. You kept the Kingston family's attention more than half way through. But — as we have discussed before — you must still condense your presentation."

"You are quite right, but the points — the supporting references — they are all important."

She tossed her head. "Of course. But we have been over this many times, my love. Your works are rich with redundant supports, perhaps twice as many as necessary. After all, in this place you are not trying to overwhelm a critic. You need only enlighten your congregants, who are engaging with you more and more each day."

"Can that be true?"

"Yes, sir, it is. I was at market Friday last and overheard Mrs. Kingston and Mrs. Reed discussing forgiveness using several of the points from your last sermon."

Mr. Collins smiled. "You know better than I how I have been insensitive to my listeners in the past. I knew not how to make myself at one with them. You have helped me do that."

They approached the path leading to the cottage. As they strolled, she said, "It is not easy to trade places with members of your flock — or anyone else, for that matter. It is not easy to tame the chaotic thoughts of one's mind into words that transmit to others the essence of those thoughts."

He walked in silence for a bit. "But you seem to possess that gift."

"Perhaps a gift, perhaps simply practice. I dwell in a privileged world between your scholarship and the simpler lives of others. I do not yet have the benefit of your schooling or your vast reading. You are many years beyond me on those counts. Neither have you had to confront the critical scholars as I have with your recent works on abolition."

He wrinkled his brow. "I am sorry for that. My education did not include much confrontation."

Mary brightened. "Oh, do not be sorry, sir. I rather enjoy it. When I presented your work as that of Joseph Weatherstone, my participation in the clash of ideas was exhilarating. It made me most happy. Some, but not all, could not see me. They envisioned a sickly old man with whiskers, I suspect. But they saw and heard the ideas, and I was the one voicing them and defending them — and, in some cases, modifying them. We can discuss those later."

Rounding the boxwood, they executed their practiced scan and proceeded to the cottage.

"You amaze me, Mary," he said. Then he paused in reflection. "No. That is not exactly correct. You did amaze me early on. But early on I did not appreciate the depth of your understanding. In my isolation, I did not appreciate that others, including women, could grasp the concepts and philosophies I struggled with. I was wrong and you have shown me that — as no other has. You have helped me to understand my wife as well. You have taught me to appreciate the dedication and caring that she and the two of you together have exercised. I appreciate what you have done more than you can know."

"Charlotte is an upright and sensitive woman. It is only natural that she deserves your respect."

They sat down at the table. Mary opened her portfolio, set aside the day's sermon papers, and laid out her annotated copies of the *Weatherstone Manifesto.* Collins laughed. "Joseph Weatherstone has lived quite a life for one of such ephemeral existence."

Mary nodded. "Yes, he has. And he has engaged some of the great minds among the abolitionists. See here — some comments from William Wilberforce and Hannah More."

William grew serious. "Wilberforce?"

"And Hannah More."

"This is all moving very fast," he said. "People will be searching for Joseph Weatherstone and will not be satisfied until they have found him."

"Or her. Do remember that Weatherstone is both of us. Aside from the Greek, he is as much me as he is you. I held my own at the gathering. As did Hannah More. As did Margaret Dashwood. The acceptance of slavery is a construct of the mind and the mind can abolish that acceptance. Slavery is not simply a matter of race or class, William. You have said so yourself, and we are ready to challenge slavery, in whatever form it takes."

She sat close by him. As she turned the leaves of her manuscript, their hands touched. Mary looked up at William, her face flushed. He stared back at her, biting his lip. She moved toward him until their foreheads touched. She kissed him. At first, his hands gripped the arms of his chair. But finally, he placed a gentle finger on her chin and nudged her head back.

William rose from his chair and addressed her, "Mary, my dearest sweet Mary. This is the realization of my greatest desires— and my greatest fears. I must put a stop to our intimacy before it is too late, before we regret our actions."

Mary looked up, tears welling in her eyes. "Are you rejecting me, then? Are we at an end?"

"No, Mary, on the contrary," he replied, managing a smile. "Oh, Mary, my dear sweet woman, I can no more reject you than life itself. But I am married and I am honor bound to be a good and loving husband. You, Mary, have in no small part made me realize the importance of my marital duties. You have inspired in me a sense of passion and longing I did not know possible. You have awakened in me a desire to listen, to care, and to attend to the feelings of my wife. You have challenged me to be a better human being in ways that I had never considered."

Mary stared down at the table, lips trembling. She put her elbows on the table and rested her head in her fists as tears flowed.

Collins continued, "But make no mistake about it. My feelings for you are strong and passionate as well. I would be dishonest to call my feelings anything but love. But for the vagaries of time and chance, you and I might have been thrown together and matched. But we were not."

"How then shall we go on, William?" she sobbed, tears still streaming down her face. "I love you. My heart aches for you. When we are apart, my mind is occupied longing for our next meeting. I know that my desires are out of place, but they are real. What shall we do?"

He sat down across the table from her. "I do not know." He smiled. "There, you see your influence on me? Before we met, before our long talks together, I would never have admitted to any uncertainty. You have changed me, Mary Bennet. Charlotte has noted the changes in me, though I have not given you the credit you deserve — to my shame. You, as well, have noted her changed feelings. For that I am thankful. I love you and, on my life, would never hurt you. What shall we do? I do not know."

Mary wiped her tears on her sleeve. "I have been foolish and impetuous. In my desire for you, I tried to impress you. I have embraced your love of learning and your imprisoned passion for justice, and have given them voice. I — we — have become a new person — Joseph Weatherstone. He would not exist but for our combined passionate minds. And now he comes to naught."

He watched Mary as he pondered. After some time, he murmured, "He does not have to."

She tilted her head.

"Do you think that we could continue our work together?" he offered. "Is it possible for two people with such passion to pursue a lofty purpose while resisting the desires of the flesh?"

In the enveloping quiet, only the tick of the clock and occasional sound of wind outside intruded.

At length Mary sighed. "Yes, we could. I do not know from where I shall draw strength, but I would rather be with you sharing a noble journey than being apart from you. On reflection, I admire your strength, William. That is part of what draws me to you. I appreciate the integrity of your convictions and hope that I may grow into that strength myself."

Mary became calm. She gave a sweet smile. "But I shall still call you William, and you will still call me Mary. We may not be intimate lovers, but we are still of one mind. That will not change."

He smiled sheepishly. "That is fair. And Joseph Weatherstone will reap the benefits of that one mind."

Mary smiled a winsome smile. Then she spread out their papers, and for the remainder of the afternoon they continued polishing the *Manifesto*.

* * *

Margaret protested. "Elinor, I do not need a babysitter. I am a grown woman."

"You are a young woman of nineteen in a rough and dangerous world. Jane will accompany you. It is only proper. I want to be assured of your safety," Elinor repeated.

"No!"

"Then I shall forbid you to travel." Elinor remained every bit as firm as Margaret.

"You do not trust me, Elinor."

"I do not trust the world, Margaret. The world is filled with those who would take advantage of a young woman traveling alone. The very fact of a young woman traveling alone raises questions enough. You shall take Jane with you, or you shall not go."

Margaret sat down on her bed, scowling, and crossed her arms. She remained so, stoic and silent.

"Very well," said Elinor. "I will be downstairs when you have cooled down and come to your senses." Elinor left the room.

In the ensuing quiet, Margaret surveyed her domain. This room had been the center of her world from the time they arrived at Barton Cottage until the abolitionist gathering. Here were her maps, her travel books, and her atlases. Here she dreamed of other worlds. After a time of contemplation, she rose and walked to her window. Winter gales roiled the surf, and a chill wind chased gray clouds. In other worlds, it was sunny and warm. Right now … this very minute. Those worlds lush and green and warm, set in sapphire seas with golden sand beaches, where the air smelled of spices.

In this world, it was gray and cold. The sea was gray and cold. The beach was no beach but a shore of stones, gray and cold, where the air smelled of … nothing she could name, but the very smell was gray and cold.

Jane had cared for Margaret since Margaret was a child and Jane a girl of fifteen or so. They loved each other as sisters and were loyal in duties and secrets as well. Each had stood by the other through a history of misadventures that were never brought to the attention of adults. But in the matter of travel, Margaret knew Jane was more inclined to Elinor's view of the world than to Margaret's.

Jane's view on the dangers arose in part from experiences she had as a servant on family business. Across all classes, there were some men who felt free to address her with crude aggression. She had defended herself well and taken full advantage of the protection of the Colonel and family. Several of her tormentors fled the area in the face of the family response. Jane enlightened Margaret on means of physical resistance. These included the techniques that Margaret had deployed with painful success against John Chamberlain. Jane approved of that.

After a couple of hours, Margaret came down the stairs to find Elinor busy making bread. Jane prepared dinners for the most part, but Elinor enjoyed making bread and produced a particularly artistic and tasty loaf.

Elinor looked up. "Are we come to our senses?"

"*We* are constrained to accept a minder in order to make the journey."

"Not the enthusiastic response I would have liked, but a step toward reason. When do you need to leave?"

"I am expected in five days," Margaret said. "The trip should take two and a half days."

"To Derbyshire? I should think it more like three or four."

"The roads are much improved, Elinor. I saw that when visiting Oxford."

"I am glad to hear of it. Jane is quite happy to go with you on your adventure. I shall give her some money for board while you visit Pemberley. You may proceed with your preparations."

* * *

Margaret packed in less than a day, putting her favorite atlas and travelogue in the bottom of her largest trunk. She went on to watch Jane pack, talking at length about the geography of Derbyshire. Jane was neither eager nor reluctant to be traveling. Rather, she looked forward to an adventure with young Margaret, wherever that might take them.

They boarded the coach for Crawley, where Margaret would book their coach northward to Derbyshire. As they rode to their first station, Jane enquired about Mary and her family, the abolition movement, and details about their future times at Pemberley.

"You should be happy I travel with you, Miss Dashwood. You did not pack for the winter weather. You will be going through your wardrobe in a matter of days, I should think."

"You are right, of course. I have had so few travel experiences. We can pick up a little more in Crawley between coaches." Margaret felt uncomfortable as Jane watched her expression.

Crawley was a busy town for its size. As a crossroad for travel in southern England, the town prospered from the heavy flow of traffic.

Margaret and Jane stepped down from the coach and had their trunks taken to a bench in the station.

"I saw a little shop about two blocks from here," Margaret said, pointing in the direction from which they had arrived. "Here is some money. If you would get me a cloak, that should make up for some of my light packing. While you do that, I will get our passage north."

Jane counted out the notes. "I fancy this is far more than I will need, Miss Dashwood."

"Then get something for yourself." Margaret smiled. "We want to arrive in style, after all. I shall stay here with the luggage."

Margaret watched as Jane went into the lane and Margaret turned toward the counter. The shop she had seen was about four blocks away.

* * *

When Jane returned from the shop with Margaret's elegant cloak and a scarf for herself, she found Margaret's trunk missing. She searched the station and area outside, finding no trace of the young woman. Returning to the bench and her trunk, she saw an envelope protruding beneath. She opened it and found a ticket and letter, which read:

> Dear Jane,
> I am sorry to abandon you like this. I know that it is not
> fair. But where I am going, you cannot follow. I will be all
> right. I have been planning this move for many years and
> know what I am doing. The ticket will get you back to
> Barton Cottage. Please assure Elinor that I will be fine and
> that I will write often.
> Margaret

Jane looked at the ticket, then dropped her arms and shook her head. "Petulant child. She will be her own ruin for sure."

Jane put on the scarf and Margaret's elegant cloak and walked over to the counter.

"Yes, ma'am. May I help you?" The clerk smiled.

"Did a young woman with blonde curls stop by a short while ago?"

"Yes, she did," he replied.

"Where was she headed?"

The clerk frowned. "Why do you wish to know?"

Jane adopted a sweet smile. "She is an old friend of mine, and I hoped to meet her during her stopover. But, unfortunately, I was detained and appear to have missed her. Can you not tell me her destination?"

"I see. She left a quarter hour ago for Plymouth."

* * *

For one of the few times in her life, Margaret felt fear. Plymouth proved a rough-and-tumble city. The population seemed mostly men, mostly sailors. Many showed little in the way of civility. She hired a cart and young man to haul her trunk from Plymouth Station to the sprawling dock area. She hesitated to ask for help from the burly men plying the docks. Along the way, many accosted her with catcalls. She had inquired first at the address Robert had given her, but the innkeeper said that Robert had left two days earlier for his ship. Upon seeing the hundreds of ships in port, she realized that finding *Lady Bridget* would be a challenge.

Margaret stopped to enquire directions from a group of women at one street corner, but they were sneering and rude and in no mood to help her kind. After traveling past three wharves, she met a merchant delivering stores to one of the ships. He said *Lady Bridget* berthed about five wharves down and two thirds of the way out on the dock. A half hour later, she stood on the boardwalk looking up at *Lady Bridget*. She paid the young man for his service, and he set her trunk down, departing with his empty cart. She saw an older woman walking on the deck above. "Hello!" Margaret called.

The woman stopped and leaned over the railing. "Yes, dearie?"

"I am looking for Captain Robert Johnson."

"Aye. And who may I say is calling?"

Margaret shouted. "Tell him it is Margaret Dashwood from

Devon."

The woman turned away for a moment, but turned back to her. "Would you be the interpreter?"

It pleased Margaret to hear that recognition. "Yes, ma'am, I am."

The woman hurried away. Robert Johnson appeared at the top of the gangplank and hurried down to the dock. "Miss Dashwood!" He looked down at the trunk. "So you will be joining us after all?"

"I am. I was afraid I would miss you."

"You almost did. We sail with the tide tomorrow morning. I had not heard from your sister and thought that you would not be going. When we were last together at Delaford, I sensed that your sister and the rest of the family were not inclined to approve your travel."

Margaret opened the book she carried and extracted a letter, which she handed to Robert. He read the note, written in an elegant feminine hand:

My dear Captain Johnson,

My sister has prevailed on us to approve her travel with your crew. I regret the tardiness of our reply but, as you must know, this is a difficult decision for all of us. I pray you will put her to useful work and return her safely home to us.

Yours,
Elinor and Edward Ferrars

"Splendid!" Robert said. "But surely you did not travel alone all this way. It is hardly a safe journey for a lone woman."

Margaret began, "I had only a little …" She gazed down the wharf, and spotted the figure of a woman, accompanied by another young man pulling a cart. Margaret grew silent.

Robert turned to the same direction and waited.

The woman came up and dismissed her helper. She squinted at Margaret. "Miss Dashwood …," she said.

"Jane …."

Jane looked at Robert, and then at *Lady Bridget*, then back at Margaret, pausing a very long, very uncomfortable time. Finally she asked, "Is this our ship?"

Chapter Eight
No Turning Back

William and Mary made considerable progress on the *Manifesto*. Collins was now satisfied that their work was rigorous in its scholarship and theology and Mary appreciated its clarity and accessibility.

In the late afternoon, they suspended their work out of fatigue.

"This is a good and meaningful endeavor, Mary," he said. "May I retrieve the additional references later in the week, after I have completed my sermon preparations?"

"Of course. And I suggest you have Charlotte look over the writing as well. Please put no pressure on her, but watch after her reaction. If we have succeeded in our task, she should enjoy reading it enough to finish without other encouragement."

"As you wish, Madame."

Mary chuckled. "I am still 'Mademoiselle.' But thank you."

They gathered their pages, putting them in proper order. Afterwards, she bundled against the late afternoon chill. "There is no turning back now, William. When Joseph's ideas are loosed, the world will tremble." Following a warm embrace, she headed off on foot for Pemberley.

* * *

Charlotte arrived by carriage about an hour later. He greeted her with kisses and an embrace, and assisted with her cloak. He set out a plate of jam and biscuits, offering her tea. Charlotte smiled.

"When you are settled, and if you are not too weary from today's adventures, you may wish to glance at our work for today. But only if you like." He set their papers on a table near Charlotte's reading chair.

Again she smiled. "That would be lovely. In a bit."

Charlotte and William sat at table together, sharing biscuits while she recounted her afternoon with Elizabeth Darcy. Charlotte allowed that she expected to receive soon proofs of his last collection of sermons from their printer in London. This volume would have the highest printing run yet, as the printer now sells out his entire production run.

"It would never have happened but for you and for Mary. I am amazed," he said.

After their small repast, she took her seat and began reading

Scripture Cries Out for Freedom. She looked up after reading the first page. "Your new title is a considerable improvement."

He sat in his chair with a Latin text and concentrated with difficulty, glancing up to watch as Charlotte read. She nodded from time to time and continued through to the end at a brisk pace. When she finished, she looked up to him. "This is wonderful. I for one am convinced. Joseph Weatherstone's arguments will soon carry the day."

William Collins smiled.

* * *

In Plymouth, Monday morning dawned gray and cold, with a brisk westerly wind. Margaret arose early in excitement. She took a small bit of breakfast meat and hurried on deck to watch a beehive of preparation. She offered her assistance, but Mrs. Dunsford recommended that she simply watch today.

"Sure, ya be handling the riggin' soon enough. We all pull our weight around here and you be no exception. But it can be dangerous work. There be many a one-handed sailor, a one-legged sailor, or a one-eyed sailor, sometimes all in one. For the present, you and your lady keep off to one side and watch."

"Yes, ma'am." Margaret turned to see Jane coming on deck and in her direction.

They moved to the rail, Margaret watching deck hands tying and untying lines, securing hatches, and making final arrangements with line handlers from the dock. Jane faced the other direction, leaning on the rail, watching the bustling dock and wharves.

"Good morning, Miss Dashwood."

"Good morning, Jane."

"Have you let your sister know your true destination?"

Margaret paused and looked down. "No. I will post her from our first stop in Jamaica."

Jane continued to scan the port activity. "I see. That will be quite some time, and I'm certain Mrs. Ferrars would be concerned by such a long time not hearing from you. Many weeks each way, if I recall our geography lessons. I would expect your family to send someone to Pemberley to find out what happened. And when that man returns and reports that you are not there ..."

Margaret stared ahead, jaw set.

"That is why I took the liberty of posting them and letting them know that I would be watching after you."

Margaret jerked her head in Jane's direction. "I do wish you had not done that."

Jane remained composed, still watching the docks. After a long time, she said, "And of course, we all wish you had not run away. There is really no other term for it, is there? You have vexed them most thoroughly. At least they will not waste time and worry thinking that we vanished on our way to Miss Mary Bennet's."

"What precisely did you tell them in your letter?"

Jane looked up at low gray clouds. "Let me think. Hmmm. I seem to be having difficulty remembering exactly. Shall we return? We could be back at Barton Cottage before the post arrives, and intercept the letter." She turned and watched Margaret for a minute before returning to her study of the port. "Or perhaps not. So, here we are, two young women who have never gone to sea setting out on a journey with no guarantee of safety or success. We do not have approval from your family. Nay, we are traveling against their express wishes. I think you shall have to await our return to read that letter."

They fell quiet.

About eight in the morning, Captain Johnson judged his ship seaworthy and ready to sail. He had arisen well before dawn and checked and re-checked every aspect of *Lady Bridget*, inside and out, fore to aft, port to starboard. He mounted the forecastle and looked aft, where first mate Mr. Dunsford waited for his command.

Captain Johnson looked up to see topsails billowing at the preferred angle. He drew in a deep breath and shouted, "Cast off all lines!" accompanied by a broad wave of his arms. On the dock, men slipped mooring lines from their cleats and tossed the lines toward *Lady Bridget*. The deck hands hauled in lines, wrapping them and securing them to capstans. *Lady Bridget* drifted into Plymouth harbor at a walking pace. Once well-cleared of the dock, Captain Johnson called out, "Come about! Come about to two-three-zero!"

The helmsman answered, "Aye, aye. Come about to two-three-zero!"

The quartermaster answered, "Aye, aye. Come about to two-three-zero!"

Lady Bridget began turning, ever so slowly, toward open sea. For a few moments, the topsail made a loud clatter while the ship faced dead into the wind. The sail caught again as deck hands altered the masts' orientations. Margaret sensed growing forward movement as

Plymouth's wharves slipped astern. *Lady Bridget* cleared Plymouth's breakwater, leaving behind swarms of service craft.

Clear of the harbor, *Lady Bridget* began her slow rocking motion. After about half an hour, Captain Johnson still stood at his position on the forecastle, scanning the horizon with a long glass. He lowered his glass and called out, "Let fall the mainsail! Set sail!"

All hands on deck answered, "Aye, aye! Let fall the mainsail! Set sail!" With practiced grace each man executed his task unfurling and securing great sheets of canvas. The ship surged ahead, kicking up foam and generating a bow wake. After a period of adjusting and re-orienting masts, the first mate called out, "Underway, making way! Full rigged and running!"

The Helmsman shouted, "Steering two-three-zero. Rudder amidships!"

Captain Johnson answered, "Steering two-three-zero, aye. Maintain course." The forward lookout came up to him and saluted. Johnson handed the lookout his long glass and returned the lookout's salute.

Captain Johnson approached Margaret and Jane. He bowed. "Miss Dashwood." She curtsied. He turned to Jane. "Miss ..."

"Jane, sir."

He nodded. "As you prefer. We are a family here, and the formal lines of land are relaxed, except at command times, such as getting underway."

She curtsied. "Thank you, sir. It is Jane Moseby, but just Jane suits me." She turned to Margaret.

"So I have known her all my life. In truth, with the many changes now afoot, I should prefer just Margaret, if you please."

Jane nodded. "We are in a new world, heading for the New World."

"Right! Jolly good. Keep on your toes at all times. We are off to a good start. Fair winds. If the weather holds, we will see land again in thirty-five to forty days."

Jane raised an eyebrow. "And if the weather does not hold?"

Johnson laughed. "Then it will take longer. The sea can be cruel. Our ship is sound, our crew seasoned, but we are always at the mercy of the sea." He glanced about. "I must make my first rounds. Mrs. Dunsford — Harriet — will begin your orientation. In the weeks ahead, you will learn your watches and duties of life in a small boat on a large sea. Each of us wants to be competent in as many tasks as possible. No one should be indispensible."

He took a moment to appear serious. The two women nodded.

"And Margaret, when you feel you have your sea legs, you can begin preparing documents for our trades in Martinique and Puerto Rico."

Margaret curtsied again as Johnson walked away and down a ladder leading to spaces below.

Jane looked down at Margaret's shoes. "Sea legs?"

Margaret giggled. "At sea, the ship is always moving beneath us — rocking, pitching. I have read that it can take some time to become accustomed to the constant motion. Until that time, one can experience discomfort, even nausea. It is called sea sickness and is not pleasant, I understand."

They both strode to the rail and gazed out.

"Seems pleasant enough," Jane said.

"Yes it does," Margaret replied.

"There is no turning back now."

"No. Shall we go see Harriet Dunsford and see what she would have us do?"

* * *

Mrs. Dunsford assigned them duties right away. Under Roger Dunsford's tutelage, they began their sounding and security watches. He taught them the numbering system for the ship's interior segments. Lamp in hand, they checked all corners and recesses of *Lady Bridget*, looking for leaks or unsecured hatches. After each check, they entered their results in a logbook and reported back to the officer on deck. Sounding and security watch changed every six hours, day and night.

They came to enjoy the smell of pine tar and pitch in the spaces below and learned the nature of their southbound cargo — fabric and machinery from Britain for islanders, which would be replaced by spices and tobacco on the return trip.

* * *

Elinor wailed as Edward returned from town. She could make no reply to his pleading, instead handing him a letter:

Sir and Ma'am,

As I accompanied Miss Dashwood on our journey, she concocted a ruse, sending me to purchase some clothing in Crawley. As I did so, she apparently took passage to Plymouth, with obvious intention of traveling with Captain Robert Johnson's party. Though she has a considerable head start, I shall endeavor to catch up with her and dissuade her from her plan. I will do all in my power to keep her safe and will communicate my results as soon as I am able.

Your obedient servant,
Jane

Chapter Nine
Learning

Mary finished gathering Mr. Collins's sermon pages and walked toward the door as congregants greeted him. She took a seat on a nearby pew and waited, looking about at the church's colorful banners and windows. She pulled tight her coat against the winter chill in the sanctuary.

A tall gentleman with long gray hair, a stranger, was the last person in line. He approached Collins as the pastor held out his hand in greeting.

"I am searching for Miss Mary Bennet," the man said without extending his own hand. His face was stern, his tone severe.

Mary started at the mention of her name, but regained her composure and continued observing him from behind.

Collins smiled as he looked into the stranger's eyes. "Good Sabbath to you, sir. William Collins at your service. May I inquire why you are seeking one of my parishioners?"

The man frowned. "I am trying to contact Joseph Weatherstone. He seems an elusive character. Your Miss Bennet has been in contact with him, and we would like to learn his location."

Mr. Collins looked around, moving a little to the side before answering the man. "'We'? Excuse me, I do not think we have been properly introduced." He extended his hand again. "William Collins, Mr. …"

"That is not important. It is urgent that we find Joseph Weatherstone."

"I see." Collins nodded. "Well, it has been nigh two and a half, three years since old Joseph came to services here. His health is failing, you know. When last I visited him, he was talking of going to Brighton … or Portsmouth. Something about the salt air cleansing his congestion." He turned to Mary. "Anna, do you recall whether it was Brighton or Portsmouth?"

"I believe it was Portsmouth, Mr. Collins." She turned to the stranger. "I remember thinking that he would be fortunate indeed to survive the trip — he was coughing something awful. But then, he had a number of strong ideas about things like salt air and herbals. Are you familiar with him, sir?"

"Humph. Joseph Weatherstone is a dangerous man. He owns to

a great many daft ideas that threaten our society. He appears to have entrusted some of his seditious writing to this Miss Bennet."

Mary laughed. "That would not surprise me, sir. Mary Bennet seems to catch the eye of many an old man — insufferable flirt, very engaging. But now that you mention manuscripts, it may explain why we have not seen her around these parts for several weeks. She made several trips to Oxford in the last year. Are you familiar with Oxford, sir?"

"No."

"There is a publisher there, or at least the office of a publisher. I recall her going on about a printer on Hyde Street or High Street. She may have carried his writings there when he was too ill to travel."

"Do you know the name of the printer?" the stranger asked.

Mary frowned. "I do not believe she said. I have a pretty good memory, so I would remember if she had mentioned it. Is Oxford a large city?"

"As I told you, miss, I am not familiar with Oxford," he grumbled.

"Right."

Collins interrupted. "I have several colleagues who studied at Oxford. It is not large. I venture none of the streets host more than a few dozen shops."

"If I should encounter Miss Bennet, what does she look like?"

Collins smiled. "Rosy cheeks and long blonde hair."

Mary nodded and added, "Usually plaited in braids."

He turned to leave, his long coat swirling with the turn. He gripped a cane, but did not appear to need it for walking.

"When she returns, may we give her your particulars that she might contact you?" Collins asked.

"We will find her." He advanced toward the heavy back doors, but stopped and turned. "Be on your guard about Joseph Weatherstone's treasonous ideas. And do mind your preaching, Mr. Collins. That old man's followers may find life … difficult … in the days ahead." He made his way out of the church and mounted a large black stallion, coming about with a sharp tug on the reins.

As the sound of the trotting horse faded, Mary raced between the ancient pews toward the front of the church.

"Where are you going?" Collins called.

"The bell tower! There are windows in each direction at the

second landing."

"Be careful!"

"Of course!" she assured.

Collins approached the door and peered out into the empty churchyard, gray and windy. He paced until Mary returned, panting from her run.

"He is headed south. I watched until he crested the rise. I did not sense he knows that I live at Pemberley. Otherwise, I should have expected him to ride east."

"I would agree … Anna."

She laughed. "That was quite clever, William. Perhaps we should be writing adventures together, instead. Safer, maybe?"

"Let us return home quickly. Are the other doors secured?"

She nodded.

They walked down the lane at a faster pace than normal, pausing twice to listen for horses. The only sound was the wind that blew fallen leaves across their path.

"Whatever his intentions, I doubt they were benevolent," she said.

Collins nodded. "True. In particular, I do not like that he would not give his name nor clarify who 'we' are."

"When Margaret Dashwood and I were in Oxford, several participants spoke of ruffians making threats, ruffians in the service of colonial slave holders. As of the meeting, no one had experienced any violence or come to harm, but then we have progressed in the cause a great deal in a very short time since the meeting. Oh, William, I fear I have brought danger to our quiet corner of the world."

As they approached the cottage, Collins stopped and drew in a deep breath. "I would be dishonest if I did not acknowledge that it seems you are a chosen target, but you have fought in your way for righteous principles, principles that deserve defenders. I, for one, have been much too meek. Whoever these people are, they can prevail only when the rest of us are unwilling to stand for good against evil."

He faced her and took her hands. "I must step up to my duties, and do what can be done to join the fight." He looked to the cottage. "For now we must warn the others. Do you suppose we have endangered that printer in Oxford?"

Mary shook her head. "Our publisher is in London. As best I know, there is no printer on High Street in Oxford, nor any Hyde

Street in Oxford at all."

He grinned. "Well, that is both fortunate and unfortunate. We have endangered no one in Oxford, but our grim visitor is likely to return to us, disappointed and angry."

Entering the cottage, they found Charlotte and Elizabeth in the dining room. They were finishing a small meal of meat and vegetables and had been talking. The small fire lent a cozy feel to the room.

Charlotte looked up. "My dears, why the grim faces?"

"We encountered a most unpleasant visitor at the church," Mr. Collins replied.

"By any chance, was it that gray man sitting at the back?" she asked.

"The very one. He asked for Mary. He and the person or people he works for are trying to silence Joseph Weatherstone, it seems. They believe Mary knows where he is."

Elizabeth frowned. "But Joseph Weatherstone is not a real person."

"They are not aware of that," he said, "but Weatherstone's ideals are very real and are powerful enough to be a peril to them."

Elizabeth turned to Mary. "Did he threaten you?"

She shook her head and smiled, looking up to William. "Mr. Collins was very quick and clever. He addressed me as 'Anna' and asked me where the old and ill Joseph Weatherstone had gone on the coast. When that man inquired about me, William described Mary — me — as possessed of rosy cheeks and blonde hair." She laughed. "I added braids and suggested that Mary might be in Oxford visiting Weatherstone's publisher. He seemed little interested in the pale, dark-haired Anna, left us, and rode off on the south road."

"But you expect him to return," Charlotte said.

Collins nodded. "Quite likely, after some time searching Oxford and perhaps Portsmouth. He seemed quite determined and was loathe to share any details of his associates, referring only to 'we' several times. I do not know how long it may be before he discovers that Anna is Mary, but I have little doubt that he will."

"Does he connect Mary with Pemberley?" Elizabeth asked.

Mary shook her head. "Not yet. He spoke of me as Mary Bennet, but appears to have learned my name from word circulating elsewhere."

"What are we to do?" Charlotte asked.

Collins shook his head. "Alas, the community — the village and the countryside — will have to prepare. The institution of slavery is not ending without turmoil. Though we thought ourselves outside the fray, the persistence of slavery's evil has come to us."

"Elizabeth, do you suppose Mr. Darcy would lend his wise counsel to our plight?" Collins asked.

She smiled, reaching out to take her sister's hand. "Indeed he will. He has not said anything to you, Mary, but he has to me. He is very proud of what you and Mr. Collins are doing. Beneath that reserved exterior, I suspect he longs to be a Joseph Weatherstone."

* * *

Eight days into the voyage, *Lady Bridget* sliced through the sea on her southbound course. About five in the afternoon, Jane leaned on the railing in her accustomed spot. She had loosened her brown hair, letting the breeze play with her long tresses. She gazed out over the expanse of ocean as it took on the hues of approaching sunset. Her face bore the trace of a serene smile as her light shawl fluttered around her. She turned, seeing Robert approaching and taking what had become his accustomed spot to her left.

He looked out, too, finally volunteering, "A beautiful evening."

She nodded. "Yes. Every time I come here, it is different. This evening, see how the waves are so dark, like carved sculptures. Not blue except where we have stirred the wake. And the waves are larger than yesterday."

"True. This is one of the reasons I so love the sea. Constantly changing her mood. So often, like this evening, ever changing her beauty." He was calm as they watched together for a while.

"Have you spent most of your life at sea?" she asked.

"Indeed. I was nearly born at sea. My mother sailed with my father, and she was quite with child with me when they made harbor in Jamaica. I was born the next day in Kingston and was back aboard ship for the return trip to England two days later."

"It may be none of my business, but where is your mother now?"

"No, you are good to ask. She died a few days after giving birth to my sister. Though her loss devastated my father for some time, the sea called him back, and in a real sense healed him. My sister and I grew up aboard ship. Kitty married a ship captain out of Portsmouth. They have two children with another on the way and they seem vastly happy. I guess it runs in our family. Father has since remarried — a gentle woman named Geneviève in Martinique. She is not a seafarer, but they are together for three or four months out of the year. They seen quite comfortable with that arrangement and I have a brother and another sister through them." He turned to her. "What about your family?"

Lady Bridget continued her rocking, filling the evening with the pleasant soft sounds of creaking wood and foaming wake.

"My mother and father died when I was very young. I barely remember them — only little snippets of time. My aunts and uncles did not have the resources to take me in."

"I am very sorry." Robert bit his lower lip.

"Do not be. Though I would have liked to know my parents, I was given over to the Dashwood family as a servant. Sometimes fortune smiles on us. They have been everything a family could be and more. To this day, I have been treated more as a child of the family than as a servant. My primary duties have been to be a big sister to Margaret and keep her out of trouble. That has been a full time task for most of my life."

Robert laughed, his face wrinkled with an all-consuming smile. "I sensed that. You show a most protective and loving friendship toward her …" He grew quiet as they continued together gazing on the water, now less distinct in the gathering dusk. "Among other things — I am not sure how to put this delicately — but you do seem to value honesty. Does Margaret's family know that she is here?"

The ship continued its roll. A school of flying fish skimmed the surface a few yards off the starboard beam. Jane lowered her gaze and stared for a while before addressing Robert. "You are a very fine man, Robert. In the brief time I have known you, I have come to appreciate why your crew loves you and why they are so loyal — and why this ship is so different from the typical vessel. You understand them and care for them. I dare say you love them as family.

"Yes, they know she is here. I wrote them a letter from Plymouth shortly before I caught up with Margaret. They had assigned me to accompany her to visit Miss Mary Bennet in Derbyshire. They were uncomfortable with Margaret's notion of traveling alone for all the obvious reasons, but I wager they also thought she might be up to some mischief — and they were correct. In Crawley, where we were to transfer to the Derbyshire coach, she sent me on an errand and was gone by the time I returned. I discovered where she was headed and rendezvoused with her — just in time."

Robert chuckled. "The picture you paint is consistent with what I have learned of her. And yet … and yet … you did not call her out on the dock."

"I do hope that was not a mistake. I am clearly complicit in her escape. That was wrong on the face of it, yet Margaret has all her life prepared for this adventure. Wanderlust is in her bones. She has always hated the cold gray damp of England and longed for warm sun and spices. It did not hurt that Colonel Brandon filled her head with stories of the Caribbean. Had it not been this time, it would have been another — and I might not have been with her. I would have regretted that more. By the way, how did you surmise that she was not supposed to be on this journey? That was hardly idle speculation."

He relaxed, leaning on the rail with his elbow. "There were a number of little clues that came together. I was too busy with preparations on the day we met to appreciate it, but on reflection, I sense that Margaret was not expecting you. She looked quite anxious as you surveyed the situation before asking 'Is this our ship?' Your exact phrasing stuck in my mind. I would have thought that peculiar had I not been distracted so. The letter she gave me, supposedly from her sister, does not ring genuine on rereading. And she avoids talking of home. That is what I have put together. So, do you share her wanderlust? Do you long to swim in warm, sapphire waters and smell the tropical breezes?"

"I like your insights, which are pretty much spot on. And the fact that you asked me about my wanderlust tells me that you already know. It sounds dull, but I am content wherever I find myself. I am happy that I may assist Margaret in fulfilling her dreams. She may do great things and will finally feel the warmth of the sun on her skin and in her soul. Even I am relishing the increasing warmth that I can feel here on *Lady Bridget* already in the week we have been underway. I know that I will enjoy our ports of call. I have not sought them out, but I will treasure being where I will be. I will enjoy returning to England when the time comes as well, if we can tear Margaret away. So, I will be satisfied. The lines have fallen pleasantly about me, and I am blessed with riches wherever I be. That does sound dull, does it not?"

Robert stared at Jane. "Not at all. I do not think I have ever met with such wisdom and serenity. And you have been living that spirit here. You have learned more about your floating home in a shorter time than anyone who has ever been aboard. As with everything else you mentioned, you seem at one with the sea. You are an amazing woman, Jane."

She colored while sporting a sweet smile. "Thank you."

He sighed. "I hate to bring our talk to a close, but I have the six to midnight watch at the helm. I hope that we may continue soon."

She nodded. "To be sure, sir. I, too, must make preparation for my watch at the same time. I will see if Margaret is ready. Her sea legs are still a bit wobbly, and she was a slight shade of green when last I saw her."

Robert could not help grinning. "She should keep her stomach filled. The hard biscuits are good for that."

"Harriet recommended those as well. Margaret resisted at first, saying she was not hungry. I insisted, she complied, and it does seem to help. I — or we — will bring our reports to you throughout the watch."

Jane made her way to the hatch as Robert watched from the rail. At the top, she paused and turned back to him. "And I feel blessed to share this voyage with you, Robert. The lines have fallen pleasantly about me, indeed."

Chapter Ten
Testing

In the room behind the pulpit, long before the beginning of services, William Collins paced the width of the chamber, muttering fragments of his impending sermon. His face was haggard, his eyes showing the fatigue of many nights of fitful sleep.

Charlotte sat on one side of the room, Mary on the other.

"Mr. Collins, you must not work yourself up so at this late hour," Charlotte cautioned. "You are ready. I have listened to your rehearsals with Mary for a full week now. Your reasoning and your principles are strong, and your words well honed. It is time to take a stand, and you are ready. Today is the day."

He paused his pacing. "You are correct, of course, my love. In all my life, there have been few times when I was more certain than I am today of the justice of today's sermon. But today is the leap. Today I put not only myself, but you and your family as well, on the front lines. If Lady Catherine reacts as poorly as I anticipate, we shall be without home forthwith. That shames me. It offends my sense of responsibility."

"If that is what comes to pass, then it is she who should feel the shame," Charlotte replied. "And if that is what transpires, that she puts us out of home, then we shall manage. Your published sermons, your lectionary guides, and Joseph Weatherstone's works are already yielding more than Lady Catherine's patronage."

"My lectionary guides?" Collins asked.

Charlotte turned to Mary. "Did we not tell him about his guides?"

Mary frowned, pondering. "We did not." She turned to William and announced, "As requested by a number of your readers, a series of guides have been written to accompany your published sermons. Your publisher sells them at the same price as the sermon series, and they have proven quite popular."

"I see," he said. "I do not recall preparing any lectionary guides."

Charlotte and Mary burst into laughter, and Collins, understanding, smiled.

"And besides," Mary continued, "I am quite certain that my sister and brother-in-law would offer you lodging should you be cast out. But do not be so certain of her ladyship's indisposition. For a subject of such strident currency, I should have expected her to comment on it. And she has not, has she?"

Mr. Collins and Charlotte both shook their heads. Charlotte offered, "Lady Catherine has taken kindly to Mary because of Mary's good friendship with Lady Anne, and I know that you realize she adores me." Charlotte gave a smug smile. "And we have never heard her ladyship mention the topic of slavery, one way or the other."

"Then so be it!" he pronounced. "Today is the day. I am ready."

Charlotte and Mary both rose, smiling. Charlotte checked his robes and picked a few pieces of lint from the fabric. Mary gathered up his sermon text and verified that the pages were all present and in order.

He shook his head. "Let us hope that the bishop or his staff do not show up. Today's service certainly will not conform to standard practice."

"Few of your recent services have," Mary said. "But then the Church has exhibited paltry interest in this little corner of the world. I don't recall an ecclesiastical visit in many years."

"True," Collins shrugged.

The three emerged from the preparation room into the sanctuary. About half of the congregants had arrived and were either seated or conversing on the side. Elizabeth and Fitzwilliam Darcy appeared at the back of the church as the trio reached the altar.

Mary leaned toward Mr. Collins and whispered, "Are we the only ones who know of today's topic?"

He nodded. "Though your sister likely knows that something is afoot."

"Good," she replied with a smile. "I shall note the others' reactions so that we can continue the conversation in the months ahead. I will also keep watch for our gray visitor."

"Yes, I was thinking about him, as well. It has been a week, so he has had time to reach Oxford on horseback and make his inquiries."

They took their seats, Mr. Collins on his chair behind the pulpit, Charlotte on the front pew, and Mary on the end of the pew in front of Elizabeth and Fitzwilliam. Mary smiled at them. Elizabeth smiled in return, and Mr. Darcy gave her a dignified nod. The sanctuary seated about one hundred-twenty parishioners and almost every pew was filled.

At ten minutes 'til the hour, Lady Catherine de Bourgh arrived. Those standing close by her bowed or curtsied as she passed. She maintained her habitual bearing walking down the aisle, Anne close behind her, and into her pew. Anne appeared in good health, continuing a trend of the past year. Anne's accomplishments with her poetry and outings with Mary and Elizabeth had brought her much joy and exercise. Lady Catherine also appreciated Anne's improved appearance.

After the standard order of hymns and readings, Reverend Collins arose and mounted the steps of the pulpit. He looked at his text and smiled to see that Mary had underlined words and phrases that merited emphasis.

"Dearly beloved," he began, "I have treasured your attention and your kind engagement over the past year as we have explored the meanings of scripture and the lessons of scripture as they apply to our daily lives.

"Today I am exhorting us all to take the calling of scripture more seriously than ever before. I have heard a calling to take a stand. I, and I alone, take responsibility for following this call. It comes from a lifetime of study and prayer. I know that my stand will provoke outrage in some of you, and I am prepared for that eventuality. I ask only that, where we may disagree, you will honor me and this community with your civility and rigorous debate.

"I pronounce this day that scripture demands in a mighty voice the denunciation of the institution of human bondage — slavery — and God's holy word calls us all to work together for slavery's abolition, here and throughout the world, now and forevermore."

The sanctuary erupted. Mary's gaze darted about the congregants, spying some angry red faces, some smiling and even cheering. She turned to Collins, who was watching her. She gave a firm nod, and he inclined his head in reply.

On the other side of the sanctuary, Lord Edward, his face red and veins bulging on his neck, stood in his family pew, outrage in his stiff stance. "By what right do you make such an outrageous claim?" he shouted, "By what right do you assail this God-given institution?"

This was the very question for which Mary and William had long prepared. He stretched his arms wide and motioned for the congregation to be seated and quiet. He waited until there was only a persistent low murmur. "Your Lordship, I have no right on my own to make any claim. I have no right to assail anything. But your Lordship, I have a responsibility to preach the truth of scripture, to plumb its depths, and speak the reality of all that is holy. This day, I will lay before you my findings. He — or she — who has ears, let them hear God's holy words and turn them over in their heart."

Mary glanced to Lady Catherine, who had turned to watch the congregation. Beside her ladyship, Mary could see a trace of a smile on Anne's face.

Collins continued, "In the coming weeks, we will study together specific stories and movements, from the peoples before the Hebrews to the end of time in Revelation. I shall depart from our established tradition and give you the scripture passages for each coming week. You will have that week to prepare your own thoughts and arguments.

"I do not approach this subject casually." He turned to Lord Edward's family pew. "I am well aware of the vast impact that abolition could have on members of this congregation. I am well aware of the wealth and wellbeing entwined in the slave trade and slave labor. I am also aware of the dangers inherent in taking a stand against slavery. In this holy sanctuary … this very building … I was threatened last week by a visitor who sought to silence me. I know that my life is in jeopardy when I stand for abolition."

A fresh wave of conversation swept over the people. He waited, arms folded. When quiet again was restored, he said, "Out of character, I will be brief today. *You* will continue this sermon before you depart, and as you travel to your homes, and in the village for the next week. What I leave you with in this hour of this day is a seed, a small truth that you must study and be ready to confront when you return. It is this: the Bible is a book of liberation. From the first chapters of the first book, it is the story of people striving to be free. From the descendants of Adam and Eve, through the Hebrew people, to the times of our Savior and His followers, the people of the Bible fought for freedom — freedom from enslavement by surrounding tribes, freedom from slavery under the Egyptians and the Babylonians, and freedom even from the shackles of death. Make no mistake; these people of the book were not English. Yet we English likewise pride ourselves that we are not now, nor have we *ever been,* slaves! We will continue next week, beginning in Genesis.

"For now, we dismiss with a blessing: the Lord bless you and keep you, the Lord make His countenance to shine upon you, and give you peace, now and forever more. Amen."

The order of service called for a closing hymn at this point, but the din of conversation drowned the sound of the organ. Mr. Collins and the organist eyed one another. Collins shrugged. The organist concluded her closing number and put away her music.

Collins made his way toward the back, stopping from time to time as parishioners either shook their fingers at him and offered protests or shook his hand and thanked him. Lady Catherine and Lady Anne remained seated as the sanctuary emptied. When the only congregants remaining were Mr. Darcy and Elizabeth, along with Charlotte and Mary, her ladyship and Anne rose and walked back down the aisle.

"Mr. Darcy, Elizabeth, if you would kindly remain while I have a word with Reverend Mr. Collins," she commanded.

Mr. Darcy bowed. The women curtsied.

"Mr. Collins, you did not consult me before undertaking this sermon."

"No, your Ladyship," he stammered.

"Why not?" she demanded.

Mary could see his hand trembling.

"Your Ladyship, I was aware of the disruption that this sermon would cause and believed that it should not be prevented."

"I see. And Lord Edwards made his displeasure quite clear," she intoned.

"Yes, your Ladyship."

"However, Lord Edwards is not your patron. I am. Though he may be on the board of this parish, he but advises me. I am the one who decides what will be preached in this hallowed space. I need not tell you that taking on this topic without consultation was the height of impertinence on your part."

Collins stood stiffly. The wind outside was the loudest sound in the sanctuary.

"By good fortune, you have chosen the correct side in this battle. My daughter and I have had a number of conversations about this very issue over the last months, and she has convinced me of the merits that abolition of slavery is a right and proper course of action. I have been in correspondence with Sir Thomas Fowell Buxton and will be hosting him in two weeks' time when he is passing through this region. I hope that you may join me in welcoming him. You, as well as Charlotte, Elizabeth, and Fitzwilliam. And Miss Mary, I hope that you can also join us. I understand that you have met him and had conversations with him. He seemed to know you."

Mary curtsied.

Lady Catherine turned, with Anne following, toward her carriage. Before entering the vehicle, she turned to her pastor. "Mr. Collins, make an appointment with me this week to go over your material. I want to be well prepared for Lord Edward's tantrums."

"Yes, m'lady." Collins bowed.

She boarded the carriage and was gone.

Darcy came alongside Collins, watching the carriage drive out of sight. Darcy spoke, "Mr. Collins, when first we met, I found you annoying in the extreme. And I was by no means the only one. We all thought you a ridiculous little man."

Collins looked down, forlorn.

"But I sense now that we have missed something, a wellspring of integrity and strength. As loath as I am to admit it, we appear to have been wrong. Well done, old man." Darcy reached out his hand and the two exchanged a firm handshake.

* * *

Margaret and Jane finished their third round of *Lady Bridget* on their early morning watch. The dawn was upon them and the sky was bright red. They had early decided on a pattern of alternating who gave the report. It was Margaret's turn.

She approached Captain Johnson and the quartermaster and saluted. "Sounding and security all secure, sir."

He smiled and returned the salute. "Seems as if your sea legs are all secure, too."

"Yes, they are, Robert. One of the things that has made a difference was getting out of our shoes." She looked over to Jane, who smiled and wiggled her toes.

"Aye, that is something the Navy discovered half a century ago. If the climate is warm enough, it feels better when our feet contact the deck and the riggings. I believe we have a better feel for our ship … literally."

Jane nodded. "It is true, and good because it seems the sea is getting rougher."

"That was what Quartermaster Graham and I were just discussing. The barometer has been dropping steadily over the last day and a half. And look at the sunrise."

"It is so beautiful," Jane said.

"Not if you are a sailor, unfortunately. We have an old saying: 'Red sky at night, sailors delight. Red sky at morning, sailors take warning.' We will be doing everything we can today to get ready for some rough seas. The two of you be particularly on watch for any loose hatches or gear, either on deck or down below. But have no worry. *Lady Bridget* knows how to ride out storms."

Robert looked into Jane's eyes. "But I would guess that you are not afraid," he said, "are you?"

She shook her head. "We are *Lady Bridget*. We will be ready."

"Right!" He smiled.

Throughout the day, the crew moved what they could from the deck to storage below. The quartermaster took his last bearings before clouds obscured the horizon. The ship began wide rolls and shuddered from time to time as the bow rose from the water and smashed into oncoming waves. Those waves began to host whitecaps as the wind pushed them.

By mid-afternoon, Harriet had given everyone detailed safety instructions. Anyone who belonged on deck would be tethered to masts or stanchions. About four in the afternoon, Captain Johnson ordered the mainsails furled and ordered the storm sails unfurled.

Harriet watched the operation with Margaret. "The mainsails are strong and true in a steady wind. But come the storm, the wind ain't as predictable, and they could tear or come loose. Even worse, they could catch enough wind to pull the ship over, or take us a thousand miles off course. Those storm sails are smaller, but much stronger. They be easier to turn and will keep us moving through the water so as not to founder."

"Have you been through storms before?" Margaret asked.

"Aye, dearie. If this becomes a storm, this be number seven or eight, I figure, all of 'em on *Lady Bridget*. Now do not you be scared none. You do as you have been taught and all will be fine. The only close call we ever had was in the second storm. Seaman name of Michael went up on deck without bein' tied off. Got hit by a big wave and was washed clear across the deck. He was barely hangin' on to the railin'. But that Robert chanced to see him, the next wave would have taken him. You do not want to go overboard. We will never find ya. Never. God was a watchin' Michael, though. Robert saved him."

Harriet looked at Margaret. "Do what I taught ya and it will be fine. You got them hard biscuits?"

"Yes, ma'am." Margaret opened the pouch slung over her shoulder to reveal a cache of hardtack.

Harriet smiled. "Good lass."

* * *

Margaret and Jane shared the midnight watch. Throughout the evening and night, anyone not on watch stayed in his or her bunks. The one exception was the gunner, who slept with the cannon, ensuring they did not break loose from their constraints. The wind's howl penetrated deep into the ship and some rolls approached forty-five degrees. Margaret and Jane adapted by grasping beams and fixtures while moving through their inspections, at times laughing at the absurd tilt of their floating home. As the two women completed each round, they continued to alternate taking their reports on deck. Robert had taken the midnight watch at the helm and seemed genuinely happy to see them at the end of each round.

Both Margaret and Jane had become adept at tying each other's tether lines. They opened the hatch for only seconds to allow them out and then secured it again. On deck, those who emerged were greeted by a roaring gale and stinging drops of water blown sideways, either rain or sea spray or both. The deck streamed with water every time a wave smashed into the side of the ship. The women were thankful for bare feet, which gripped the deck better than shoes. They were thankful as well that, after three weeks sailing south, the wind and water were warm.

At about four in the morning, the bale on hatch number seven came loose, the hatch opened, and water began pouring into the compartment whenever a large wave overtopped the gunwale. Margaret and Jane raced to the main hatch.

"I can go out and secure it," Margaret said.

"No. My turn." Jane said and began placing the line around her waist, which Margaret tied with the quick and careful skill honed by long practice. "If the bale is broken, I may have to keep securing it. Get back under it once I am out. I will let you know what I find and we can decide whether we need to get someone out to fix it."

Though the sky roiled with storm clouds, moonlight penetrated the clouds enough to maintain a ghostly glow. Jane made her way toward hatch number seven, holding on to posts and fixtures near the centerline of the ship. On reaching the hatch, she found the bale bent, but intact. She was able to close the bale, though the loose rattle told her that it would probably spring open again if struck by a wave.

Jane looked around. The ship seemed in a calm spell for the moment. She opened the hatch a moment to see Margaret below.

"The latch is loose, but it should hold. I will go up to the forecastle with Robert. The forecastle is above the waves, and I can see the hatch from there. I can get right to it if the hatch pops open again. Keep on our rounds but do not come out if everything is all right. If something goes wrong, get someone to tie you and come out, but only in an emergency."

"Are you sure you will be all right?" Margaret called.

Jane looked toward the forecastle for a moment and then turned back. "I will be fine. If he can stay out here, so can I." Jane secured the hatch as tightly as she could and made her way up to the forecastle.

"Early on your rounds?" Robert greeted her.

She laughed. "Hatch seven popped open. I secured it, but I should watch it."

"Is it broken?" he asked.

"No, the bale is bent a little. Probably got slammed by a wave. I can see it from here if it opens again."

"You will stay out here?" he asked.

"If that is all right. Margaret is continuing the watch. She will come out only if there is trouble, and then with help tying her tether."

"I would not mind the company. It is a good fifteen feet above the main deck here, so we do not get much from the waves. It is wet, to be sure, but safe."

"Do you get tired standing all this time in one spot?" she asked.

"With the ship tossing in a gale and the wind flapping every piece of fabric? No, not at all. Are you well tied?"

"Absolutely," Jane showed him her tether. "Harriet taught us, and Margaret and I have done it about a hundred times."

Robert laughed, barely audible above the wind. After a while, he turned to her. "I said I would not mind the company. Actually, I very much cherish some company. As you surmised, this watch is the loneliest. It may be my imagination, but I fancy the wind is dying down and the sea is a little less rough. When Mr. Graham is up in a couple of hours, we can have him check the barometer and see if it is rising. I would wager we are past the worst of the storm."

For the remainder of the watch, they talked of home and of ports they would visit. Both agreed that Margaret was enjoying the voyage now and that she was serious about her trade responsibilities. Toward the end of the watch, the clouds became thinner and more ragged. Robert and Jane tried to predict when a hole racing through the clouds would open to reveal the moon, and cheered when it did.

"How have you found your life aboard, Jane?" he asked.

"Most satisfactory, Robert. I remember tales of intolerable life for women aboard sailing ships, but such is not the case with *Lady Bridget*. As you promised that first day, we are family here, and we enjoy an admirable respect. I cherish the results of my labors."

"Your favorable observations please me. Alas, those tales are still true on other ship on the sea, perhaps most."

By six o'clock, the seas had calmed noticeably, and the dawn began gray.

"That is so beautiful," Jane said.

Robert smiled. "If you are a sailor, yes."

She nodded. "I am a sailor."

The watch was relieved and they made their way to the main hatch.

"The bale held," she said as they passed hatch seven.

"So, it did. We will have Jimmy take a look at it in a couple of hours."

As they arrived at the bottom of the ladder, the ship lurched and Jane fell forward. Robert reached out, caught her, and held her tightly in his arms. She looked up to him, her cheeks coloring. She began to open her mouth, but then closed her lips as she looked into his eyes.

"Neither am I," he said.

She looked at him quizzically. "Neither are you what?"

"You were going to say, 'sorry,' but then you thought you were not sorry that we were thrown together."

She reached up with her hand and pulled his head to hers and kissed him.

Chapter Eleven
Off Course

On Tuesday morning, Reverend William Collins sat in an exquisite chair in the center of an elegant rug facing Lady Catherine de Bourgh's grand writing desk. Her ladyship finished penning a note as Collins waited, hands folded in his lap. She folded and addressed the missive, pressed the warm wax with her seal, and then called in her manservant and handed it over to him with instructions for delivery.

As the servant departed, she turned to William. "Reverend Collins, I had the opportunity to spend the afternoon yesterday with Lord Edward. He seemed … uncomfortable … with your sermon of this Sunday past."

Collins looked at her, giving only a flick of a nod.

"His Lordship and I have known each other, oh, forty years or more. I have always found him annoyingly accepting of moral compromises in a variety of matters. The fact that you have elicited such a passionate response from him does you credit. He would not be so uncomfortable if he could dismiss your arguments."

"Thank you, your ladyship," Collins replied.

She frowned and continued, "Mind you, my original intent for this meeting was to reprimand you, or worse. You acted as a loose cannon, Mr. Collins. As you are well aware, I have great responsibilities for this estate, for this parish, and for the welfare of my family. A rogue individual in my employ could be as costly as he could be brilliant. I do not appreciate that sort of uncertainty."

Collins bowed. "My humble apologies, your ladyship."

"That was my original intent." She waved her hand. "However, between savoring Lord Edward's annoyance and Anne's delight, I find it difficult to maintain my customary unpleasantness."

"I would not describe your ladyship as unpleasant," Collins protested.

She laughed. "Not to my face, no. Let me tell you a secret, which you are bound to keep as my confessor. I know that I am not possessed of native charm. I do not enjoy soothing conversations. I am not skilled at using wit and vivacity. On the other hand, I am possessed of wealth, and power, and connections, and I most certainly know how to employ those. The image of unpleasantness is one that

I cultivate with great care. There you have it, Mr. Collins. You have escaped my displeasure this time through a fortuitous combination of good scholarship, bold preaching, and the entertainment of irritating Lord Edward. I must also extend what protection I may offer regarding this threatening man you encountered. That you have kept knowledge of Charlotte and Mary shielded from him is quite noble."

"Thank you, ma'am. I am your humble servant."

She regarded him a while and then continued, "Now my curiosity is piqued, Reverend Collins. I have sat through — one might say suffered through — your regular sermons for nigh on four years. I remember very little of them until recently. For the first two years, I doubt that I was awake through half of them. They began to reach me beginning last year and yours of last Sunday was memorable. Pray tell, what has changed?"

"I have a muse, ma'am."

She could not help smiling. "A muse? Is our dear Charlotte your muse?"

"No, ma'am, my beloved Charlotte has been a great and wonderful supporter of my development, but Miss Mary Bennet has challenged me both to improve the quality of my craft and its accessibility, and to take the stands that morality demands."

"I see. So, you are letting your life be governed by strong-willed women, myself included."

He bit his lip, unsure how to respond.

"You are wiser than most men, then. There is another matter you have kept from me. A little bird told me that you are deriving some income from the publication of your sermons and the scholarship that goes with them."

Collins paled. "Your ladyship, I myself have only very recently become aware of that fact. My sermons and notes on them were curated and edited without my knowledge. The success of their publication was a complete surprise to me. I assure you, I had no intention of profiting at the expense of the estate, and would offset my patronage as appropriate, of course."

"What? Do you think I am dissatisfied?" Lady Catherine looked surprised. "No, indeed! Your success confirms my wisdom in selecting you to lead this parish. If this enterprise does not interfere with your ministerial duties, I have no objections. In point of fact, my daughter, Anne, has purchased several of your tomes and assures me they are better than the original sermons themselves."

"Thank you, ma'am. You must know I treasure Anne's good opinion, given the quality of her own writing."

Lady Catherine donned a mischievous smile — the first time Collins had seen such. "Which brings up a final point before I must attend to other matters. You seem to concur that Anne's writing has substance and quality. She should be published and am willing to provide any needed resources, but she is, as always, too shy and timid to pursue the matter. If you and, perhaps, your muse would lend a helpful hand, it would please your patron."

Collins rose from his seat and bowed graciously. "Your Ladyship, it would be an honor."

* * *

William, Charlotte, and Mary enjoyed a late lunch at Hunsford Cottage.

"She was really that pleased?" Charlotte asked after William concluded his retelling of the morning's meeting with Lady Catherine de Bourgh.

"Indeed. She said the sermon demonstrated good scholarship and bold preaching." He smiled in Mary's direction.

Charlotte laughed. "I meant her pleasure in annoying Lord Edwards."

"Yes, that as well," Collins replied with a smile.

Turning to Mary, Charlotte teased, "I believe you are acquainted with Lord Edward's son, John. As a matter of coincidence, we happened to be discussing your rapport with him the day we first conspired to establish our little publishing empire."

Mary looked down. "Yes, rapport. I am forbidden the hospitality of their estate, which I take as a badge of honor." Turning to William, Mary continued, "And Lady Catherine is continuing your patronage even with the revenues of your work?"

He nodded. "She says that as long as our adventures do not interfere with our service to the parish, she considers it a good mark to have a man of reputation in her employ. I protested that the two of you should be receiving much of the credit. She agreed that was noble and correct, judging that having one person in possible danger from that gray man was enough. I was as surprised as I was grateful for her wise insight."

"Ah, speaking of which," Mary responded, "Fitzwilliam has

received word back from his associates in Oxford. Our mysterious gray visitor appears to be a man named Douglas Marshall in the hire of a secret society of plantation owners. According to Fitzwilliam, they employ him for his menacing presence, though he does not appear to have actually committed any violence. Mr. Marshall departed Oxford for Portsmouth after making numerous queries about our phantom printer. My brother-in-law has sent queries to friends in Portsmouth to keep watch for Mr. Marshall's appearance there. I am actually keen to return to Pemberley this afternoon. He told me there would be a surprise waiting on my return."

"Thank you for your company, my dear," Charlotte said. "Let us get together later in the week. Mr. Weatherstone's publisher is eager to get the *Manifesto* in print."

Mary glanced at William, who nodded. "Yes, that would be excellent. We can deliver the manuscript next week. We have polished enough and need only read it through once more."

After sweets, Mary gathered her portfolio, gave Charlotte and William each a kiss on the cheek, and proceeded home at a fast walk.

* * *

Mary caught sight of an elegant carriage at Pemberley's front entrance with groomsmen attending to the horses. She hurried into the great hall.

"Mary!" sounded an excited voice from a side room.

"Georgiana!" Mary squealed and ran to embrace her. The two laughed as they hugged, dancing in a circle.

Mary stepped back. "Or should I now be calling you Lady Brougham?" She made an exaggerated low curtsy.

"Do and I shall not speak to you again!" Georgiana pouted, crossing her arms. "Except at public gatherings, of course." She giggled.

Tilting her head as she surveyed her sister-in-law, Mary finally asked, "Am I seeing what I think I am seeing?"

"Indeed you are!" Georgiana beamed. "You shall be an aunt by summer's end. Dy came here especially to make our announcement to Brother before word got out."

"I remember a time when Fitzwilliam was less than comfortable with the idea of Dy as brother-in-law," Mary reminded her.

Georgiana smiled. "True. And it would have been a continuing discomfort were not Dy so charming, a quintessential gentleman. As is, their friendship has never been stronger and I do believe Brother will be deliriously happy at the prospects of doting on a young niece or nephew. I know Elizabeth is — she was the first to greet us when we arrived."

The two stood looking at each other and smiling.

"But in addition to our announcement, his Lordship has matters to discuss with you, dear sister and future aunt. I understand that you have had some adventures of your own, and you have attracted the attention of the Home Office," Georgiana said as they began walking toward Georgiana's old room.

"Oh?" Mary frowned. "All I have been doing is editing sermons and lectionary guides."

"Uh huh," Georgiana said. "Well, some very well-connected plantation owners have complained to the Home Office about a certain Miss Mary Bennet, who they believe to be an agent for the great Joseph Weatherstone. To be honest the Home Office regards those complaints as a nuisance. Most quarters of the office regard abolition as inevitable and timely. But they have become quite curious about Mr. Weatherstone. It seems they are finding it difficult to locate any records of Joseph or his family on this Fair Isle." She raised her eyebrows.

They began climbing the stairs to the second floor. "Imagine that," Mary replied. "And Dy's interest is …?

"He works for the Home Office, of course, but his first desire is the safety of his sister-in-law."

* * *

Margaret and Jane completed their fourth round on watch in the afternoon. They stopped at the hatch to the quartermaster's room, where Robert and Mr. Graham were deep in discussion over the ship's charts. It was Margaret's turn to report. She rapped on the door frame and announced, "Sounding and security all secure, sir."

The two men looked up and smiled. Robert spoke. "Excellent. How goes the repair on hatch seven? Come in, the two of you. Take a look at where we are."

As they approached the chart table, Margaret replied, "Jimmy completed the repair about an hour ago and says the damage was nothing to worry about. Still, he put on a larger bale for added safety."

Graham nodded. "That is comforting. Look here what else the

storm has done to us." He pointed to a straight line beginning in
Plymouth and then to a break, then to another line well off to the
right. "The storm blew us a good three hundred miles southeast of
our intended track. Between currents and the trade winds, we are
considering reversing the direction of our original journey, especially
since the top yardarm on the second mast suffered damage in the
storm. There is a particularly good shipwright on Martinique, which
would have been our final stop otherwise. Plus, Fort-de-France
provides a safe and friendly harbor."

Jane perused the charts. "Is that where your stepmother,
Geneviève, lives?"

Robert smiled. "Indeed it is. That was part of our consideration.
Geneviève will see that we receive fair treatment by the shipwright."
He turned to Margaret. "And she will introduce you to some of the
merchants for whom we will need your interpreter skills."

* * *

During the remaining voyage, Margaret had added duties in
the galley to her routine. Jane added time in the sail loft, inspecting
the spare sails for impending rips and mending the heavy canvas.
With the ever-increasing intensity of the tropical sun, Margaret's
hair bleached to a bright gold and Jane's complexion tanned to a
handsome bronze. Both women grew stronger with the constant
physical labor that was part of their floating home.

Lady Bridget altered course, arriving at Fort-de-France,
Martinique, forty-six days after leaving Plymouth, dropping anchor
in the harbor several hundred yards from shore. The crew lowered two
of the ship's boats into the water and deployed a sea ladder. As the
advance party rowed toward the dock, they could see Geneviève on
the dock, waving and jumping up and down in excitement.

Margaret leaned close to Jane and whispered, "She is much
younger than I expected."

Jane chuckled.

Robert turned to Margaret. "Well, Miss Dashwood, your time to
shine is upon us."

The party climbed the short distance to the boardwalk,
and Robert led the others to Geneviève. Margaret began her
interpretations.

*"Geneviève, I apologize for our early arrival. A storm altered our
course and caused damage to* Lady Bridget, *the repair of which I would*

entrust only to your local craftsmen."

Geneviève Renée Trudeau Johnson was beautiful — tall and poised. Her face was pretty and quick to smile. In her flowing white dress, she glistened in the bright Caribbean sunlight. A broad-brimmed hat of woven reeds protected her delicate features from the blazing sun. Two young children, also attired in white, looked up smiling at the newcomers from behind their mother.

"Robert, you know that you are always welcome at any time and for any reason. I hope that you remember your little brother, Jacques, and your little sister, Marie."

Robert kneeled down on all fours, face to face with the children. *"I am glad you told me who they were. I would not have known. They have grown so. Let me see. Is Jacques twenty and Marie sixteen?"*

The children laughed, while shouting *"Non, non, non!"* in unison. Jacques was quick to correct. *"I am eight and Marie is four!"*

Robert hugged each and kissed them on the head. Then he rose and continued his conversation with Geneviève. *"May I introduce our party? Two new members of our crew family are with me. I am being made intelligible by our interpreter, Miss Margaret Dashwood. Margaret's partner in mischief is Miss Jane Moseby. And you must remember our excellent quartermaster, Mr. Graham, and of course Harriet Dunsford, who is in charge of everything that matters."* As he introduced each member, Geneviève hugged them and planted a kiss on each cheek.

Finally she turned to Robert. *"Please bring your ship alongside the dock. The water is more than deep enough, and it will make the repairs and cargo transfers so much easier. The main inn here is half empty, and I will make sure they do not overcharge you. I expect that after … how many days?"*

"Forty-six," he replied.

"Forty-six? Oh, my. After forty-six days, I am sure your people would like some time in beds that are not moving all the time."

He nodded.

She clapped twice. *"And then, this evening we will have a big island feast to honor my son and his nautical family."*

He embraced her. *"Merci, merci beaucoup!"*

Chapter Twelve

Labors of Love

Georgiana and Dy's visit was to be short, but joyful.

Lord Brougham arranged a private meeting over tea with Mary, Fitzwilliam attending by mutual agreement and desire.

"So, my dear sister-in-law, I have watched your growing stature in the abolition movement with considerable pride. You can imagine how pleased I am when my own reputation is elevated as people discover our family ties," Dy said.

"Thank you, sir," Mary said.

"I am all sincerity, my dear, for you have achieved this by your own integrity and scholarship. There is one aspect of your new circles of influence that has me and my colleagues fascinated, though, and that is your close association with the great Joseph Weatherstone."

Mary glanced over to Fitzwilliam, who occupied himself studying details of the crown molding surrounding the room.

Dy laughed. "Do not worry, your secrets are aggravatingly safe with your reticent brother-in-law. There are many reasons I would not wish to play cards against him. Also, be assured that your secrets are safe with me. Fitzwilliam and I have known and relied on each other through thick and thin for most of our lives — actually, the entirety of our adult lives. He will vouch for my ability to keep mum."

He turned to Darcy, who nodded.

Satisfied, Mary asked, "What do you wish of me, then, sir?"

"Right! The Home Office is keen to avoid any further trouble around the slavery issue. I can tell you in complete honesty that we are committed to the abolition of slavery throughout the Empire. The process will, of necessity, be more deliberate than many of your compatriots desire. It will also be fought in the strongest terms by many of the wealthiest and most powerful families in the kingdom. I know that is not news to you," Dy said.

Mary lowered her head. "Indeed, I have become aware of that."

"In an effort to keep the issue from tearing our society apart any more than it already has, we have been meeting with everyone we can persuade to sit down with us. I myself have talked with over a dozen colonial plantation owners, as well as with William Wilberforce and Hannah More."

Mary eased back in her chair.

Dy watched her with a smile. "It must please you to know that they remember you as erudite and well-informed. But the highest praise came from Sir Thomas Buxton, who gave a glowing account of your representation of Mr. Joseph Weatherstone at the Oxford meeting. He told me that you have been most prompt and courteous acting as an intermediary between the two."

"That is too kind of him," Mary said.

Dy could see that Mary was not going to reveal any information of consequence through simple conversation. "I have since had the good fortune to read some of Weatherstone's writings myself. Like you, he is erudite and well informed … remarkably like you. Given my pledge of confidentiality, would you be willing to introduce me to him?" He waited as she pondered a very long time. "Or is that a moot point? Might I already be talking to him?"

She could see Fitzwilliam nodding out of the corner of her eye. "You are, sir, or at least half of him."

"Half?" he asked, close to laughter.

"Yes, sir," she continued. "Joseph is the pen name of a collaboration between myself and an exceptional scholar. I came to know of those writings while editing other works. My colleague's work was solid — erudite, as you said. As with the other writings, it was much in need of editing for clarity and accessibility. I have already discovered that those — our — anti-slavery writings have come to the unhappy attention of some slave-owning colonists. Did Fitzwilliam apprise you of an unpleasant visitor in their employ we had here?"

"He did inform me of a visitor — a Mr. Douglas Marshall — but your brother-in-law would not reveal the nature of your relation to Mr. Weatherstone. Now that I have a clearer picture of this puzzle, we in the Home Office can be useful to you preventing any violence."

Dy looked at Mary. "Masterful job of constructing this charade, by the way. Do not be surprised if we try to recruit you for the Home Office."

She laughed. "I do not see them fancying women in their employ!"

He grew serious. "I am delighted that you see it that way, for it means our cover has been effective. The Home Office, as well as His Majesty's secret service, employee a number of your fair sex, who provide us with much of our best intelligence. For the present, though, I would ask that you keep Mr. Weatherstone's identity and 'whereabouts' vague. I sense that his powerful moral authority is all the greater as a ghost than as a flesh-and-blood advocate. We in the Home Office can be ... helpful ... in providing his 'locations' to parties who may wish to do him harm."

Mary gave a sigh of relief and crossed her arms. "I do enjoy working with our future niece or nephew's father."

"Splendid! You can be of most assistance to us by continuing your fine writing, keeping your other writings separate, and continuing your correspondence on behalf of Mr. Weatherstone to your colleagues in the movement. Someday, his true identities will be revealed, I do not doubt — perhaps when the idea of slavery has been repudiated throughout the Empire."

He began gathering some papers he had in his lap. "Is there anything else I should know?"

She frowned. "Do you know the identity of the other half of Joseph?"

"No, I do not. It is just as well that I remain uninformed. If he — or she — is as clever as you are, then the work is in good hands. There is little that my knowing would contribute to the cause."

He stood to leave. "It pains me to leave this wonderful house and the company therein. Alas, Lady Brougham ..." he chuckled as Mary closed her eyes, "... and I have many pressing engagements between here and London. I wish safety and success to you, your collaborator, and Mr. Weatherstone. In my dotage, I will have the honor to say that I once met him, or at least half of him."

They all laughed and made their way to the dining room for light refreshments before their departure. Mary hugged Georgiana, promising to write and extracting a promise of regular updates on her future niece or nephew.

As the carriage drove out of sight, Mary turned to Fitzwilliam. "Thank you, brother, for your unwavering integrity. Knowing of your support has made great things possible that would otherwise be very difficult."

As they returned to the house, he said, "You have earned it, sister. You and Joseph's other half."

* * *

On the following day, Mary recounted her time with Lord Brougham to the great relief of both William and Charlotte. The two women completed the final, smooth draft of *Scripture Cries Out for Freedom*. William remained at table, reading one of the books he had not had the opportunity to read. They had edited and recited the manuscript to the point that there was very little for him to contribute.

When they had reviewed the last sheet and placed it in the waiting box, Charlotte tied the box shut. She looked up to Mary. "William and I shall travel to London tomorrow to deliver this into the hands of the publisher. Though it hardly seems fair to you, Mary, I agree with you that it is wise that as few people recognize you as possible. We shall be gone only five days at the most. As I promised, I will look into the school situations in London, though I am not sure anymore if I should be suggesting you as a student or a teacher. Who would have imagined, eh?"

Charlotte handed Mary a key. "Thank you for your offer to watch after the house. Of course Constance will attend to all the details and she is quite fastidious in her duties. You will not need to do anything beyond checking that the chickens and rabbits have been given fresh water. Actually, I had best gather the eggs now." She rose and headed out the back door.

Mary turned to William. "You know that I shall miss you. My love for you does not grow dim. I am grateful that we must work in Charlotte's presence, lest my impetuous longing should burst forth unconstrained."

He folded his hands on the table. "And I shall count the hours 'til our reunion. Oh, Mary, dear sweet Mary, our bittersweet time together is what I live for. Someday, a writer will tell of our love as one of the great pure meetings of soul and mind."

She gathered her notes and kissed his cheek, tears welling in her eyes. "Until we meet again, God go with you."

He helped her with her cloak and she left through the back door, giving Charlotte best wishes for their journey and asking that they bring back a good book to read as might be recommended by some of the publishers in London. Mary also reminded Charlotte to carry some examples of Lady Anne's poetry so that they might move forward with her publications.

* * *

The great island feast would be grander than anything that Margaret or Jane had ever experienced, even finer than any event she had attended at Delaford. After availing themselves of luxurious baths at the inn, Margaret and Jane found that Geneviève had sent each of them light, flowing dresses appropriate to the island climate. She even provided broad hats similar to hers.

After they had dressed for the evening, Margaret gazed at Jane. "What?" Jane demanded.

Margaret kept smiling and pulled Jane over to a full-length mirror. "Jane, you have always been very handsome. I guess I have known that since I knew what 'handsome' meant, and I have been an ungrateful wretch in not having had the sense to tell you. As I see you here, in that dress, your hair falling about your shoulders, I see that you are very pretty, beautiful, in fact."

Jane colored. "You are much too kind," she protested, but gazed at her reflection in the mirror, turning one way then the other, to inspect her appearance. "Our host has quite the knack for making a girl presentable, I must admit."

They left the inn and strolled through the town, ascending the hillside to Geneviève's home. All along the route, heads turned to watch them. Children waved or ran up to chat with them, as Margaret interpreted. Each turn of the road brought new fragrances of flowers and tropical soil. The Johnson home was large by island standards, made of heavy stone painted white, with the front veranda commanding a sweeping view of the harbor. The aroma of a whole pig roasting over a fire and spicy sauces and fruits replaced the fragrance of flowers. Geneviève arrived at the door to welcome them and gave the two women an abbreviated tour of the house.

Margaret's heart raced at the large open windows drawing breezes throughout the house. The thick, white stone walls displayed bright paintings and bright decorative pottery. Most of the furniture was rattan or other woven reeds, while potted tropical plants lined the windowsills. If there were an image defining English gray and cold, this was the absolute, complete opposite.

Margaret exchanged greetings in French with the cooks as they completed their tour through the kitchen and out into the wide stone patio in the back of the house. There Margaret saw the roasting pig and a long table set with plates and glasses and flowers. The gardens beyond were a paradise of orange poincianas, purple jacarandas, and the multiple hues and fragrances of frangipanis. In the palm trees overhead, she first heard and then saw multihued parrots.

As the women emerged from the house, Robert was talking with some of the early guests, his back toward Margaret and Jane. He turned in their direction. Geneviève had provided appropriate attire for him, as well — a loose white shirt and cotton pants, with a white hat to protect him from the sun. When he caught sight of Jane, his expression was first a stunned trance, transforming by degrees into a radiant smile. He eased over to them and took Jane's hand. "You look amazing, my dear," he said.

She blushed as she looked down. "Thank you. You look quite dashing yourself."

* * *

Over the next half hour, dozens of guests arrived with their families. Margaret was free to roam the party, observing the deference paid to Geneviève. Margaret's French was put to the test and she was pleased with her performance. In particular, she enjoyed deciphering the chatter between Jacques, Marie, and their young guests.

Once the last guests arrived, they took their seats at the table. Geneviève placed Robert and Jane together near her while Margaret shared a span with several young families. Geneviève called for attention and made formal introductions of the *Lady Bridget* family and the local families. As she did so, dishes were served and wine was poured. After introductions, Geneviève commanded, "*Bon appétit!*" and the feast began in earnest.

Margaret learned from her tablemates that Geneviève managed a substantial portion of the commerce of Fort-de-France, and that she had the respect of all the merchants and townspeople. Captain Johnson, Robert's father, had likewise earned their admiration as a fair trader and good husband. Margaret sampled all of the dishes, returning again and again to the pork.

In the course of the meal, she recognized the names of several merchants from her preparations during the voyage. She did her best to associate faces with names and to learn some of the details of their families. She learned that Geneviève had a strong aversion to the concept of servitude. All of the people attending them were independent caterers, part of a loose business community that Geneviève had helped establish.

* * *

As the party wound down, guests departed with thanks and compliments. Most of *Lady Bridget's* crew left for the inn and rest.

With still an hour of daylight remaining, Jacques and Marie came up to Robert and Jane with entreating chatter. Robert looked to Margaret.

"They want their big brother to take them down to the beach to pick up seashells," Margaret interpreted.

"That is a very good idea," Geneviève agreed. She pointed over the railing to a broad, sandy stretch down at the bottom of the hill. *"They will show you the way. We do have some lovely shells here, and Jane would enjoy the stroll. Have them back by sundown for bedtime."*

The four headed down the road toward the beach, their words untranslated, their excitement needing no translation. Margaret and Geneviève watched as Robert and Jane walked slowly arm in arm while the children danced about them, pointing out one thing or another.

"They are made for each other, are they not?" Geneviève asked in unaccented English.

Margaret started. "Ah, so you speak English — quite well. That is unexpected."

Geneviève laughed. "It can be supremely useful to know a language without showing it. In the cutthroat business of trade, I can find out the truth without tedious investigation if the traders think that I do not know what they are saying.

"You will be here for about a week while we get your yardarm repaired. As you stroll the markets in the next few days, do not let it be known that you understand French. Act like a classic difficult Englishwoman who expects everyone to speak English. Be listening to their own conversations, and you will find out the true cost of goods and services. I have already seen that you can be a good observer, that your French is quite good. I also hear that you are a credible actress, even able to become a stowaway."

"You heard that, did you?" Margaret asked.

Geneviève laughed. *"Oui,* Robert told me. I hope that you will devote time tomorrow writing to your family back in England. The ship that carries the post will be here in two days. Our port is the last stop before Europe." Geneviève eyed her sternly.

Margaret nodded. "I will. I promise."

"Good. Now back to my original question. It would appear that my son Robert — I cherish him as my full son — and Jane are of one heart. I know only the little that Robert has said and my brief observations at dinner, but I sense an aura of kindness about her, as well as practical good sense. She is quite pretty, in addition. Do I sense correctly?"

Margaret smiled as she replied, "It is no wonder that Robert's father fell in love with you. You are a keen observer, as well as charming and beautiful. I can confirm your senses. Jane has been my guardian angel since I was a small child. When facing adversity, she is clever and persistent. When facing heartbreak in others, she is kind, with a gift for healing. When facing threats or injustice, she can be fierce and courageous. Given who I am and what I have done, I doubt I would be alive today but for her interventions. And, as you have observed, their hearts beat as one when they are together."

"Excellent. That brings me great joy," Geneviève concluded.

They continued to watch Robert, Jane, Jacques and Marie examining the beach. The children were as likely to bring a treasured shell to Jane as to their brother.

"One thing I am curious about," Margaret continued. "We were not expected here for another month, but you met us on the dock. You had arrangements made with the inn, and this magnificent feast. How did you do that so quickly?"

"Very good. You are the first to ask. In days gone by — not so much anymore — pirates were a dreadful problem here. Their raiding parties caused enormous loss of life and property. So we station permanent lookouts up on the mountain." She pointed to the high peak above the harbor. "They can observe the ships far, far out to sea. If we do not recognize the ships, we alert the town and have a well-armed volunteer militia hidden all about town by the time they drop anchor or try to dock. If we do recognize the ship, as we did with *Lady Bridget*, then we have our joyous island welcome ready."

"Excellent. I had heard about pirates. They were one of the reasons my sister and brother-in-law opposed my voyage. Piracy was one of the matters that Robert and his father were taking to parliament."

Geneviève agreed. "Yes, I urged them to do that. They are wise to pursue the matter. We have largely brought an end to piracy here by our own actions, but it is still a problem to the west, particularly around Jamaica. As I listen to the seamen and traders coming from that area, I cannot help but think that something is peculiar about British enforcement to the west. Just a sense."

Letter Home

Wednesday, the 5th of February 1805
Fort-de-France, Martinique

My dear sister and brother,

I am writing to you from the veranda of the home of Geneviève, wife of the senior Captain Robert Johnson. Please know that Jane and I are safe and well.

I am certain that you must believe me the most horrible of sisters, headstrong and foolish. I exhibited the worst of ingratitude and impudence when I chose to run away by myself and cast my lot with the crew of Lady Bridget. As you doubtless already know, Jane accompanied me, for which I will be forever grateful. Please be aware that she had <u>no part</u> in my scheming and that she tracked me down in Plymouth and chose to remain with me from her deep well of family loyalty. Jane has become one of the most respected members of our crew, and I do believe she has won a special place in the heart of our captain.

You were right, dear sister, to be concerned for our safety at sea. The ocean is enormous and is no dreary, safe English countryside. Even in the first underway days, I succumbed to the dreaded seasickness. And yet, our beloved mentor, Harriet Dunsford, the quartermaster's wife, has taught me how to manage that. By contrast, Jane seems to have taken most amiably to life afloat and was not affected by the mal-de-mer. She and I have worked hard and contributed our fair share to the running of our vessel. I dare say, you would be amazed by my growing strength and endurance.

On our way, Lady Bridget sailed through a fierce storm lasting several days that blew us far off course. I should have been frightened, but with our good instruction, the competence of the captain and crew, and Jane's enduring calm and companionship, I never feared for our survival.

We have put in at Fort-de-France, on the island of Martinique, for repairs and trade. Geneviève, our Captain Johnson's stepmother, is one of the most gracious and beautiful woman I have ever met. Her kindness and hospitality are an inspiration. She has given me a great deal of encouragement to use my French, and I find myself wonderfully at home in the language, particularly when speaking with Geneviève's adorable very young son and daughter. Those children, in turn, adore Jane and Robert. Tomorrow, I shall put my language skills to the ultimate test as I wade into the local market, gathering intelligence for our provisioning negotiations.

Once our ship is repaired and our trades completed, we shall set sail for Jamaica, and then will return safe home to England. While I have already admitted to being a most dreadful sister, I cannot truly regret my impetuous decision. The warm, spice-laden breezes and the sapphire seas are more vivid and more wonderful than even my wildest dreams. Please forgive Colonel Brandon for his part in stoking my wanderlust. Tell him I see firsthand that he told the truth. I doubt that I could ever again be as happy in England as I am in this tropical paradise.

Know that we are safe, dear sister and brother, and that we will take all precautions. I will write again from Jamaica.

Your horrible, dreadful,
but contented sister,
Margaret

Chapter Thirteen
The Work Begins

Mary continued chatting with Charlotte and William as they boarded their carriage for the trip from Hunsford Cottage to the station for their trip to London.

"We shan't be long gone, Mary," Charlotte assured. "London is a city of immense interest, but the noise and commotion wear on my country sensibilities."

Mary smiled. "Aye, the times I have visited, it seemed as if I were in a maelstrom. Still, I do envy the opportunity to converse with the publisher and to visit those grand bookstores on Charing Cross Road. Perhaps another time. Who knows where our adventures will take us?"

She and Charlotte exchanged final hugs. Mary embraced William. "Take good care as well, sir. I know you will return with fresh new ideas and inspirations."

He kissed her on the cheek and they were off.

Mary waited, watching them disappear down the lane and the sounds of hoof beats faded. "Do take care, William. And Charlotte, as well," she whispered. She turned about and began to wander the grounds. A promise of spring showed in corners of the garden. Charlotte had planted imported Dutch crocuses, which were only now peeking through the ground, showing a hint of purple. On the far side of the fallow ground, two witch hazel bushes had opened their precocious flowers — a gift to Lady Catherine from the botanist Peter Collinson, who had recently imported them from the Americas.

Thoughts of the Americas brought Margaret Dashwood to mind. Mary had received only a single letter from her since that monumental time in Oxford. Margaret had shared in confidence her resolve to travel to the Americas, or at least to the Caribbean, despite her family's objections. Mary wondered if those plans had come to fruition. How strange, she thought, that she felt no draw for such travel. This meager push of English spring was enough. The fires of ideas were more than sufficient substitution for blazing sun and sapphire seas. Mary hoped that Margaret had indeed begun her journey and that she was safe.

Constance had already finished her chores, and made her way home some time before the Collinses' departure. Mary turned toward the cottage, noting that the chickens were emerging from their coops to scratch for the fresh grain that Constance had scattered. Their young maid was efficient and attentive to the animals' needs.

Mary took the key from her coat pocket and entered the cottage. The interior was still warm from its recent occupancy, fragrances of the last meal still hanging in the air. She wandered from room to room, feeling an uncomfortable sense of trespassing. She admired what Charlotte had done to construct an atmosphere of dignity with her décor, a feeling of "rightness." William had been, early on, unappreciative of these refinements, but admitted to Mary how his appreciation was growing. Again, Mary examined her feelings for William, arguing with herself as to whether they were feelings of true love or merely the infatuation of a young woman — she thought for certain that she was no longer really a girl.

She harbored no jealousy of Charlotte. She did not consider Charlotte a rival, but a partner. She sensed Charlotte's growing love and respect for William, and judged that good. Why must nature force upon them such exclusivity of relations? Mary sat in her accustomed chair at the table, the chair she occupied when she and William transformed into Joseph Weatherstone, the chair where she and Charlotte edited those magnificent, world-changing tomes. She sat in solitude, no sounds save the occasional gust of wind and ticking clock. Her meditation continued half an hour or so.

At last she frowned and looked about the well-appointed dining room. "You are asking the wrong question, Mary Bennet. The question should not be '*why must* nature force upon us exclusivity?' The real question should be '*does* nature force upon us exclusivity?' I do not recall anyone's asking that question. I certainly do not recall an answer." She rose from her chair and began pacing the rooms, running her hands along the edges of cupboards, tables, and chairs, agitated. At last she made her way to William's study, his library. Entering, she inhaled the magnificent fragrance of books, the hundreds of books, which represented to her the true power in the world.

Mary had little doubt that the answer to this essential question hid in one of the hundreds of books now surrounding her. It was, after all, a theological and philosophical question. She sat down in William's chair, realizing that, despite her diligence and scholarship to date, her education and experience were woefully inadequate for the task on which she now embarked. She turned to his desk, spying the pile of notes she had penned. She smiled, picking up the top third of the stack. She opened several, remembering her feelings as she had opened her mind — and heart — to him.

The content of the missives included a good bit of critique of William's preaching. Even in the solitude of the library in the otherwise-empty cottage, she blushed at her brash pronouncements. Still, he had taken them to heart in many cases. Though indelicately worded, the critiques were correct for the most part. Her heart raced to see that on several occasions he had underlined portions of her writing and made notations to check one reference or another.

Midway through the sampling, she saw that he had written in the margin "Mary, Mary, Mary" in a hand unmistakably his, but written with much more care than the manuscripts she had edited after joining collaboration with Charlotte. Mary found herself breathing rapidly at the idea of William thinking of her as he toiled, alone, in his sanctuary. It occurred to her that he had preached several times on the meaning and sanctity of marriage. He had preached those sermons before she began her work with Charlotte, and thus she had not seen the manuscripts from those Sundays. She had read the printed copies in books and considered how dreary the editor in Oxford must have found them.

Yet, she was certain that she would have commented on them. She set aside the more recent notes, careful to maintain their order and appearance. She browsed through her early, even brasher, letters until she found three commented on William's sermons about marriage. Mary was gratified that her own detailed nature included writing the dates on each of her notes. She rose from the seat and made her way to the shelves containing the bound copies. The three sermons of interest resided in the second and third volumes. She took them to William's desk and began re-reading those early pronouncements. In keeping with his early approach to preaching, they covered marriage, but not love; duty, but not passion or romance. Mary noted with some satisfaction that the editor had done a rather perfunctory job — correct but simple, leaving out many of William's original notations. With considerable pride, she realized that her own work surpassed the Oxford editor's work.

After reading the three sermons, she pondered how they had been processed before her collaboration. She and Charlotte had been very careful to preserve William's original manuscripts without additional markings so that he would not be aware of their joint efforts. Mary and Charlotte had forwarded to the London publisher only Mary's smooth drafts. She hoped that the Oxford editor had returned his originals.

Mary stood up and began to search each of the shelves until she located the papers, tidy and in order as expected, each tied with a ribbon. She retrieved the three chapters, marking their locations for their, and took them to his desk. As she had hoped, each ponderous piece was endowed with generous notations, from Greek characters that existed in the original literature to page numbers in specific books. Realizing that the editor had ignored these notations further diminished her opinion of him. It was little wonder that the volumes that resulted from her collaboration with Charlotte were outselling the earlier works by a wide margin among scholars.

Mary had little difficulty finding and retrieving some of the references specified in the margins of his writing. She began having difficulty reading the writings and realized that the hour was late and the day fast fading. She stacked the books to the side of his desk and arranged the papers to continue later. She scurried through the house, ensuring that doors were bolted or locked. So absorbed had she been in the studies that she did not realize how the temperature inside the cottage had fallen. Her hands were stiff with cold and she shivered in her wrap, which had been adequate during the earlier part of the day when the Collinses departed. She finally locked the cottage door and half-walked, half-ran back to Pemberley.

Elizabeth was waiting for her, quite concerned by her long absence. "I was about to send a servant to see if you were in danger."

"I was working on the edits to the latest volume and lost track of time," Mary said.

Elizabeth scowled. "You should have brought them here. It is getting quite chill outside, and I feared that you could have been out in the dark on your way back. We have enough concerns for your safety."

Mary nodded. "You are quite right, sister. In the future, I will be sure to pay attention to the time. Still, it was most advantageous to have access to Mr. Collins's library while doing our work."

After a warm meal, Mary went to bed. Memories of the marginal notation "Mary, Mary, Mary" caused her to smile as she drifted off to sleep.

* * *

Jacques and Marie returned from their beach excursion filled with excitement. They presented Geneviève with an assortment of colorful shell treasures. Margaret continued to translate among the children, Geneviève, Robert, and Jane. They had not discussed keeping Geneviève's English prowess secret, but Margaret sensed by Geneviève's sweet smile that she appreciated the discretion.

After bidding the children a good night, Margaret, Jane, and Robert left the house, promising to return for meals regularly during their stay. The three strolled down the hill to the inn. Jane and Robert told of their adventures with the children, and Margaret set forth her plans for the following days, including the admonition to not reveal her knowledge of French. The inn was a short distance from the waterfront, and they observed a spectacular sunset on the ocean.

Jane turned to Robert, smiling. "Red sky at night, sailors delight."

Back at the inn, Jane and Margaret prepared for bed. Margaret reviewed the notes she had on the vendors they would encounter the following day and went over how she was to be a "classic difficult Englishwoman."

Jane laughed as she said, "That cannot be so hard!"

* * *

After breakfast, they set off for the market. Jane carried a small basket for purchases and Margaret reveled in the bright colors and bold fragrances of fruits she knew only from books.

At their first encounter, she eyed mangos, big and plump, bright red. She looked up at the vendor's sign — Jean Oualou. In a forced heavy English accent, she asked the man at the stall, "How much for the mangos?"

He turned to the woman behind him, presumably his wife, who was unpacking a crate of green coconuts. He confided to her. *"Watch this. I wager I can get her to pay five times the price."* He turned back to Margaret, smiling. *"Deux francs.* Two francs."

Margaret smiled in return and handed him two coins. She gave the mango to Jane, who placed it in her basket as they moved down the street.

"How much was it?" Jane asked, eyeing the beautiful fruit.

"About four shillings," Margaret said.

Jane smiled. "That is quite good, then."

Margaret smirked. "If he knew I understood French, it would have cost about nine pence."

Jane's expression darkened. "Then he cheated us. Are you not going to demand the proper price?"

Margaret laughed as she replied. "No, indeed. Your first impression that it was a good price would be correct in London. We will be paying whatever they ask today. Two days hence, we will be meeting with them to provision us for the voyage to Jamaica. Two days hence, as if by magic, I will be speaking like a native."

They visited Louis Dupré's spice shop, where they paid seven times the real price for cinnamon and three times the real price for ginger. They purchased two flutes for Jacques and Marie at Mme. Lessaire's shop for two and a half times.

As they approached the end of the street, Jane looked downcast. "They are every one overcharging us. This is most unseemly."

Margaret shook her head. "Geneviève told me to expect this as long as I was a classic difficult Englishwoman. By all appearances, we are quite wealthy. And there is no love lost between France and England, even here."

Jane nodded. "I suppose." Then she brought her face up alert. "Remember Geneviève said we will be having fish for the noon meal. She asked us to get a good flounder or tuna."

They strode up to a fishmonger and surveyed the catch. Two men stood behind the rack.

Margaret announced in loud, stiff English, "I need a good flounder or tuna!"

The burly man at the back kept a straight face while telling his coworker, *"Sell her that big one on the side. It is two days gone. The cat would not even touch it."*

The front vendor picked up the fish and held it forward. "Five francs," he said.

Jane and Margaret eyed the specimen, which was very pretty.

Margaret reached for her money, but paused for a moment and began a conspicuous twitching of her nose. She leaned forward — close to the fish — and smelled it. She threw back her hands with great drama and twisted her face. "That thing is horrid!" she shouted. She looked up at the seller's sign. "Come, Jane, we shall not be buying anything from Pierre Lepeu!"

The expression on the face of the man in the rear changed to alarm. *"Do something! Quickly! She will report us to Geneviève!"*

As Margaret and Jane turned to walk away, the front merchant ran up to them. In stumbling English, he pleaded, "Forgive me, Madame. I must have picked up the wrong fish. Please return so that we can make a proper selection!"

The two women eyed each other, all seriousness. They eased back to the stall with the burly man nowhere to be seen.

The merchant presented several alternatives. Margaret sniffed each one, nodded, and selected two large flounders.

She reached again for her money, but the seller waved his hands. "With my compliments, for the grievous mistake with the first one."

Margaret looked at Jane and nodded before returning to Pierre. "That is very kind. I will give a good word — how do you say it? — *bon mot* — to Geneviève for you."

They walked away from the relieved seller. It was all Margaret could do to keep from bursting out laughing as she interpreted in her head the argument behind her. Jane kept her eyes ahead and smiled. The word "*idiot*" did not need translation.

* * *

With shopping finished, they made their way up the hill and presented their purchases to Geneviève, who guided them again to the kitchen.

"The fish are beautiful. How much did you pay for them?" she asked.

"Compliments of Pierre Lepeu!" Margaret responded.

Geneviève registered surprise. *"You drive a hard bargain."*

Margaret shrugged. *"Just followed my nose."* She laughed.

Geneviève looked to Jane and then back to Margaret. *"Do we trust her?"*

"With our lives," Margaret replied, nodding.

"My dear Jane," Geneviève began. "We should like to welcome you into our sisterhood."

Jane began to laugh a joyful laugh.

"Of course, you are sworn to secrecy the same as your fellow traveler, even from my fine 'son' Robert."

Jane bowed low. "Of course."

Margaret and Jane recounted their morning dealings with the merchants. While Margaret had dealt with their purchases, Jane had observed the interactions between the people in the shops and had taken note of the inventories therein.

Geneviève particularly enjoyed the recounting of the fish purchase. On reflection, the *gratis* offering of the fish almost offset the overcharges of the other items. "I will make a certain show of smelling his wares in the future," Geneviève said, laughing.

The three remained in the kitchen as the noon meal was prepared. Through Margaret, Jane conversed with the cooks, exchanging thoughts and tips on meal preparation.

Robert arrived with Mr. Graham and Harriet. Again, through Margaret's interpretation, they related the progress of repairs and their satisfaction with the cargo crew that Geneviève had recommended.

Jane smiled a serene smile, watching as Margaret performed her duties with great professionalism.

Chapter Fourteen
Emerging from the Chrysalis

Mary returned to Hunsford Cottage the following day, eager to continue her research. She devoted the first half of the day to editing the next sermon in the series that she and Charlotte curated. The other half she devoted to her own research on the exclusivity of marriage.

William had preached the sermons she now edited after she had begun her collaboration with Charlotte, but before they revealed their collaboration to William. It pleased her to note the increased sensitivity of his writing and relieved to see that he maintained his rigorous documentation. With the advantage of time and familiarity, she recognized thoughts and even phrases from her letters to him woven into his sermons from time to time. Even his vocabulary evolved as he took into account the feelings of his congregants and as he wrestled with the nuances of some ambiguous passages. Those scriptures with uncertain meaning were almost always accompanied by voluminous references to conflicting authorities.

His spelling and paragraph structures still brought smiles to her lips. She and Charlotte would not soon be out of work.

Her marriage research proved far more challenging. While William's preaching on marriage had acquired more emphasis on love, loyalty, and mutual respect, he had little, if any, interest in marriage relationships beyond the single husband of one wife. She located the books he referenced on marriage, a minute subsection of his library.

Most of the books clung to the narrow topic of responsibilities within marriage. Only two discussed alternate relations. Mary learned that the proper term for marriages involving more than one partner was polygamy, from the Greek "many marrying." This included polygyny, meaning "many" and "female," and polyandry — "many" and "male." Both works judged that polygamy was confined to Hebrew scripture. For these authors, the concept that monogamy was the only acceptable form of marriage relied on only three lines in the entire Christian scripture, two in the book of Timothy, and one in Titus. All three passages dealt with qualifications of deacons or bishops, not ordinary adherents to the faith. They made no mention of these relationships beyond their Biblical context — nary a mention of social or legal acceptability. But then, William and his peers were theologians and not lawyers.

Try as she might, Mary could not find a specific point in history when plural marriages became unacceptable. She vowed to continue her reading, and made careful notes of the references she found in two volumes against the day when she might have access to a more complete library.

Having exhausted William's books on the subject of exclusivity, Mary turned her full attention to editing his sermons. By the time William and Charlotte returned from London, Mary had completed her work on four additional sermons.

* * *

Charlotte was keen to inform Mary that their publisher intended to reprint William's earlier sermons, with Mary now as the editor of a revised series.

"When Mr. Prentice, our publisher, asked what accounted for Mr. Collins's sudden improvement in scholarship during the third year," she said, "I explained that the improvement was due to a combination of his increased experience and growing empathy, but also to the serious efforts of his fine new editor. Mr. Prentice told me, 'Well, by all means, keep it up.'"

Charlotte's and William's biggest news, however, was that Joseph Weatherstone's *Scripture Cries Out for Freedom* had entered its fourth printing, with each run larger than the previous printing. The manifesto had become a staple in the arguments raging — regardless of one's stance — over slavery. Charlotte laughed at the shocked look on Mary's face as she related that partisans were burning copies in public to show their support of bondage.

"But, Mary, my dear, that means they have paid good sterling to acquire some extraordinarily expensive firewood. Joseph's work is appearing in print far faster than they can burn it."

Mary mused on this peculiar turn of events. She took great comfort knowing that she would be spending more time with William as they refined his earlier sermons and produced additional missives from Joseph.

Mary's excitement rose further when Charlotte presented her with an entire box of best quality writing paper, explaining that royalties and advances from their efforts now permitted a more professional and lasting relationship with her pen.

As promised, while in London, Charlotte made inquiries of

several universities on Mary's behalf. In each case, her presentations were met by initial polite dismissals. Still, the scholars' attitudes shifted quickly when they learned that Mary was Weatherstone's editor, at which point, they indicated a desire to meet with her with the understanding that there were no women teachers in the universities.

Mary found herself facing the prospect of achieving precisely what she had set out to accomplish. She might soon emerge into the great world of ideas, in the vanguard of the struggle for freedom ... but without William.

Charlotte watched with amusement Mary's stunned silence. "You did not appreciate your immense talents, dear child. But those publishers did. To a person, they commented on your clarity of editing and the greater ease of reading." She studied Mary. "I see that I have presented you with quite the dilemma. Let us allow these decisions time to mellow. We must soon talk with Elizabeth and Mr. Darcy as regards your future."

* * *

As spring gave way to summer, two volumes of Mr. Collins's sermons took form during the now-regular weekday visits —*Volume 1, Revised* and *Volume 7*. A third work began to take shape during Sunday discussions between Mary and William. Using the ponderous title *The Way Forward, or Rising from the Ashes of Slavery*, the two worked to produce a plan of practical action, with the goal of easing the transition to a post-bondage empire. As neither had any actual experience with slave owning, nor any benefit from the trade, they felt free to exercise their imaginations unencumbered.

Their weekday work was serious and efficient. Mary arrived soon after breakfast each day and occupied the dining room table with her writing, shuttling between the table and library. When Charlotte was at home, Mary enjoyed conversing with her and enjoyed looking after the noon meal with Constance when Charlotte visited parishioners. Both Mary and Charlotte listened to early versions of William's weekly sermons, and felt free to give strong, but good-humored, critiques of his efforts.

Their sermon reviews worked to the benefit of the congregation. His weekly homilies often generated conversations after services, sometimes lasting an hour or more. For the first time in decades, the sermons elicited laughter on occasion, and even a fleeting smile from

Lady Catherine.

At the end of each weekday's work, Mary embraced Charlotte and William as she departed. After their Sundays alone together, William and Mary extended their parting embrace with gentle kisses.

* * *

The repairs to *Lady Bridget's* mast approached completion when Robert hosted a meeting with the town's merchants to provision *Lady Bridget* for the remainder of her voyage. He explained that, as his agent, Margaret Dashwood was authorized to conclude contracts and make payments for goods and services. The sturdy hall had served generations of merchants, portraits of forebears decorating the stone walls. The suppliers sat on long benches lining the sides, and a large, heavy table occupied one end, with chairs for the negotiators. Robert stood in the back, arms crossed, enjoyed a light breeze in the open doorway.

The merchants smiled and exchanged comments among themselves, joking — in French — about the "bargaining prowess" of the young English woman, Margaret, and her "maid," Jane. Robert finished his introduction and took a seat on the side of the room. Margaret donned a sweet smile and began her part of the meeting in clear, fluent French. The smiles of the merchants vanished.

"As you have said, the young English woman appeared to have no idea of the price of anything on offer in this fair town. Indeed, the young English woman would have had no idea — had she not had access to the sales records for our past five voyages to Fort-de-France. The young English woman would not have recognized that she was being overcharged by as much as five-fold, were she not able to understand the language.

"But the young English woman does understand, and her very able assistant takes excellent notes regarding the commercial relationships in Fort-de-France. The young English woman does not have patience with protracted negotiations about prices, so let us proceed using real numbers, and we can all return to our businesses in short order.

She turned to Jane. "If I may have our price proposals, Miss Moseby."

With dignity, Jane handed Margaret a sheaf of papers. "Yes, Miss Dashwood."

"Monsieur Oualou, we enjoyed the fine 40-centimes mangos you sold to us for two francs. You offer to sell us twenty crates at a bit more than one franc each fruit — believing that I was unaware the fruit

would last only three to five days before spoiling. We will take two crates at 40-centimes each fruit. We both know that is a very generous offer to pay full honest retail, yes?"

Oualou nodded.

"In addition, we will purchase twenty crates of limes at 10-centimes each fruit. My assistant and I will personally inspect the limes, since they will last two weeks, but only if they are, in fact, fresh. We wouldn't want any over-ripe fruits, would we?"

He agreed.

Margaret continued her list through dried papaya and coconut and an assortment of root vegetables.

"Monsieur Oualou, you no doubt notice that I am paying full retail. I will not demand wholesale prices on this voyage as long as we do not linger in our negotiations, and the produce — on inspection — meets our expectations of quality. You may not experience that courtesy on future voyages, since I see that you charged double on previous negotiations. Do we understand each other?"

"Oui, mademoiselle," he said, taking her list, and departing.

She turned next to a grim-faced Louis Dupré.

"Oh, monsieur, do not look so downcast. Your exquisite spices will soon be offered for sale to the finest shops in London. We require more kilos than you sell in a normal year, and will offer the same retail prices as with Monsieur Oualou — this time. I realize that is a large order, but I am sure you can get the quantities we need from Monsieur Cartier on the far side of the island before we sail."

Louis blanched. *"You know Cartier?"*

"No." She laughed. *"But, I heard your wife say that Monsieur Cartier could provide what we needed. I still prefer to deal with you — for now."*

"Ah." He took his list and left the room.

In like manner, she purchased flatbreads and hardtack, specifying that they would inspect it for dryness and observe the crating to guard against worms infesting the stores.

She purchased cured beef and salt pork.

With each negotiation, Jane handed her a list, which Margaret relayed to the supplier.

The final vendor was Pierre Lepeu.

She smiled a wicked smile. *"So, Monsieur Lepeu, we meet again. I must say, we very much enjoyed those fine, very FRESH flounders you last provided us. We baked them with a lemon glaze and a hint of red pepper and herbs, fragrant and delicious."* She paused, awaiting his reply.

"I am honored that you enjoyed them," he said nervously.

"You must be relieved that you corrected Emmanuel's error before we left the market."

He shook his head as he muttered, *"She knows Emmanuel? Of course she knows Emmanuel."*

"While we so wish that we could take your FRESH fish with us, alas, we cannot. But you can supply us with the dried fish on this list, no?"

He took her proffered list and looked it over. *"Oui, mademoiselle."*

"And it would be good to keep Emmanuel away from the selection task."

He smiled. *"Oui, mademoiselle."*

She rose, and they shook hands. *"Au revoir, Monsieur Lepeu."*

"Merci, Mademoiselle Dashwood."

The room was now empty of vendors. Margaret and Jane hugged.

Jane turned to Robert and handed him their master list with total prices.

His eyes grew wide. "I understood almost nothing of what you said. How on earth did you get these prices?"

Margaret and Jane laughed again. Margaret replied, *"C'est un secret."*

Chapter Fifteen
Everything Changes

On a pleasant July morning, Mary and William sat at table constructing *The Way Forward*. After opening Hunsford Cottage's windows to invite in buoyant summer air, Charlotte sat finishing a smocked baby gown for a parishioner who was due to give birth in August. She smiled as she listened to Mary and William in mental battle collaborating as the two minds of Joseph Weatherstone.

"I believe, Mr. Weatherstone, that three full chapters challenging the scriptural legitimacy of slavery are entirely too much. They would occupy a third of the new work and they cover the same ground that *Scripture Cries Out* has already covered; and they do not contribute to the forward direction we desire in our new work."

"On those three points you are correct, Miss Weatherstone. But if the challenge were unnecessary, then we would not still be engaged in a national battle over slavery, would we?"

Charlotte watched as Mary folded her hands on the table, preparing for the ritual fight that characterized their working pattern. Mary remained placid, while William looked mildly exasperated, sensing that he was losing the intellectual exchange.

Constance brought fresh tea for everyone.

"Thank you, dear," Charlotte said, as she and the servant exchanged knowing looks.

Mary continued, "Have we presented these points before, Mr. Weatherstone?"

"Yes."

"In what work?"

"*Scripture Cries Out*, of course. Why …?"

"And, are people reading *Scripture Cries Out*?" Mary raised her eyebrows.

William tried to scowl to mask his smile. "Yes — except those who burned their copies."

She stifled a laugh. "True — except those who burned their copies. And, Mr. Weatherstone, that great treatise is now in its fourth and largest printing. I rather doubt that anyone reading our current work will be unfamiliar with the first."

"Hmmm," he said, folding his arms. "I acknowledge that your arguments are compelling. But I still believe that the scriptural arguments are inseparable from the practical paths we propose."

They sat for a period until he started, glancing at the clock. "I must away to visit Mr. Patterson to discuss arrangements for his father's funeral. Shall we continue this matter later?" He rose from his seat at the table.

"Indeed, sir." She nodded. "May I suggest a third possibility, Mr. Weatherstone? I can work to refine the first three chapters, to condense them. You will recall that we discarded over fifty pages from *Scripture Cries Out*, and you were unable to identify what I had removed when you first read the polished text."

He thought but a moment. "Right! I am forced to admit that Joseph's work would likely not be in its fourth printing in its original state. I do not know how long I shall be away with Mr. Patterson, but I think you ought to proceed with your scheme."

He bowed to Mary and gave Charlotte a kiss on the cheek as he left the cottage.

Mary's gaze lingered after him as he left, and then she returned to task, pulling out several fresh sheets of her new paper to begin Joseph's revised opening. A gentle breeze wafting into the cottage gave the room a pleasing freshness and comfortable feel. Songs of birds in the garden and the rustle of leaves blended with the lively bustling sounds of pots and pans emanating from the kitchen as Constance prepared lunch. The rich aroma of beef barley soup completed the feeling of happy comfort. Mary began to write.

"It is wonderfully amusing watching the two of you working together as Joseph," Charlotte said after a bit. "It is as if I am watching a dear old couple who have labored together for decades. When you bicker, it is good-natured and honest. Sometimes he prevails, sometimes you prevail, but always it is with good humor. The result has been a very productive Joseph."

"Thank you, Charlotte," Mary said. "You know that I value your good opinion. I am so much in debt to you for making all this possible. When I remember last October, when I was at the depth of frustration with that ridiculous school, with little prospect of fulfillment, I could not have imagined my current circumstances."

Charlotte held out the almost finished baby gown.

Mary nodded in admiration. "It is exquisite. She will love it!"

"Well, Mary, you have earned your current satisfaction. You have exercised the qualities we extolled that bright autumn afternoon.

Without benefit of further formal schooling, you have found respect and distinction in the highest circles. You have garnered both praise and ire from some of the most powerful personages of the Empire."

Mary paused her writing and gazed out the open window, across the garden to the fence where a pair of magpies frolicked. "Has it really been only nine months? It seems like many years ago," she murmured.

Charlotte looked toward the kitchen, ascertaining that Constance was immersed in meal preparation. She let the gown rest in her lap and watched Mary as she toiled, alternating her attention between documents and new writing. "Do you love him?" Charlotte asked.

Mary bolted upright, her expression one of shock. "I beg your pardon?"

"William. Do you love William?"

Mary colored. "William and I have a most proper relationship! We are colleagues — thoroughly honorable and proper."

Charlotte tilted her head. "Oh, my dear, I know that. Many people, I sense, mistake my ability to hold my tongue for a lack of observation. Be assured I am attentive to any signs of impropriety, and I have seen nothing to suggest that. That was not my question, now, was it?"

"No." Mary shook her head. "You asked if I love him."

"Well? Do you?"

Mary's gaze returned to the garden fence where the magpies continued their play. "I often believe that I love him." She turned to Charlotte. "At other times, I believe my feelings are little more than the infatuation of a silly girl, a silly girl captivated by a fine mind and sturdy character. You must trust me when I tell you that I would never do anything to hurt you."

Charlotte set the gown aside and moved to the table, sitting across from Mary, who was fighting tears. "Mary, dear Mary, I know that. I have not accused you of anything improper. I wanted to know because it is important. As I said, I am not unobservant. I watch the two of you labor together, and I see the clear admiration you possess, one for the other — the admiring smile, the turn of the head. It is rather sweet, actually. He probably does not notice, but I do supervise Constance when she cleans his library — it does not clean itself, you know. I see the treasured collection of your notes, and I know that he values them above anything else in that room. And, of course, you two share your minds in a way quite removed from my experiences. I do not feel inferior in that, only different. My needs and priorities dwell in other areas.

"I believe that you do love him; that you love him for good reasons, Mary. There is not a great gap between our ages, and your level of maturity exceeds that of most young women of your age. That is true. Our honesty with each other may prevent misunderstandings."

"Thank you for your remarkable observations and confidences," Mary replied, now at ease. "I marvel at your understanding of my feelings and realize that you possess great wisdom. I have for so long felt alone with my impossible longings, even ashamed at times. If it does not seem presumptuous, perhaps it is fair, then, for me to ask, for I have likewise wondered — do *you* love him?"

Charlotte pondered the question for some time. "Indeed, that is a fair question, though my answer will likely seem wanting. I respect Mr. Collins. I have been faithful to my vows, and I have not an eye for anyone else. I do not dislike him. When I married him, it was for the security that marriage provided for myself and for my family. By virtue of birth and connections, he could give us the material protection we needed. As you will recall, he and I married very soon after your sister rejected him. In the first year, our relationship could charitably be called loveless.

"You know that your sister and I considered him a ridiculous man at the time. You observed, no doubt, that Lizzie was quite pointed in her evaluation. And, in so many ways, he *was* ridiculous —pompous, haughty, and insensitive. He presented a terrible face of the church to our parish, and I was the one left to offer what pastoral care I might.

"You and I have shared enough that I can share with you that we had no marital relations in that first year. But I cannot lay all faults with him. I was distant because the thought of intimacy with that Mr. Collins held no appeal for me."

Mary had folded her hands before her on the table. "I am sorry."

"Well, but then you came along. At first, my intent in this collaboration had been to provide you an outlet for your talents as a favor to Lizzie. And, I thought, in the off chance that you were competent at your tasks, it would add to our financial security. We know now that we shamefully underestimated your skills and energy. We underestimated your passion and moral authority, as well. You and William have helped to move our society forward in historic ways, even to the extent of creating, in Joseph Weatherstone, a phantom more powerful than some of the greatest men in our society.

"Furthermore, with you by his side and informing his thoughts, Mr. Collins has become a better person, more attentive, more caring. He and I have even had relations, though not often. His flock appreciates the transformation, Lady Catherine appreciates it, and he has even impressed your brother-in-law — no small accomplishment. Perhaps the crowning achievement is that your sister Elizabeth agrees that Mr. Collins is no longer a ridiculous man."

Charlotte continued, "But do I love him? I cannot in truth say that I do. Respect, yes. Admire, yes. I am faithful to him, and he to me, he has fulfilled my expectations, and he seems satisfied with our marriage. But, true love may be beyond our grasp."

Mary sat in silence, hands still folded.

"I suspect, too, Mary, that you hold close the thought that; had circumstances and time conspired otherwise, you instead might have been Mrs. Collins."

Mary lowered her head.

"On one of my visits to William's library, I noticed some papers you had left behind regarding plural marriage." Charlotte sported a mischievous smile.

Mary colored anew. "I was curious and did what research I could with the resources available."

"Diligent, as I would expect of you. And what have you found?"

"This conversation has taken a most peculiar turn, Charlotte."

"Humor me, please, for I have been curious myself upon occasion."

"Well," said Mary, "I know the scriptures well and have studied the commentaries here and what I have found is that marriages of strictly one man and one woman are a rather recent convention and quite narrow in scope. In Christian scripture, the requirement seems meant for certain church leaders. In the commentaries, the conclusions usually are that polygynous marriages were advantageous long ago when deaths of young men, in battle in particular, were more common and disproportionate, and poverty even more extreme than today. It was a simple expedient for the needs of society."

As Mary continued an exposition of her finding, her hands became animated accompanying her explanations. Charlotte, in turn, folded her own, listening with quiet interest.

"Today, the civil law does not recognize plural marriages in Europe. It is still practiced in Arabia and other foreign lands and our society supposedly regards the practice as barbaric. I say 'supposedly.' It is, of course, ironic, given the number of prominent men in Britain and on the continent known to have mistresses, often with their wive's tacit approval. The practice carries with it the implication of wealth and power. Some of those relations have produced children who are cut off from inheritance, but who still benefit from connections to the men in question. In a very practical sense, we still condone the Old Testament patriarchy, yet without any legal backing to safeguard the vulnerable members of those relationships."

They paused their discussion when Constance appeared with lunch. The day's fare included the anticipated beef barley soup as well as fresh apricots from the garden.

After the meal, Mary returned to writing and Charlotte to the gown.

"I am delighted that we had our conversation, Mary. I sense that we trust one another and that we all three hold the good fortunes of the others in our hearts."

Mary breathed a sigh of relief. "I agree with you, Charlotte, and I am so happy that we are able to enjoy such good company as friends and colleagues."

Mary continued her writing and Charlotte continued her sewing. After an hour or so, Charlotte whispered, "Mary, I would not be offended if your relationship went further."

* * *

Both the senior and younger Captains Johnson took a keen interest in recent studies regarding preservation of food for sea voyages. From childhood, the younger Robert hated the worms and decay that so often infested their seagoing fare. From time to time, he would go hungry rather than face the putrid food.

On the senior Captain Robert Johnson's second voyage to Fort-de-France — the voyage on which he proposed to Geneviève —she introduced him to Mulambo Katanga, and the two formed an instant bond. Johnson admired Katanga's intuitive grasp of the science of preservation and engaged his services on every voyage thereafter.

Part of the secret of the Johnsons' relative prosperity in the shipping business was their lower cost of provisions and their generally healthier crew.

Margaret and Jane supervised the preparation of *Lady Bridget*'s provisions. Margaret likewise enjoyed Monsieur Katanga's insights, especially since her French allowed her to revel in his tales of slaves one-upping their masters in the bad old days. She urged him to expand his business to other islands, even to England.

With his perpetual jovial laugh, he explained that he was quite happy as he was. *"Any more success, and I shall have to work!"* he explained.

She laughed. *"I know how industrious you are. You do not fool me."*

* * *

"I am in a quandary, Jane." Margaret said as she gazed from the writing table on Geneviève's veranda to the harbor below.

Jane looked up. "Well, then, all is normal with you. I am relieved." She returned to folding the finished laundry.

Margaret tried to ignore Jane's comment, but could not help smiling. "I am writing the first of my series of reports on slavery in the Caribbean, and I hesitate to write it under my own name."

Jane looked up. "But there appears to be no slavery here."

"I know, though there are still vast differences between the classes, in part a vestige of the past. And, yet, there is thriving commerce, wealth, and general calm. I know that slavery is not abolished throughout the French colonies, but in the area around Fort-de-France, it has effectively ceased. Much of the credit must go to Geneviève and Captain Johnson, of course. I intend to use this region's success for comparison with the other locations where slavery still exists."

"Pardon me, Margaret, but it appears that your story is already quite well developed, and that you are able to describe the situation here. What, then, is your quandary?"

"Right," Margaret said. "I have almost finished my writing, but I do not believe that my work will be published, much less taken seriously, when they see that a woman wrote it."

Jane paused folding, moved to the table, and examined Margaret's work for several minutes. "That would be a pity. I have seen your works before, and this exceeds by a good measure your prior efforts — quite polished. You should present your work under a *nom de plume*."

Margaret scowled. "I thought of that, but I cannot imagine such a ruse would work. It would not take very long to be discovered, I should think."

"Then you must solicit a sponsor, an unimpeachable scholar — such as your very good friend, Joseph Weatherstone?"

Margaret dropped her head into her hands. "But he is not real, Jane — you know that." When she raised her head back up, she saw Jane smiling. "You are right, of course, Jane. I shall forward these to Mary Bennet, who would be more than happy to bring them to light. So, then what will I use as a pen name?"

"Hmmmm. What is the manly equivalent of Margaret?" Jane asked.

She thought a moment. "I recall it is Gareth."

"Oh, I dare say I like that. And Gareth's last name might invoke your Dashwood free spirit. What say you to Speedwell?"

"Gareth Speedwell … Gareth Speedwell … I like it! So it is. 'Observations on the State of Slavery in the Caribbean Region,' by Gareth Speedwell, Esquire. I certainly think that he should be Esquire."

Jane laughed. "Most certainly. Nothing less than Esquire would do."

* * *

Dearest Mary,

Much has happened of consequence since our exhilarating days together in Oxford. I hope that all is well with you and that you are finding fulfillment in your fight for freedom. I am engaged as a productive member of the crew of Lady Bridget, which sailed from Plymouth and England's dreary winter only a few weeks after our sojourn at the abolition meeting.

I am writing to you from the port of Fort-de-France on Martinique, where I have had the opportunity to observe an economy once dependent on slavery, but that has moved on to an economy founded on commerce ruled by quality of goods and skills of trading. I have had the great good fortune to meet an observer, a British citizen, named Gareth Speedwell. His writing bears a strong resemblance to my own in the same way that Joseph Weatherstone's writing bears a resemblance to your own. If Gareth's writing pleases you and seems of value, I would ask that you present it to

Mr. Weatherstone to see if he might pass it on to publishers friendly to the movement, as suggested at our Oxford meeting. I regret that our missives could not be more immediate and intimate, but the sea is vast, and our thoughts of necessity travel slowly across the great Atlantic. I hope at this voyage's end, we may be free to meet again and share our adventures. With sisterly affection,
Margaret Dashwood

* * *

Observations on the State of Slavery in the Caribbean Region
by Gareth Speedwell, Esquire

I, Gareth Speedwell, a citizen of England, with good fortune and privilege not of my own making, have been blessed by providence to observe the disparate communities of some of the islands of the Caribbean Sea. Free of the burdens of weather and the social conventions of my native land, I have been able to let loose my thoughts amidst the intoxicating warmth, colors, and fragrances of these islands. Inspired by the writings of Wilberforce, More, and Weatherstone, I have endeavored to observe the practice and consequences of slavery in this part of the world where it is still an active practice.

My current port of call is Fort-de-France, on the French Island of Martinique. By virtue of its size, Martinique's agriculture is able to provide food, including tropical fruits and meat from livestock, for its population, supplemented by a bounty of fish and shellfish from the surrounding sea. The primary land crop is sugarcane, destined both for export as sugar and in the form of rum. Planting and harvesting sugarcane requires an immense amount of labor and was the province of slaves for the first century of French settlement. Because of the brutal nature of work under a tropical sun and the cruelty of the slave masters, bloody rebellions had occurred here with some frequency. The cost of providing security for the landowners, and for each leg of commerce, of necessity, are added to the production cost of sugar and other exported crops.

The citizenry of the Fort-de-France area elected to eliminate slavery some fifteen years ago and instituted a regimen to compensate landowners for their direct monetary loss — the original price of the slaves — over a ten-year period. While the program is judged a success by the local citizenry, the effects of the slave trade can linger here.

One of my favorite activities in Fort-de-France is strolling the market. While several former slave families have set up shops there, they often struggle with their businesses, as one would expect given the lack of training and family histories in commerce. Those that have done well tend to be the produce and meat merchants, whose slave labor experiences give them an advantage handling their products and evaluating and preserving product quality.

One merchant I note in particular, Monsieur Katanga, has done quite well not only selling cured meats, pork and beef in particular, but also maintaining a successful venture that provides curing services for other merchants. Monsieur Katanga was responsible for the drying ovens and smoke houses on the Delacour plantation when he was a slave. The skills and constructions associated with this occupation are scarce anywhere, and his family is the only one on the island able to provide these services. As such, his family does not compete with other merchants or landowners, and he provides an essential service. Thus Compagnie Katanga has integrated well into the Fort-de-France commercial community, and he is both respected and prosperous. His situation may provide a model for transitioning from slave-based economies to free economies.

As a side note — Compagnie Katanga provides curing and preservation services for ships' stores as well. Merchant vessels are finding that their savings from avoided spoilage exceed the cost of his services five-fold.

I shall update you, dear reader, from my next port.

Gareth Speedwell, Esquire

Chapter Sixteen
Uncharted Waters

July gave way to August, and August yielded to September. In late September came formal publication of *The Way Forward*. The printer labored in secrecy to prepare an initial press run far larger than any of Weatherstone's previous works. Profits from those early runs had allowed their London printer to acquire new presses that produced the books faster and could use a thinner paper. As a result, the new work fit in the pockets of both supporters and opponents.

The first run of *The Way Forward* arrived in bookshops on the last Tuesday of September and was out of stock by Friday. Several bookshops took the precautions of hiring guards, first against disturbances by pro-slavery partisans, and then against disappointed customers when the shops' stocks ran out.

Word of the book's fate took several weeks to reach Hunsford Cottage in Derbyshire.

As they enjoyed a quiet Sunday afternoon following services, Mary presented William with Margaret Dashwood's note and the enclosed letter from Gareth Speedwell, Esquire. A measure of their satisfaction this afternoon derived from discussions at the end of William's Sunday morning service. He had laid out comparisons from scripture between the responsibilities of slaves and those of paid laborers. For the second time in a month, Lord Edward had agreed with some of Reverend Collins's points and told of changes his family was making in anticipation of movements afoot in society that seemed inevitable. Lady Catherine observed their exchange with amused detachment, but kept her comments to herself.

William mused, "This Speedwell fellow writes quite well. I am surprised I have not heard his name mentioned before. He claims to be from a family of means, but in all my travels I have not encountered any Speedwells of note — no Speedwells at all, in fact."

"True." Mary observed. "Margaret's letter is wanting in detail, though I get the distinct impression that Gareth Speedwell is a close cousin of Joseph Weatherstone. He writes in a cursive as graceful as Joseph's."

William studied her, and then the letter for a while and smiled. "I see."

Mary continued, "Given that Gareth's observations support so many of our common aims, I shall forward a copy to Lord Brougham that he might pass it to *The Times*. That should keep the trail of custody sufficiently difficult to follow."

They sat at table, reading again Gareth's tales of his tropical paradise and plantation life. For the first time since early spring, their hands touched. A blush rose to her cheek, and she turned toward him.

Taking a deep breath, she said, "William, I have denied my passion these many months, but my desires have only grown. It is too much!"

Instead of retreating as before, William returned her embrace. "Mary, oh, Mary!"

Mary pulled away, rose from her chair, and stood before him. The room was silent save for the tick of the clock as they gazed at one another. He watched as she began to unfasten her dress, and then he reached out with one hand to caress her.

* * *

Warm mid-afternoon sunbeams washed over Mary and William. With the door closed, a small fireplace warmed his spare room to a most pleasant temperature. They talked with one another in the chamber, the only other sound the clock. Each noted the hour from time to time, but for the most part they gave attention to each other.

"I am the most vile of scoundrels," he said.

Mary chuckled. "Not the most vile by any stretch, sir. We British are renowned for our vile scoundrels, are we not? I really do not think that you rank among them."

He frowned. "Do not make light of what we have done … what we are doing. I have gravely sinned."

She propped herself up on her elbow. "'Most vile,' 'gravely sinned.' We are not at the bottom of some pit, William. You love me. I love you. Love is not of Hell, William, it is of Heaven."

He waved his hands in agitation. "Do not minimize this — do not trivialize it. We have committed adultery. You and I. Adultery!"

She sat up beside him, mellow light painting perfect soft shadows over her smooth round form. She pushed the sheets aside. "I think not, but what is the penalty for that?"

William grew irritated. "Eternal damnation!"

"Really?" She raised her eyebrows.

"Do not plead ignorance with me, young lady. You know very

well the price — eternal damnation of our souls."

"Where does it say that?"

"What?"

Mary drew her legs to her chest and rested a cheek on her knees. "Where is it prescribed that eternal damnation of the soul is the price of adultery, if this it be? I know that it is not English law. And even if it were, His Majesty, to the best of my knowledge, has dominion over neither Heaven nor Hell to enforce it."

"It is God's law!" William raised his voice.

"Where does it say that?" she demanded.

He looked shocked. "I cannot believe we are having this discussion. 'Thou shalt not commit adultery.'"

She turned her head to rest her chin on her knees. "A good answer, but not to the question I asked. Nowhere in Hebrew Scripture does it say that eternal damnation of the soul — or damnation of anything else — is the penalty for adultery. The penalty for adultery is death by stoning."

His face reddened. "Now you are being legalistic and trite!"

Mary remained serene. "No, my love. I am asking a completely pertinent question, the answer to which you have never given serious consideration. You know the texts better than I — you likely even know them in their original languages. The penalty for adultery was death by stoning. Which they carried out how many times?"

He paused, pondering her question.

"The answer is exactly never, sir. And in Christian Scripture? It is condemned without penalty."

He looked at her for some time. "I will need to examine this."

"Please do." She looked into his eyes for a while. "Would you send Charlotte away?"

"Absolutely not!"

"Good. If you had said 'yes,' I would agree that we have gravely sinned, that we were the vilest of people." She waited in silence. "Instead, I perceive that your affection for her has grown these many months. You have become more attentive to her needs and desires, have you not?"

"You are changing the subject. This is about you and me."

She lay down again, running her hands across his chest. "On the contrary. We cannot commit adultery in the eyes of God unless Charlotte be wronged. In the times of the patriarchs, you would be marrying me as well, and Charlotte and I would be partners ... or rivals. As we are already working so well together, and her happiness seems only to increase, I am certain it would be the former."

He reached over, moving a stray lock of hair away from her face. "We are not living in the times of the patriarchs. Our present law and customs make no provision for any relation other than a man and his wife. Nothing else."

She caressed his cheek. "Nothing else. No blessing, no curse."

He closed his eyes for a moment. "But there will be a curse. When word of our relations gets out, my life's work is destroyed." He opened his eyes and turned to her. "It does not matter. I know that many people still think me ridiculous."

"I beg your pardon, sir?" Mary sat up again. "Why do you say that?"

"I overhear conversations."

"Of late?"

He likewise sat up, his brow wrinkled. "Now that you ask, no. But I overheard conversations last year. The pain was real and persists. I have dedicated my life to the pursuit of the divine and I am serious in my studies. You, of all people, know that."

"Then take comfort in this, William. You have changed in the course of the year. You have changed and for the better." She moved close beside him, took his head in her hands, and kissed him on his lips. She pressed his head to her breasts. "You have emerged into your pastoral role; you are trying to gain favor with Charlotte, with me. But whatever the cause, you have become a more caring and sensitive shepherd. I like that. We all do."

Mary returned to her side of the bed, glanced at the clock, and began to dress. "Elizabeth and Charlotte will be calling for tea at Pemberley in half an hour. Either they will finish in time for Charlotte to walk home before dark, or Elizabeth will have our carriage bring her here."

William dressed, and together they made the bed.

"I am quite serious, sir. I expect your answer about adultery. I posit that we have not committed adultery — in the eyes of God. Charlotte is your loyal wife, and I should be your wife as well, if only English law recognized such. Given that English law does not recognize plural marriage at this time, then I am your lover, your mistress. Examine your library, sir. If you find that we indeed have sinned, then I shall be gone forthwith and shall banish myself from you forever."

"What if you should become with child?"

"Then we would make arrangements. Charlotte and I have discussed this. We know what we are about," she said.

"Pardon?" he asked.

"Since midsummer, Charlotte and I have discussed the scripture as it relates to plural marriages. You should join us in our conversation. You are so very grounded in scripture, but this area is a blind spot for you, as it is for most religious scholars. Still, from you I expect an answer."

"As you wish, Madame."

Mary laughed. "Alas, I am still 'Mademoiselle.' But thank you."

Once William's room was in order, they retired to the dining room and returned to deliberating how best to publish Margaret's letter and Gareth's report for the better part of an hour. Afterwards she bundled up against the late afternoon chill. "There is no turning back now." Following a warm embrace, she headed on foot for Pemberley.

* * *

On Tuesday, Mary labored at the table and Charlotte enjoyed reading the first galley proof of Lady Anne's second volume of poetry.

"My, you are immersed in your work, Mary. With *The Way Forward* finished, and Mr. Speedwell's missive on its way, I should think you would give yourself the opportunity to rest," Charlotte said.

"We are working on a supplement to *The Way Forward*, much as we did with Mr. Collins's lectionary guides. It is part of my offering to him to keep the book shorter," Mary said.

"Excellent, my dear. He seems most comfortable putting his trust in your writing. Did you make a lot of progress with the text on Sunday?"

Mary looked up, sensing a peculiarity in Charlotte's tone. "Yes, we did. Why?"

"Oh, I wondered. I thought you must have been quite busy … distracted. When tidying up around the bed in our room yesterday, Constance found this." Charlotte held up one of Mary's handkerchiefs.

Mary bowed her head.

"Mary, Mary, that red color does not become you. We have talked this through. I told you that I would not be offended, and I am not."

"I know that we discussed this, but I am still feeling a certain discomfort, a feeling of guilt. Have you confronted William?" Mary asked.

"Heavens, no." Charlotte replied. "Nor are we now engaged in a confrontation. To be truthful, I have rather enjoyed the past days. I believe that William is feeling profound guilt. He has been quite attentive to my wellbeing, and I do not wish that to end. I know that must sound rather mercenary, but I entered into our marriage as a practical matter. True, our affection has grown in the last year, but ours is still a marriage of convenience."

Mary nodded. "Well, then I shall be circumspect in regards to our relationship." She paused a moment. "And, I shall keep better track of my handkerchiefs."

They both laughed, and returned to their individual endeavors.

* * *

Margaret marveled at the difference in comfort she felt as *Lady Bridget* cast off from the pier in Fort-de-France and caught wind to sail westward. When Margaret left Plymouth, the nautical language had been as strange to her ear as German or Italian. Now, it was no more mysterious than French. In the same way, she smiled at her strength as she heaved to with the other members of *Lady Bridget's* crew family. She had little opportunity to ponder the matter, but thought from time to time how her transformation challenged the lines that delimited the sexes back home.

In addition to the sounding and security watches, Margaret and Jane added occasional watches at the helm and lookout. She mused how shocked Elinor would be if she saw Margaret's tanned complexion, most un-English-lady-like. Margaret hoped that she would never look like an English lady again.

The passage from Fort-de-France to San Juan proved routine. Though Captain Johnson and Quartermaster Graham worried forever about storms — this being hurricane season —, luck favored this leg of their voyage. During anchorage in San Juan, they emptied two holds of English cloth and tools and replaced them with casks of rum and boxes of spices.

Margaret and Jane joined with others of the crew for a day and evening in San Juan. Margaret found the port exciting and exotic, but lacking the feeling of community she had enjoyed with Geneviève and family in Fort-de-France.

In the early morning of the fifth day in San Juan, *Lady Bridget* finished loading provisions and set sail for Jamaica, 700 miles to the west, and their final stop before heading back to England.

In the evening, in the hour between supper and the eight-to-midnight watch, Margaret sat, unnoticed on a capstan, observing Robert and Jane at their favored spot at the rail. Her admiration of Jane had deepened in the months since that fateful cold morning in Plymouth. It was as clear to Margaret as it was to Geneviève that Jane and Robert were meant for one another. Whatever social conventions would conspire to keep them apart on return, Margaret vowed to herself to fight for Jane. To Margaret, Jane was family, every bit as much as Marianne or Edward.

In gathering twilight, Margaret breathed fragrant tropical air and listened to the creaking of *Lady Bridget* as the ship rocked through the Caribbean. Other than an occasional dolphin or flying fish breaking the surface, the sea rolled before them, gentle, deep blue, and warm with a sheen of red sunset colors. Margaret did not want to return to England, did not wish to see gray ever again.

The ship's bell struck the hour. Jane and Robert ended their conversation with polite gentility, and Margaret left her capstan seat to assume her watch. Margaret was as contented as she could ever recall.

* * *

Morning dawned with bland sky and fair winds. If their weather held, *Lady Bridget* would make Queenstown by evening or early morning the following day.

Through the morning, Margaret and Jane set to mending and reinforcing the main topgallant sail, torn by the storm during their journey from Plymouth. If they were able to complete the task before port, the entire collection of reserve sails would be sound and finished.

"It brings me great joy to observe the quiet affection between you and the captain, Jane."

Jane smiled. "It brings me great joy to experience that affection. We have talked a great deal of what will happen when we return to England. Will society there act to prevent our happiness?"

"I am sure that his family will be most supportive. I know only a little of the senior Captain Johnson, but cannot imagine his objections. And, after me, you have no greater champion than Geneviève." Margaret paused, and then laughed. "Well, perhaps Jacques and Marie!"

Jane laughed. "How true. They are adorable. I suppose it is a measure of my affection that I realized that I would be their sister-in-law should we marry. Robert is quite prepared to flaunt the disapproval of society, but I know only too well the cost of being of low birth. Were it not for the love and protection of your family ..." She shook her head. "I cannot imagine my life."

Margaret set her needle to rest in the canvas and tilted her head. "Then you shall be my sister."

"Society would see through that charade right away."

"No, no. I mean legal and proper. We shall adopt you. Mother would be keen to agree, I am certain."

Jane laughed.

"Please, Jane, I am quite serious. We have been more sisters than most sisters my whole life. This will work, Jane. If I live past my initial reunion with Elinor, that shall be my first order of business on our return."

Jane nodded. "This could work. Though it be only a matter of legality, my heart leaps at the thought of telling the whole world 'I am her sister.'"

"It is settled, then. And we would start planning a grand wedding for Captain Johnson and Miss — would it be Moseby or Dashwood? I do not think you need change your name when you are adopted."

Jane laughed. "Your flight of imagination is running far ahead of events. We must first complete this voyage. And before that, we must finish our work on the topgallant sail."

"You are right, Jane. But the thought of this future brings new urgency to our work here. For the first time since we left, I have reason to want to return."

In late morning, Captain Johnson stepped out of the quartermaster's room as the lookout called, "Ship off the starboard bow!"

"Very well," he said. "Can you see her flag?"

"No, sir. I cannot see a flag. And she appears to be turning toward us."

The Captain joined the lookout and accepted the looking glass. He watched for several minutes. "I do not like the looks of this. Go alert the gunner. Mr. Graham! Unlock the armory!"

Margaret and Jane watched as the deck buzzed with activity. The Captain approached them, carrying two rifles. "Do you know how to shoot?"

"I have, sir, with Colonel Brandon on several hunting occasions," Margaret replied. "And Jane was my loader. Whatever is the matter?"

His face was grim. "Pirates."

Chapter Seventeen
Battles — Derbyshire

As late October winds howled beneath roiling gray clouds outside Hunsford Cottage, the drawing room atmosphere was the precise opposite. Well-caulked windows, tight fitting doors, and a small fire kept their room cozy. Charlotte read a romantic novel in the warm yellow light thrown by the lamp on her side table while William labored, reading and writing in the glow of two lamps at his table.

In mid-afternoon, Charlotte looked up to see William staring out of the window, pen idle in his hand. "My dear," she murmured, "you seem at a loss."

He started and took a sharp breath. "I have much to consider with our new endeavor, a companion volume for *The Way Forward*."

"Ah, I thought you were reveling in the recipients of this morning's sermon. You still interpret texts during your homilies, but in a way that encourages active engagement. Well done, sir."

"Thank you. I only pray that such a spirit might spread from this place."

"Indeed. But you seem most distracted from your present work. If you are making progress, it is only within your mind. You are much more productive when Mary is here."

"She will visit later this afternoon to deliver what new material she has written," William said. "But I do have much on my mind, and I am in some turmoil."

"Oh?" Charlotte asked.

He pushed his chair back and turned to face her. "I am honor bound to confess my shame to you — that I have been unfaithful."

She turned the book over in her lap and folded her hands. "I see."

He bowed his head as he spoke. "Charlotte, I have had relations with Mary Bennet. Our passion for one another overcame my restraint. I was weak and unwilling to resist. I must be true to you and confess my sin, and beg your forgiveness."

"Thank you for your honesty, William. You have both been most careful to avoid bringing dishonor on this house. I recall Mary's term was 'circumspect.'"

William's look was pure perplexity. "I do not understand. I

hoped only that I might earn your forgiveness. I did not imagine such a tepid reaction."

"William, my dear, dear William, Mary and I have discussed this matter for many months, long before your bedding together last month. We have an understanding."

He shook his head. "This is most unexpected! I prepared myself for your anger, for whatever I would need to do in contrition. I was not prepared for what would appear to be acceptance."

"Indeed, my love. But much gratitude should be given to Mary. Since July, she and I have talked at length about plural marriages — in accepting cultures as well as in our own country. As you know so well, she is dogged in her studies on this or any other subject and is a most engaging discussion partner. She told me of your resulting arguments over meanings of adultery in light of scripture and our society. You still owe her your findings, and I shall be interested in them as well.

"I find myself siding with her reasoning, though I do not have your deep background. I should enjoy having her a member of this household. We work together well, and I treasure her companionship when you are away. Given that our society still has no formal recognition of our circumstances, she and I have decided we prefer her title be 'mistress,' should your relationship ever be discovered. That title evokes a more dignified and committed status than 'lover,' and far better than the Biblical 'concubine,' even though Hebrew scripture accepted the description and the status. She shared with me many passages addressing these matters.

"Finally, I have enjoyed your guilt-driven attention of late. I hope that our present honesty does not alter that."

William went to Charlotte, knelt and took her hands. "Charlotte, I do not deserve such a wise and loving wife. I realize more than ever that I do love you. I am blessed beyond belief. Whatever becomes of our relationships with Mary, I will labor with all my heart to give you the attention you deserve."

There was a loud rap at their front door.

"That cannot be Mary," said Charlotte. "It is still early and not her way of knocking."

The rapping repeated, louder and more insistent.

William opened the front door a crack to behold the hulking figure of Douglas Marshall, wearing the same gray cape and broad black hat worn in their last encounter at the back of the parish sanctuary. William tried to close the door, but Marshall had put his boot forward to block it. He forced the door open with ease and pushed William backward with the tip of his cane.

"You lied to me, Mr. Collins. We do not appreciate deception. I have wasted many months of my employer's time following your false leads. My patience is now at an end, sir. Tell me now — where is Miss Mary Bennet?" He continued to poke with his cane, at last forcing William into the chair next to Charlotte's.

"Tell me what you wish to know, Mr. Marshall," Charlotte shouted as she rose.

Both men turned to her in surprise.

"How do you know my name?" Marshall scowled.

Charlotte shook her head. "Mary and I have had regular correspondence since she and I confronted one another. She tried to seduce my husband — among others. Her circle of liaisons includes an embarrassing number of well-placed men and you have come to their attention this past year."

William stood up next to Charlotte, clearing his throat to speak.

Marshall frowned and turned to William. "You will remain silent, Mr. Collins. I wish to talk with your wife."

William glowered, but complied.

"Now, Mrs. Collins, tell me this. What does Miss Mary Bennet look like?"

"A peculiar question from a man who has spent months searching for her. You must know that you were searching for a bold blonde-haired hussy. You can tell when she is on the prowl. She normally puts her hair up in braids, but will comb it out when she wants a man's attention. And do not let those pink cheeks fool you — it is all rouge. Most offensive for those of us married to her quarries is how she dresses to show her breasts. I am embarrassed to watch men's eyes for they certainly are not looking at her face!"

Marshall frowned, and, after a while, grunted. "Humph! Why are you corresponding with her?"

"Mr. Marshall, I have no wish to talk with that minx! So, I write instead. She tried to steal away my husband, as she has so many others. It is bad enough that I must see her in church. She has Lady Catherine under her spell, so I cannot banish her from our sanctuary. Even more aggravating, we must rely on her as a conduit to Mr.

Weatherstone. As you have observed, Joseph is a wily fox and always on the move. She is particularly attracted to powerful men like him."

He shook his head. "Why are you maintaining contact with Joseph Weatherstone?"

"Sir," she said, with an air of incredulity, "do you not know? Mr. Weatherstone is a major benefactor of our church. His patronage is second only to Lady Catherine's. And you are aware, no doubt, of the great wealth that his publications have generated. That is likely another factor that attracts Mary to him. Joseph likes to give her pretty things. She once showed me a necklace he gave her — fit for a princess. She boasted that she wore it while they made love. He may be old, but he is not dead yet."

As Charlotte regaled Marshall with complaints about "Mary Bennet, the Blonde," Mary arrived at the cottage and saw his black stallion tied to their post. "Oh, dear," she murmured and crept to the corner of their cottage, away from windows, and then inched around, peering into each window as she approached it. Even before reaching the drawing room window, she could hear Charlotte and Douglas Marshall's conversation. She peeked in and saw him from the side, his cane still pointing in menace between the two. She crouched, crawled beneath the window, and made her way to the kitchen door that led into their garden.

Mary was relieved to find it unlatched and pulled it open slowly, fearing any noise that the hinge might make. She tiptoed in and removed her shoes so as not to make a sound. The cottage's stone floor was icy and she winced on first contact. The drawing room conversation was quite audible now. She searched for something heavy enough to be effective in a fight, but light enough that she could handle. She eyed frying pans hanging beside the stove. One of them would suffice, but she feared making a noise removing them from their hooks. She spotted the iron poker rod that Constance used for stoking the stove and picked it up. Perfect, she thought, and tiptoed into the hall toward the drawing room. Recalling the room's arrangement, she expected that Marshall would have his back to the hall, but could not count on his not turning around. She would need to make full use of surprise should he see her. She raised her arms and positioned the poker behind her, gripping it with all her strength. She was grateful to those who elected to leave the stone floors bare.

As she crept into the doorway, William and Charlotte both spied her, but concealed any sign of recognition.

"Douglas Marshall, your mission is doomed!" William said in a loud voice.

"I told you to hold your tongue!"

"You cannot silence truth! Justice will prevail. It is only a matter of time."

Marshall swung his cane back to strike William. "I said …"

Mary took three long strides and brought the poker down in the center of Marshall's hat. He crumpled to the floor, cane flying in one direction, hat in the other. Though he made no movement, Mary raised her poker again, ready to strike if needed.

"Charlotte, fetch that length of rope from the garden shed!" William shouted and began checking the prostrate figure. He found a small pistol in a side pocket, removed the round from its chamber, placed the pistol on the windowsill behind a curtain, and then took Marshall's cane and slid it under the dining room cabinet. Only then did he check for a pulse.

"Mr. Marshall is alive," William said as Charlotte returned with rope. William began tying Marshall's legs, and then his arms. "We need to get help right away. Pemberley is the closest house with strong men available. Could one of you take his horse and ride to summon help?"

Charlotte shook her head. "I have rarely ridden. I do not think I would fare well."

William beckoned to Mary and whispered, "He may be able to hear … Anna."

"I have ridden Narnia for years, but she is very tame. I doubt that I could manage that stallion," Mary said.

"Then I must go, though I worry for you should he awaken."

"I whacked him once. I can whack him again," Mary replied, gripping her poker.

The three agreed. William rose, donned his cloak, and headed out the front door. They heard Marshall's stallion snort and stamp, but then his hoof beats at a gallop.

Mary adjusted her grip on the poker, raising it to her shoulder at the ready as she stepped back far enough to be out of any reach.

Charlotte looked at Mary. "Well done, Anna, well done. The last thing he remembers is our description of that flirt Mary Bennet. I rather think Douglas Marshall was taking a fancy to her himself."

* * *

Mary and Charlotte both sat uneasy waiting for Mr. Collins to summon help. Charlotte secured a heavy skillet from the kitchen at Mary's suggestion and practiced her swing.

"I suppose, Anna, it is our Christian duty to hope that we have not killed him."

"You are right, Charlotte — that will take some practice."

They murmured, avoiding the mention of names, for about 40 minutes before hearing hoof beats and a wagon's clatter.

William entered the cottage with Fitzwilliam. As always, Mr. Darcy was dressed as a gentleman and tipped his hat as he greeted them, "Mrs. Collins, …" he paused and smiled, "Miss Anna."

She curtsied, returning his smile.

Darcy turned to examine Marshall as four Pemberley men entered the room. Mary recognized two of the gardeners and two stable hands, all very strong.

Fitzwilliam first examined Marshall's head. "My, my, that is going to hurt for some time." Then he examined the bindings. Raising his eyebrows, he asked, "Who did the tying?"

"I did," William replied.

"Well done," Fitzwilliam said with a smile. "You are a man of many talents indeed. He was not going anywhere like this. You have him trussed up like a Christmas goose!"

Marshall made a weak stirring, groaning as he tried to move.

Fitzwilliam motioned for Mary to leave the room, which she did. "Douglas Marshall, you should lie still, sir. You have had a nasty fall. We are taking you for some medical attention and a place to stay."

"What happened?"

"As I said, sir, you had a nasty fall. Perhaps you fainted? Do you have a medical condition?"

Marshall strained against his bindings. "Release me at once!"

Darcy shook his head. "That would be unwise in your condition. We will get you medical attention."

"Where are you taking me?"

"To jail, sir. Our constabulary runs a fine establishment, one of the best. They may even have heat."

Marshall raised his head. "Oh, no, you will not. Where is my horse?"

"He is residing at one of the finest stables in all England." Darcy looked up, beaming, to the two stable hands. "I dare say your stallion has never received such exquisite care. They will spoil him rotten. But do not concern yourself — I shall not charge you for his board. Shall I bill The Colonial Society?"

Marshall laid his head back down, wincing. "Just let me free. I shall be on my way."

"I am afraid we cannot do that."

He ground his teeth. "Aghh! Why not?"

"Because then we would have to shoot you."

The four Pemberley men carried Marshall, still bound, to the wagon and placed a blanket over him against the cold wind.

Mary returned to the drawing room, and thanked her brother-in-law.

He chuckled. "It was a rather amusing diversion, truth be told. I must visit Hunsford more often. After we have settled Mr. Marshall in his new accommodations, I shall come by to pick you up. It is already growing late, and I do not fancy you walking back to Pemberley in the dark, though I have no doubt you would relish the experience."

"She is most welcome to stay with us this evening," Charlotte offered. "We had planned a great deal of work on our publications, and Mr. Marshall's unexpected visit has disrupted our work. Mary can stay in our guest room."

Darcy bowed. "That is most generous. Thank you. I am quite sure those arrangements would please her."

Mary nodded.

Darcy eyed the poker still in Mary's grip. "And I shall be cautious never to cross my sweet sister-in-law." He turned to William and Charlotte. "By your leave, my friends." He bowed and left the cottage.

Mary waited until the sound of the wagon faded before turning to Charlotte. "When did you acquire a guest room?"

Charlotte smiled sweetly and turned toward the kitchen to return her frying pan and Mary's poker.

* * *

When Constance arrived on Monday morning, she found Mary at the table, working on her manuscript. Mary had been careful to occupy only a small area of the tabletop with her work.

"Good morning to you, Miss Bennet. You are here early. Such diligence!" Constance said.

"Charlotte and William had a visitor yesterday and the day was quite disrupted. It was that nasty Douglas Marshall fellow, the one who had previously threatened William and me."

"Ah," Constance said. "That would explain the festive crowd gathered around the jail as I passed through town."

"Charlotte and William distracted him, I used your stove poker to strike him, William tied him up, and Mr. Darcy brought men from Pemberley to carry Mr. Marshall to town. It was a most peculiar Sunday. The hour grew late and Charlotte invited me to spend the night here," Mary said.

"That sounds frightful," Constance said, shaking her head. "Perhaps I can hear the whole story after I prepare breakfast. It sounds like a gripping tale and you are a great teller," Constance said.

"Thank you." Mary smiled.

"Will you be staying for breakfast?"

"If it is no trouble."

"It is no trouble at all," Constance replied. "And will you be staying with us for a while?"

Mary looked up to see Constance trying to suppress a smile as Charlotte entered the room.

"Constance has been my loyal confidant for these many years." Charlotte said. "She is the one who retrieved your handkerchief from the bedroom. In addition to her discretion, I have relied on Constance as a reliable source for sage advice."

Constance nodded. "I love this family. I have loved them since first I began here, and I am most happy for the joy that has grown in the past year since you began working with Mr. Collins."

Mary and Charlotte followed as Constance returned to the kitchen to prepare the meal.

"Constance also works with the town's midwife. She and I have talked about the fact that I have not conceived, despite my recent intimacies. She is not convinced that the difficulty is with me. If we were to have children, though, Constance would make an exceptional governess."

Constance smiled. "Thank you, ma'am. I do enjoy working with children. Charlotte and I have even discussed the idea of adding another room or two to include a nursery. This house's previous occupants have for a long time been older couples or confirmed bachelors."

William returned as the table was being set. "I had a good visit with the Goodlettes. I do not think that Thomas is long for this world. I have seen it before. By good fortune, his loving family surrounds him and he can look back on a life well lived." He turned to Constance. "Have they told you of yesterday's adventure?"

"Only the basics, sir. I look forward to Miss Bennet's spirited telling at some point."

William chuckled. "I stopped by the constable's office on the way back. Mr. Marshall is not sharing any information about his employers and he is not expecting any mercy from them. So, he may remain incarcerated here for some time."

* * *

In late November, Mary worked on the next volume of sermons while Charlotte knitted warn wraps for some of the poor families of the congregation. Outside Hunsford cottage, a light snowfall had clothed the land in white, and some flurries continued.

In mid-morning, Mary set down her pen and gazed through the window at the pristine landscape. "Charlotte, I believe that I am with child. I have no experience to guide me and few other friends to consult, but I think it is so."

"I see," Charlotte said. "Nor do I have any experience in this realm. But I know of one who does. Would you object to talking with Constance? She continues to work with the midwife and is quite knowledgeable."

"I would be most grateful, Charlotte."

When Constance brought tea, Charlotte asked, "Constance, Mary believes that she may be with child. Would you be willing to guide her?"

"It would be my honor, ma'am." Constance bowed. "If it is so, would we follow our plan to retire to Brighton through our confinement? Were it summer, the town would be crowded, but in wintertime it should be quiet."

"If you are still willing."

"Yes, indeed I am." Constance smiled.

* * *

William returned from Thomas Goodlette's wake in late afternoon. He found Charlotte, Mary, and Constance at table, writing and engaged in cheerful conversation.

"Good afternoon, ladies. Your gathering seems most festive. To what do we owe this merriment?"

Charlotte answered, "We are making plans for our sojourn in Brighton in the new year. We shall be away starting in January."

"Brighton? In winter? That strikes me as anything but festive. Why?" he asked.

Charlotte stood up, smiling, and approached him. "We desire peace and quiet to prepare for the arrival of your child."

His face shown with a smile. Stepping forward, he embraced her. "Charlotte, my love! This is most joyous news."

Charlotte returned his embrace for a moment, but then placed her hands on his shoulder. "But you should direct your joy to the child's mother."

His smile changed to confusion as Mary stood up.

"I am with child, William."

"Oh, Mary, my dear Mary. We cannot pretend that this outcome was not predictable." He looked at her with a soft smile. "I know that you will be a loving mother. And I pledge that I will be a responsible and loving father. Are you contented, Mary?"

"I am."

He looked to Charlotte and Constance. "Do I also sense that the two of you are supportive of her as well?"

"We are," Charlotte replied.

He smiled. "Then I join in celebrating this joyous news." He reached out and embraced her.

Charlotte and Constance clasped hands and smiled.

William became serious. "Of course, when word of what to us is joyous news spreads, my position here and our situation will be at an end. I know that I must accept that — I am responsible for my actions and their consequences. Though the loss of this parish will bring a measure of regret, we shall continue with another situation. Of course, that possibility is due to the diligent work that you — Mary and Charlotte — have labored over for these many months. We will do well."

"Oh, do not be so anxious, Mr. Collins," Charlotte said. "With proper preparation, we believe that our special family — it is well within the scriptural meaning of family — will be received with love here. That is why we have developed a plan. That is why we will sojourn in Brighton. Let us explain."

They gathered about the table, and William leaned forward with eager interest.

"Constance is contributing her considerable skills," said Charlotte. "She examined Mary and believes that she will not be showing until January or February. The three of us shall travel to Brighton and there reside, with Mary registering as Charlotte, me registering as Mary, and —" She laughed. "Constance registering as Constance. We shall return after our confinement with 'my' son or daughter. Then we will celebrate the child's baptism and introduction here."

William rested his chin on folded hands. "In the past, I might have objected to the deception inherent in this plan. Today, I am changed. I appreciate the expedience of the charade. Setting aside the moral questions raised, which do weigh on me, I should expect it to be quite a challenge to maintain such a secret."

"We have pondered this at length," Mary replied. "As we discovered during Douglas Marshall's visit here in October, Charlotte is a wonderful storyteller, skilled in constructing a consistent and compelling picture for others. In fact, Charlotte will be practicing her story-telling skills while we are enjoying Brighton. I have urged her for some time to write stories from her vivid imagination, stories quite unrelated to our own scholastic endeavors. I will be her scribe and editor. At the same time, we will rehearse our conversations regarding the child. It may prove unnecessary to practice any active deception. Our little world here need only observe a loving mother and doting friend, ignorant of which is which."

He shook his head. "I smile remembering your brilliant performance during that invasion, Charlotte, but maintaining a narrative over years and decades? That is difficult to imagine."

He sat in thought for many minutes. "But … I owe it to you all to try. Should the story fail, then it would be as I suggested earlier. And, I do believe that Joseph Weatherstone and Gareth Speedwell would both support this plan." He looked around the table. "Then it is settled?"

"It is settled," Charlotte said.

"It is settled," Mary said.

"It is settled," Constance said.

Chapter Eighteen

Battles — Caribbean

Captain Johnson handed one rifle to Margaret and the other to Jane. "We have enough arms for a rifle for each crewmember. Here's hoping we won't need these— we shall try to outrun the pirates' galleon. Mr. Graham has us on course for Queenstown and the pirates are at a distance, it appears their sails are in want of repair, and they're broad of beam, so we may have a small speed advantage, even though they be a bit closer to port.

"We need only get within ten or fifteen miles of Queenstown, and we will likely meet up with the picket ships protecting the harbor. We're hoisting our grand ensign so that they may know who we are. Once those pirates catch sight of a Navy vessel, they'll haul away.

"For now, go see the gunner, get your powder and rounds, and load your rifles. Take a position along the railing behind the forecastle. If that ship gets within cannon range, they'll target the sails to disable us. We're ready to return fire, but have only two 18 pounders. I am going to the bridge to watch for a picket ship. Have you what you need?"

"I am ready," Jane said. "They shall not take *Lady Bridget*."

The captain smiled. "Not without a fight."

"They shall *not* take her, sir." Jane was adamant.

He gazed at her and nodded. "You are right! They shall not." he said, and climbed to the bridge.

Jane handed Margaret her rifle and left to get their ammunition, returning in a few minutes. "Colonel Brandon would approve. Our gunner is well organized and insists on the quality we've come to expect." She took one of the rifles and began loading it.

"You have not yet reproached me, reminding me that you would not be here, in peril, had I not rebelled." Margaret said, swapping rifles.

Jane smiled. "When we finish with the fight, if it come to that, be assured that I will remind you — and quite often." She loaded the second rifle, set the powder and rounds against the bulkhead, and looked at Margaret. "And yet … had you not rebelled, I would never have met Robert, so I am not disposed to reprimand too harshly."

"Will we survive this encounter, Jane?"

"Yes!"

"You seem so certain." Margaret raised her eyebrows.

"There is really no point in thinking otherwise, is there?" Jane said, gazing to sea, squinting to make out the pursuing ship. "We are here, and nothing will alter that. We shall focus our minds on the tasks ahead and pay no mind to what might have been. Are you ready, Margaret?"

Margaret pressed her lips together and nodded. "I am."

* * *

Through the noon hour and into the early afternoon, *Lady Bridget* sliced westward through the sea. At last they could see the galleon in detail, its black sails tattered and torn. While it had closed the distance by half, the menacing ship was now astern and keeping up with difficulty.

A cheer rose on *Lady Bridget* when the lookout called, "Ship dead ahead. She's English flagged, a man-of-war!"

Captain Johnson smiled and altered course toward the English ship.

Margaret observed him. "The captain seemed perplexed when he looked back."

Jane frowned. "That's because the pirates are not turning about. They *must* see the man-of-war, yet they are continuing to pursue us. That is nonsensical. We may yet need these rifles."

When *Lady Bridget* had closed to within a mile of the English frigate, the frigate turned broadside and fired two cannons.

"What the devil?" the captain roared when the two rounds fell short. "They're firing on us! They cannot have missed our ensign."

He adjusted course to move out of the gap between the frigate and the galleon. The galleon kept pursuit and the English frigate fired again, one round glancing off *Lady Bridget*'s hull. Their luck did not hold with the third volley from the English frigate — one round pierced the foretopsail and another splintered the mainmast above the topsail yard.

Lady Bridget's crew could see boarding ladders at the ready on the pirates' *Jacqueline Fouck*, her name now readable in aged and peeling paint. Margaret joined her crewmates firing on the pirates. Her first target was the lookout, who fell immediately into the sea. Swapping rifles, she fired next at the helmsman while Jane reloaded. The shot missed the helmsman, though she could see splinters of wood fly from his wheel. She swapped rifles again and took a second shot, which struck the helmsman in his left side, sending him staggering from the wheel.

"Margaret!" Jane shouted, pointing to an archer on the forecastle of *Jacqueline Fouck*. "He means to set us alight!" The archer dipped his arrow into a bucket of flaming pitch and was preparing to draw his bow.

"Oh, no he is not! Not our sails!" Margaret fired and hit the archer in the center of his chest. He fell backward, overturning the blazing bucket. Two of the pirate crew rushed to put out the flames, and Margaret downed one of them.

Now at close range, *Lady Bridget*'s gunner fired at *Jacqueline Fouck*'s cannon ports. They could hear screams as his first round rebounded through the lower deck. His second round hit one of the *Fouck*'s cannons as it prepared to fire. The resulting blast ripped open their side. They abandoned the remaining ports and the *Fouck*'s crew rushed to prevent fire from spreading to the powder stores.

Other members of *Lady Bridget*'s crew family had similar success. While the pirates returned volleys, they had fewer arms and they were of lesser quality and accuracy. With the helmsman disabled and its bridge deserted, *Jacqueline Fouck* drifted to *Lady Bridget*'s starboard side, and the remaining pirate crew swarmed *Lady Bridget*. Some secured lines to keep the ships bound together as others — wielding pistols, knives, and swords — encircled the crew. The last pirate to die fell by Captain Johnson's sword, but three of the larger pirates finally subdued him.

A shudder ran through the coupled ships when the frigate, *HMS Lancet* sidled to *Lady Bridget*'s port side and the *Lancet*'s crew bound the ships together with line. The pirates did not lower their weapons as a squad of Royal Marines boarded *Lady Bridget*, led by a bony-faced lieutenant.

"What is this treason!?" Captain Johnson demanded.

"Hold your tongue, Captain Johnson," the lieutenant barked. "You are under arrest for fomenting rebellion in the colonies, to wit, encouraging revolt among the slaves."

"That is preposterous! By whose authority do you charge me?"

"That would be by my authority," a high voice sounded from behind. Everyone turned to see a portly, bespectacled man emerging from the *Fouck*'s captain's cabin. He dressed in ruffled finery, including a broad satin sash affixed with an elaborate golden medallion.

Robert seethed. "Governor Tarkington."

They saw, emerging from the cabin behind the governor, the pirate captain, a tall, wiry man, dressed all in black, save a scarlet scarf. A whip dangled from his belt. Scars and pockmarks festooned his grim face, and a scruffy light beard tried with little success to cover his damaged visage. A broad-brimmed black hat, with an incongruous white ostrich feather, rested atop long, tangled black hair.

Tarkington fumed watching *Jacqueline Fouck*'s crew struggle to position a gangplank between the two ships. Once in place, he tiptoed across, looking for all the world like a bulbous high wire artist. Stepping down onto *Lady Bridget*'s deck, he panted from the exertion.

Tarkington's breath smelled of brandy.

"You are late in arriving, Captain Johnson. We expected you some weeks ago."

Johnson's jaw clenched. "We diverted to repair storm damage."

"Ah. No doubt cavorting with your French conspirators." Tarkington looked up at *Lady Bridget*'s severed mainmast and fallen sails. "A pity you won't be able to avail yourself of their services … ever again. I see that the *Lancet*'s gunners are more powerful than Atlantic storms. You have fallen, despite the damage you have inflicted on poor Captain Stanford's ship and crew."

Captain Johnson's face blazed red. "You are in league with these bandits, and you shall hang for that treason!"

Tarkington laughed, and with him the Marines and Captain Stanford. "Fierce words from a man bound by three strong men, surrounded by Royal Marines, his crew captured, and his ship too damaged to sail. How ironic that you would invoke 'treason,' since that is the very charge you will face at trial, and for which *you* shall be hanged." He turned to the Marines. "Take him away!"

Jane surged toward Robert, only to be held back with difficulty by two men from the *Fouck*.

Governor Tarkington headed toward *HMS Lancet*, where another gangplank stretched.

"Not so fast, Tarkington!" Captain Stanford shouted. "What about us? These bastards killed half my regular crew and wrought grave damage on my ship. We have a pact, sir. How are we to be restored?"

Tarkington surveyed *Lady Bridget* and *Jacqueline Fouck*. "Frankly, Captain Stanford, even with the damage our navy inflicted on this vessel, she is in far better condition than your rats' nest." He waived his hand. "*Lady Bridget* is yours — the ship, the crew and the contents. Do with them as you please. Your blackbellies should be able to make her whole again." He looked about. "Lieutenant Jasper, you will remain aboard to make sure there is no mischief from this traitor's crew."

"With pleasure, your lordship." Jasper bowed.

Tarkington turned and waddled across the second gangplank to board *Lancet*. Its crew withdrew the gangplank, untied from the ships, and *HMS Lancet* moved away, turning toward Queenstown.

Margaret observed Jane, a single tear making its way down her cheek — Jane's face grew red with fury. Margaret listened to the men from *Jacqueline Fouck*. In addition to English, several spoke proper French. She inclined her ears to the crowd of black men at the railing, who had remained aboard that ship. They spoke what seemed a number of languages that she did not recognize, though a few also spoke French.

Captain Stanford, his face twisted in pain, pressed his eyes closed and held his head as he made his way to the gangplank. "Search the ship and see what she has. I am retiring to my cabin." He looked at his blood-soaked deck, with a dozen or more bodies lying where they fell. "And clear them away before we invite some infection."

Lieutenant Jasper waited until Stanford had closed his cabin door before turning to his captives. "Hear me, you traitors, this is the way I work," he shouted. "Your women will separate to the *Fouck*. The men shall remain here in the service of the *Fouck*'s crew while we prepare to turn *Lady Bridget* over to them. If any man of you causes trouble, then I will select one of the women to receive thirty lashes. If any woman of you causes trouble, then I will select one of the men to receive thirty lashes." He waited, watching their grim faces. "Are … we … clear?" After a long silence, he repeated, narrowing his gray eyes. "Are … we … clear?"

The crew of *Lady Bridget* mumbled with resentment their understanding.

"That's more like it," Jasper continued, coming as close to a smile as he seemed able. "You wenches, your first assignment is to clear the decks of the dead. Then you will swab the blood you spilled."

Jasper conferred with the senior surviving member of the pirate crew aboard *Lady Bridget.* "Get your blackbelly carpenters over here and get ready to repair the mainmast."

One by one, Margaret, Jane, Harriet, and the other women made their way across the gangplank and gathered by the far railing under the watch of several men with pistols and machetes. One of the men called to a woman among the black men. She was tall, with gleaming ebony skin. Margaret had not noticed her earlier, for her hair was the same short tight curls as the men and her tattered clothes draped over her form. "You, woman, make yourself useful and lend your hand cleaning up!" he shouted.

She appeared to not understand until a large black man near the front of the group spoke to her in French, "*That white devil says you need to help clear the decks of bodies. It may be a good thing to help them. Stanford's crew is cut in half, and he lost some of the worst ones. These women may be useful.*"

"*Oui, Jacób,*" she replied, and took graceful strides toward the women.

As the pirate in charge turned to the men, Margaret saw that none of the pirate crew were watching or listening and whispered, "*I speak French. I am Margaret. How can we help you?*"

The woman flashed a momentary smile and checked again that they were not watched. "*I am Justine,*" she whispered back. "*Let us get on with the task. We can talk in whispers in parts of the ship away from those bastards' ears.*"

Several of the black men were escorted to *Lady Bridget,* where they began examining the damage to the mainmast. Margaret, Jane, and Harriet followed Justine toward the forecastle, and began very, very slowly moving bodies to the railing, making a great show of exertion.

Margaret translated between the women.

"*You seem an accomplished actress, Margaret,*" Justine said.

"She is a frightful deceiver, which has proven useful from time to time," Jane said.   Margaret frowned and pouted, but translated with accuracy nonetheless.

Harriet and Justine chuckled.

"*What do we do with the dead men?*" Margaret asked.

Justine shrugged. "*Into the sea. It is sad in a way, but there is no other choice."*

The first body was one of the two who had raced to extinguish the flaming overturned pitch bucket. *"I killed him,"* Margaret said.

"Merci. He was especially cruel. I think, perhaps, he had no soul."

They lifted him to the railing and gave a final push. All four watched his body hit the water, the sea turning crimson with the blood dripping from the deck and the lookout Margaret had first shot. The waters writhed with a dozen or more large sharks.

"Dinner time, fishies!" Justine shouted with glee. She turned to the others. *"I'm sorry to seem so cold, but they have treated us as no human should ever be treated."*

They turned next to the body of the archer, whose dead hand still clutched his shirt at the center of his chest, an expression of quiet resignation frozen on his face. Flames had burned off portions of his pant legs and shirt, his skin blackened and blistered.

"I shot him as well," Margaret said.

Justine raised her eyebrows. *"You seem to have killed the most dangerous of our bandits. Since I have been aboard, I have seen him set seven ships alight. He was young and uncaring, and it mattered nothing to him that he was destroying the lives and livelihoods of hundreds of souls."*

After making their show of "weak female" struggles to heave the second body over the railing, they returned to the deck to find the helmsman alive, breathing with difficulty.

Justine frowned. *"A pity you hit Timothy. He is not cruel like the others —one of the reasons they did not trust him with a gun."* She turned to Margaret to translate. *"Do you want us to try to save you, Timothy?"*

He gave a small nod and Margaret continued her interpreting. "I should like to return to England … to my home … to escape this hellish nightmare."

Justine turned aft and shouted, *"Médecin! Médecin!"*

Jane shook her head, looking down at Timothy. "I don't think there is medicine strong enough to mend the damage we've done to him."

"Médecin is French for doctor. The word for medicine would be *medicament,"* Margaret explained. She turned to Timothy. "I'm sorry I had to shoot you."

"It is but the latest damage I've sustained since they captured me and brought me aboard this Devil ship," he said between gasps.

A large, heavyset man climbed the short ladder to their deck. "*What have we, Madame Justine?*" he asked.

Justine replied. "*Timothy was hit in the fight. While he is alive, he has lost a lot of blood. He says he wishes to live.*"

The doctor nodded and spoke in English, "Well, young Timothy, it looks as if I will be putting you back together again. You recall the price?"

Timothy nodded. "I have kept my bargain. Madame Justine is my witness."

The doctor looked to Justine for confirmation.

"*He has. Timothy is one of the honorable ones.*" She turned to Margaret, Jane, and Harriet. "*Doctor Katanga extracts the pledge of a life debt before he will provide treatment. The man must not take another innocent life — ever again.*"

"*And if he violates the pledge?*" Margaret asked.

"*Then the next time he is wounded — and there is always a next time — he will not be given treatment. I believe this is the third time that Timothy has been saved. And he has kept his pledge.*"

"He is not yet saved. That looks a most serious wound!" Margaret said.

Doctor Katanga turned to Margaret and laughed a deep, jolly laugh. "Child, you shamefully underestimate me! I have mended far worse than this — as that day off Antigua, eh, Young Timothy?"

The helmsman gave a weak smile. "It is true. I was very near death. I continue to walk with a limp."

As they talked, another one of the slaves, a young man, joined them. He was frightfully thin, with patches of hair missing and a mouth lacking at least half the proper number of teeth. He carried a large black leather bag. Margaret watched a shiver passed through his body. The doctor spoke to him in a language Margaret could not identify. The young man replied with a stutter, seeming at home with the doctor's requests.

The doctor took a short rod with a double hook on the end that the young man had extracted from the bag. He mixed sprinkles of powders from several bottles into a white paste and applied it to the rod. "Now, young Timothy, this is going to hurt a great deal, but it is necessary. I must remove the round and cleanse your wound."

Timothy shut his eyes and grimaced. "Like Antigua?"

Doctor Katanga thought a moment. "Actually, no. Not so bad as Antigua. I am able this time to add a pinch of opium for the pain, which I could not do that day, and I have something special." He held out his hands to Margaret and Jane. "If you kind ladies will please take hold of his hands and squeeze them tight while I remove his damage. And, young Timothy, if you will look upon their beautiful faces, it will blunt much of the agony."

Margaret watched the terror in Timothy's eyes and felt him grip more tightly to their hands as the doctor inserted the rod, made a few twisting movements, and withdrew it. They heard a 'thunk' on the deck.

"Got it!" he announced with pride, holding up the round. He spoke again to the young man caring for his bag. From a different set of bottles, the doctor produced another paste, which he applied to Timothy's wound. He took a swatch of cloth and applied a few drops of two different yellow liquids to the cloth. He rubbed it together and stretched it over the wound, holding it in place, counting backwards from thirty. Katanga examined his handiwork and nodded with satisfaction.

"Madame Justine, can you find a place to hide young Timothy for a day or so lest the miserable scum try to put him back to work?"

"Yes, doctor, of course."

The doctor returned the items to his assistant, who replaced them in their proper spots in the bag. He dismissed the young man and took a deep breath.

Jane and Harriet helped Timothy to a hatch and disappeared inside.

"Remarkable!" Margaret said. "That was most impressive!"

Katanga shrugged. "We do what we can. I learned a lot before we were re-enslaved and I have had ample opportunity to practice aboard this barbarous ship. I must innovate all the time and experiment because there is no choice."

"Your English is exquisite."

He laughed. "Thank you. I had to learn and keep up with my languages to follow the medical books. I had access to a number of useful volumes in Queenstown before the dark days returned."

"How is it that you are aboard a pirate ship? You said you were re-enslaved? You were free?"

An angry frown clouded his face. "Yes! We were all free. Then that bastard Tarkington came into office in Queenstown and made alliances with *Jacqueline Fouck*'s Captain Stanford and the crew of *Lancet*, especially that Devil's spawn Lieutenant Jasper. For his cooperation and coordination, Tarkington receives one-third of the haul, and Jasper gets a tenth. Tarkington ordered the constabulary to stand back while they took us — all free people — back into slavery."

Margaret's face turned red with anger. "Is there nothing we can do?"

Katanga shook his head and switched to French so that Justine could understand. "*Tarkington is ruthless. The consequence of challenging him is death. His second in command arrived the year after Tarkington and was appalled by what he found. Lieutenant Governor Hooker is doing everything he can to shield the population, though he knows it will be certain death once Tarkington discovers. The whole population of Queenstown trembles in fear of Governor Tarkington.*" He looked up. "*You can ask Madame Justine.*"

Justine twisted her face in anger. "*True. Tarkington is like a plague on the land. Many of us resisted when first he came to office. We refused to go back to slavery. Sadly, his is a special level of cruelty. He burned and looted the house that Jacób and I lived in. He burned our fields.*" Her jaw clenched. "*He murdered my child, my precious Annabel.*"

Jane and Harriet returned from below.

"We have him resting and can tell them we threw his body overboard." Jane offered.

"Thank you," the doctor said.

"*Again, is there nothing we can do?*" Margaret repeated. "*We have thinned their ranks and now outnumber them.*"

Katanga and Justine turned together to check aft. He raised a finger. "*Keep your voices down. We may be greater in number, but they are heavily armed. Jasper has two fine English pistols, and I have seen on Captain Stanford's table in his cabin eight or ten loaded pistols at all times. That is why he bars his door when he sleeps. There will be no rebellion so long as Stanford and Jasper are alive.*"

Margaret folded her arms. "*When we are finished with this, I shall get word back to England. This travesty shall not stand.*"

Katanga and Justine eyed one another. Justine spoke, "*I'm afraid that is wishful thinking and likely terribly wrong. You are young English women in the presence of vile and brutal men. You are no more free than are we. When he is hungry with lust, the Captain will have his way with you. He will be brutal when he relieves his lust, and when he tires of you, he will turn you over to his men for their sport. When they also tire of you, when you are bloodied and bruised and broken, they will throw you overboard — alive — for their amusement. We have seen it maybe a dozen times — young women aboard the ships the Fouck captured. Some of our company tried to put a stop to it. Some were shot, others beaten to within an inch of their lives."* She turned to Katanga. *"The good doctor's assistant — we call him 'Chitter' because of his damaged speech — was one they beat when he defended some of the young women — helped them escape, actually. The good doctor was able to save him, though I fear Chitter has suffered life-changing damage."*

They heard a cry *"Médecin"* from aft.

The doctor shook his head. "I must away. Do the best you can to stay out of sight. Do what you can to appear unappealing." He got up and headed aft.

The four women resumed the grim task of clearing bodies into the sea, where swarms of sharks awaited their feast.

After a while, Margaret asked Justine, *"Has Captain Stanford had his way with you?"*

She shook her head with a rueful smile. *"My husband, Jacób, is most clever. He spread the story that I have a hideous disease of my female parts that causes a man's member to rot off. The captain won't go near me, seeing me simply as another slave laborer."* She grew stern. *"Someday, Stanford, Jasper, and Tarkington will face justice. I only pray that I will be alive to see it."*

They returned to their slow removals.

* * *

In the late afternoon, Captain Stanford unbarred his door and emerged. He called to Lieutenant Jasper: "I am lonely. I have a powerful hunger for some female company."

Jasper flicked his head toward the forecastle. "There are three up forward who should suit your fancy, sir." He motioned for two other men of the crew to join them.

At the top of the ladder, Stanford pointed to Margaret.

"You! The wench with the yellow curls," Jasper commanded. "The captain wishes you to join him in his cabin."

She looked with disgust on Stanford's pockmarked face and greasy hair. "I do not wish to join him. I decline."

Jasper laughed. "It is not for you to decline. You will come now!"

"No!"

Jasper motioned with his hands and the two following pirates moved toward Margaret. She backed up and struggled as they grabbed her arms.

Jane landed a hard kick at the legs of the man closest to her, and he fell with a shout. The commotion attracted the attention of more of the crew, who joined in subduing Jane and dragging Margaret toward the captain's cabin. Margaret wrested one arm free for a moment, and drove her fingernail into the eye of one of her captors. He screamed and fell back and another took his place.

Jasper ordered the men holding Jane to tie her to the foremast. "Shall we kill her?"

He thought a moment. "No. We'll save her for later."

Margaret continued to struggle as her handlers forced her into the cabin, finally punching her with enough force to send her sprawling on the floor, dizzy.

Captain Stanford entered and motioned for the others to leave. He barred his door and turned to Margaret. She rose and faced him, her face red with fury.

"I admire a spirited lass, but you are mine now, and I am going to rip that spirit right out of you." He moved toward her and grabbed her shoulders.

In an instant, she drew her leg back and brought her knee forward into his groin, much as she had once done — as Jane had taught her — to John Chamberlain, Lord Edward's son. This time, she used far more force.

He doubled over, squealing. "You she-devil! You sea witch! I will teach you for resisting me." He reached on his table and grabbed a dagger. Stanford brought his arm back and slashed the knife down toward Margaret's head in a broad, sweeping movement.

Margaret leapt back, almost avoiding the blade. She felt a burning sting when the knife tip grazed down her forehead and eyelid, and a little deeper down her left cheek. She felt warm blood springing from the cut.

Stanford paused, writhing in pain from her kick.

Margaret reached to his table. With blood obscuring the vision in her left eye, she grabbed his half-empty rum bottle, hauled back, and swung the bottle toward his head.

Until that day, the women Captain Stanford had encountered

were pampered French and English passengers of the ships he had plundered. However, Margaret — like Jane and Harriet — was a hard-working crewmember of *Lady Bridget*. For months she had done her fair share of work hauling barrels and crates, climbing ladders and rigging. In the hands of the English Margaret of cold, gray Barton Cottage, the rum bottle would have landed a painful blow to Captain Stanford's head. In the hands of *Lady Bridget*'s Margaret, the rum bottle shattered against his skull. The shards protruding from the handle raked across his face, leaving behind torn ribbons of flesh.

As Margaret began her backhand swing, Stanford dropped his dagger. He leapt backwards, though not so quickly as had Margaret.

As powerful as hauling barrels and crates had made her forehand swing, months of heaving on lines and sails gave even more force to her backhand. She felt momentary resistance when the virgin blades of broken glass, sharper than any surgeon's razors, pierced his throat. She felt another brief stiffness of the glass continuing through his windpipe. A fountain of blood erupted from his neck, showering her with hot red liquid.

Captain Stanford fell to the floor, writhing and clutching his throat, unable to speak. He struggled less than a minute, and was then still.

* * *

Hearing the loud commotion from the captain's cabin, the men tying Jane abandoned her to join the crowd outside. As soon as they departed, Harriet and Justine undid her ropes. The three raced to the crowd.

Margaret lifted the bar on the door and stumbled out. The men jumped back at the sight of her face running with blood and her clothing drenched and dripping red. Jane pushed forward, knocking one of the men over. Jacób and Justine joined with other slaves blocking the crew's access to the cabin and allowing passage for Jane. Jane forced Margaret inside, glancing only a moment at Stanford's sprawling body before turning to examine Margaret.

"Keep your hand away from your face, Margaret! Don't squeeze your eyes shut. We'll get the doctor. Don't cry. Don't do anything." She paused at the Captain's table for a few seconds before guiding Margaret back out. Jane called, "Medicine! Medicine!"

Through her daze, Margaret corrected, "*Médecin! Médecin!*"

A confusion of shouts sounded from the back of the crowd as Lieutenant Jasper pushed his way through. He caught sight of blood-covered Margaret. "What have you done!? I'll kill you myself! I'll rip your head right off!"

The sight of Jasper rushing toward her, his powerful, grasping hands stretched wide, paralyzed Margaret. Still, she jumped at a roar to her right. She observed, as if in a slow moving dream, a cone of red and gray erupt from his head to her left, mixed with pieces of skull. His head and his body followed and he toppled to the deck.

Jane turned to the crowd pulling another of Captain Stanford's pistols from the pocket of her dress and handing the spent one to Harriet. She screamed, "Does anyone else think that they can trifle with my sister!?"

No one needed translation. Jacób motioned with his hands and the crowd moved back. One of the men knelt, looked up to Jane for assurance, and approached the Lieutenant's sprawled body. Jasper continued to bear his final hideous snarl.

"*Is he really dead?*" Jacób asked.

"*She emptied his brains. But he's an English officer, so I've seen them prance around with less.*"

A grim laugh ran through the crowd.

Doctor Katanga made his way toward the front. He paused,

looked down at the Lieutenant, and raised his eyebrows. "*I'm good
…*" Then he shook his head. "*… but not that good. The Devil can have
him.*"

He turned to Jane, who had a crazed look on her face while
she held the pistol. He glanced over at Margaret. In their native
language, he conversed with Justine and Jacób. Satisfied, he returned
his attention to Jane. "It is over. Justine and Jacób assure me that the
Fouck and *Lady Bridget* are now in our hands. You may wish to lower
that pistol so that I may attend your sister."

Jane lowered the pistol, and Doctor Katanga sent for Chitter to
bring his bag. The doctor and Jane helped Margaret into the cabin
and had her sit on the bed. He glanced at Stanford's body and shook
his head. "Did you kill the captain?"

"No. I did," Margaret replied.

"Ah, and Lieutenant Jasper?"

"I did," Jane replied.

"Hmmm. I am finding it necessary to revise my understanding
of English women. Perhaps this is a good time to remind that I am
your friend."

Jane finally relaxed and chuckled.

He turned his attention to Margaret and examined her face. She
could see him with her right eye. "This is bad. This is very bad."

Chitter entered, carrying the doctor's bag.

"Still, I've fixed worse. I can probably save your eye." He began
extracting bottles of powders and liquids from his bag. "You must
help me. As difficult as it will be, you must relax. You cannot put
force on your eyelid. It is barely holding together and any pressure
will split it. That would be much more difficult to repair. Do not
move your head. Only say 'yes' or 'no'. Do you understand?"

Margaret whispered, "Yes."

He hummed as he sprinkled and mixed a paste. Chitter stood at
respectful attention in the doorway.

"OK. Remember, Miss Margaret — you must not squeeze
your eye or the lid may break forever. Again, relax." He turned to
Jane. "Miss Jane, please squeeze her hand. Squeeze so hard that it is
painful." He continued to swirl the paste in a small dish until he was
satisfied. He dabbed a generous portion on his finger and began to
move toward her eye.

"Is this going to hurt?" Margaret asked.

"Oh, yes-a mum. It's a going to hurt like the very fires of Hell. You will think that there are flames coming from your eye."

She took a deep breath. "Do we have to do this?"

He shrugged. "No. Of course not. We can leave it alone. In a day, the pus will ooze from your eye. Then the flies will come and the worms will eat out your eye. That is the nature of this injury. No eye, but no pain."

Margaret wilted. "Do it."

Jane looked to Doctor Katanga as he glanced up at her. She caught a twinkle in his eye and a fleeting trace of a smile. She returned the smile as she gripped Margaret's hand.

He applied the paste, easing the edges of the slice together and filling in the area around her eye. He applied a thin streak down the cut on her forehead and on her cut cheek. Margaret tensed on first contact of the mixture, but remained calm while he sculpted the paste and smoothed it. Finally, he drew a leather patch with leather drawstring from his bag and tied it around her head. He counted silently to thirty, examined his work and nodded. "I am finished."

"What?" Margaret asked. "That was it? That was not so painful."

Jane was laughing. "Oh, Captain Margaret. Do you remember climbing that big tree outside Norland Park, despite your mother's forbidding you? You slipped on a branch and slid down the trunk, skinning your leg something terrible. You were wary of my iodine, so I made a big fuss about its hurting, and that you were too much a child to take it. You were surprised that it was not so very bad. Today is no different. Had the good doctor said, 'it will not hurt much,' then it would have certainly felt like the very fires of Hell."

Margaret shook her head. "I'm surrounded by tricksters."

Katanga gave another deep laugh.

"What have you applied to my eye?" Margaret turned to look around with her free eye, adjusting to the new vision.

"Oh, a variety of substances I've observed to cure over the years. I used a plaster base to immobilize your eyelid until it can knit together. I mixed it with a little rum. The water sets the plaster and the alcohol prevents infection. I have added a pinch of opium to reduce the pain, and I also used some quassia bark to ward off the flies, and scrapings of the blue mold from limes, which prevents the necrotic pus. Then I added a special ingredient to speed the healing of the cut on your eyelid."

"Special ingredient?"

"You do not want to know," he said.

"Perhaps I do."

"Very well. I added ground up dried donkey testicles."

"Oh."

"I have observed that this ingredient speeds the healing so that the cut should be healed and strong by the time the plaster begins to crumble. It is an old folk remedy from my ancestral land. I've never seen it in the modern literature, though I sense that it works. That is enough for me. The leather patch holds my medicine close to your eye so the healing can progress."

Margaret thought for a bit. "You have a wonderful understanding of medicine, sir. I met a man on Martinique — also named Katanga — who has a similar familiarity with food preservation."

"Ha!" He laughed. "That would be my cousin Mulambo! He works with Miss Geneviève. They are partners. Did you meet her?"

Margaret grew excited. "Indeed we did. I hope that she will soon be Jane's mother-in-law."

"Ah, that is wonderful! It reminds us, though, that we have much to do, and quickly." He turned to Jane. "Your fiancé is in the clutches of that bastard Tarkington, who will try to have him hanging in a day or so. We must move right away to rescue him. With Captain Stanford and Lieutenant Jasper now resting peacefully, we have command of both ships secured."

The doctor addressed Margaret, "The men will follow you, Miss Margaret, especially since you are restoring their freedom."

"I am?"

"Yes, I heard Miss Jane call you Captain Margaret. You are the new captain of *Jacqueline Fouck*. Law of the Sea — the captain is the law. If you restore their freedom, it is restored."

"How can that be?" Margaret asked.

"Many years ago, Captain Stanford killed the captain of *Jacqueline Fouck*. He took the ship and was the new captain. You killed Captain Stanford, so now *you* are the captain. True, it is not a pretty line of succession, yet that is what we have. Now, we should stop wasting precious time and begin planning our rescue.

"Before we begin, it is important that Captain Margaret have the former captain's blood washed away. A few of my medical peers remain unconvinced, but most are quite certain that many diseases are propagated by contact with bad blood, and Captain Stanford led a life certain to produce bad blood. Use seawater — it serves nicely to wash the blood away. Do keep the water away from her face, though. We want time for my medicines to work."

Outside the cabin, the doctor departed to treat other casualties, and Jane accompanied Margaret toward the forecastle, with Harriet and Justine. The air about the ship was filled with a light, fragrant smoke.

Harriet smiled. "While you were being seen by the doctor, our crews have come together. Mr. Graham and their quartermaster, Mr. Mattson, have gotten on well. Even as the two ships 'ave been adrift together, God's been smilin' on us. They got a position fix, and we've actually been driftin' toward Queenstown. Their charts showed a shallows we was passin' over, and we dropped *Lady Bridget*'s anchor. The *Fouck*'s anchor, like so much of their ship, ain't workin' very well. So here we are. Once the two of us was anchored, we could feel a nice breeze.

"Now, it only seemed right that we celebrate with our new friends. Our cook's set up cookin' on deck. We broke out some of the good stores we got in Fort-de-France, and we're tryin' to host a little island feast like Miss Geneviève's feast. Our new friends are overjoyed. After seeing their stores, we suggested throwing them overboard, though I'm not sure that's fair to the fishies. The *Fouck* never availed themselves of Mulambo Katanga's meat preservation services, that is certain. Several of the slaves — do we call them slaves or have you restored their freedom? — had been cooks in Queenstown, and together are cookin' a banquet fit for the king with our cook. You can smell it already! Some of the men are fisherman, and they've already caught some flounder and snapper for the banquet. Those mangos and limes you acquired will be put to fine use."

"Marvelous!" Margaret said. "And I am powerfully hungry. I suppose that I should declare their return to freedom as the first order of business after I am cleaned up."

"*Then we must make you presentable.*" Justine said "*You must look the commanding part of a captain. I will assist. Before the dark times, I owned a lovely little dressmaking shop in town. I'm quite good, if I say so myself.*"

Margaret turned to Justine. "Splendid! I have an idea for my uniform. Hear me out."

As Margaret detailed her idea, Justine and Harriet began laughing.

Jane shook her head and folded her arms, though she could not hold back a smile.

When Justine finally stopped laughing, she wiped a tear from her eye. "*It is no wonder your 'sister' treasures you so. Your scheme is most crazy. I like it, and I will give you my finest effort.*"

The three women lowered buckets into the sapphire sea and drew up water. Margaret braced for an icy bath, only to revel in the warm Caribbean seawater.

She raised her hands. "This is wonderful! We're definitely not in England any more!"

After six buckets, the red stains in her clothing were mostly gone, and the water running from the deck into the sea was clear.

At first they could hear the sound of sharks, attracted by the rinse, thrashing in the water below. Then they heard laughter rising from the railing of the forecastle. About half a dozen of the *Fouck's* crew had gathered in amusement to watch Margaret's fully clothed shower.

"*You lazy scoundrels!*" Justine scolded, shaking her finger at them. "*This woman has saved us all. She killed Stanford, so she is now captain. Show proper respect!*" She put her hands on her hips, addressing her husband. "*And you — you should know better. Get these layabouts back to useful work!*"

Jacób threw up his hands. "*Yes, ma'am.*" He bowed to Margaret. "*My apologies, Captain.*" He shepherded the other men away from the forecastle and back to tasks getting the two ships ready for sail.

"*Idiots!*" Justine shouted. "*Why are all men such idiots?*"

"Now, now," Jane said, "not all men. Captain Johnson is quite the consistent gentleman."

"And my brothers-in-law, Reverend Ferrars and Colonel Brandon, are the finest of men," Margaret added.

"Can't complain about my Mr. Dunsford," Harriet said. "Or your Jacób."

Justine smiled a little. "*Perhaps. My Jacób is mostly a fine man. Perhaps I remember the idiots more than the fine ones.*"

The women turned Margaret around several times, and, satisfied that the blood was barely visible, headed back to the captain's cabin.

"Let us now get you changed from these wet garments. We have much to do to get you ready. Still, I think we can." Justine said.

* * *

About an hour before sunset, the food was ready, and served in generous portions to both crews. An informal "council" assembled on the half deck between the main deck and the forecastle — Mr. Graham, Harriet, and the gunner from *Lady Bridget*; and from *Jacqueline Fouck*, Doctor Katanga, Justine, Jacób, Mr. Mattson, Timothy the helmsman, and Seaman Jeffers, who had been captured by the *Fouck*, respected because he spoke in three of the languages in addition to English and French.

Jane emerged from the cabin and motioned for the doctor. "Margaret asks if you would be willing to translate so that she can address the crew in English?"

"Very wise," he said. "Captain Margaret understands the symbols of power. I would be honored."

Jane opened the door wide and Margaret emerged onto the half deck wearing the black clothing that had, until recently, belonged to Captain Stanford. Justine had needed only a few adjustments to the shirt and pants, the boots and red sash fit well, and Margaret wore his hat at a jaunty angle, giving good display to the ostrich feather. Rather than the whip he dangled from his belt, she wore his sword. Margaret stood tall above the main deck, her hands on her hips. The eye patch completed what should have been a frightening appearance, were it expected.

Instead, on catching sight of her, the crew of the *Fouck* burst out laughing. She remained calm, glancing over to see Justine's rising irritation. Margaret held up her hand in a motion for Justine to wait.

She nodded to the doctor. "Gentlemen of *Jacqueline Fouck*, Doctor Katanga informs me that by law of the sea and tradition, I am your new captain."

Another round of chuckles mixed with quieter laughter followed.

"Some of you find this amusing. Perhaps some of you believe that I am not up to the task."

A hush fell over the crew.

"Don't accept my assertions. We should ask others if I am able to conduct myself under trying circumstances. We could ask Captain Stanford." She paused in the silence. "Alas, he is no longer with us."

She looked toward the sea. "We could ask Lieutenant Jasper." Another pause. "But he, too, has departed the ship with the former captain. We could ask the merchants of Fort-de-France." She turned to Jane. "My beloved sister can attest to my ability to conduct business with a organization of arrogant men."

A murmur ran through the crew.

"And so, by the law of the sea and tradition, I am your new captain. My first task is to inform you that you are all now, by right, free citizens and equal under the law. As your captain, I so declare."

After a stunned complete silence, Jacób put his hand on his chest and shouted, "Long live Captain Margaret! Hip, hip, hooray!" The others joined him.

Margaret waited for the cheers to die down. "I am hungry now. Let us eat."

The banquet turned festive. The crew filled with food, instruments were brought from below and music, singing, and laughter filled the evening.

Jane shuttled between the council, the serving line, and crewmembers from both vessels. She paid particular attention to Chitter. He had been reluctant to make his way into the food line. She brought him a plate heaping with fish and beef, each glazed with a mixture of mango, lime, and herbs. She told him through Doctor Katanga, "I mean to see you up to proper weight. You are far too valuable a member of this crew to waste away."

He smiled a shy smile. Earlier she had found his smile, with its broken and bent teeth, somewhat frightening. Now, she saw only profound gratitude.

In the setting sun, the council finalized their plans for the coming day. The two ships would proceed separately to the dock in Queenstown, arriving in the pre-dawn darkness. Two parties would assemble on the pier, one bound for the Governor's Palace, the other for the jail to rescue Captain Johnson. It was decided that British women should lead both parties. Harriet would lead the party to retrieve Governor Tarkington, and Jane would lead the party to the jail. Justine would accompany Harriet with the doctor interpreting, and Jacób would be Jane's second-in-command with Jeffers providing the language bridge.

"So," Justine said, "Stanford and Jasper have received justice. Now it is time for that scum Tarkington to receive his."

"And Sergeant Randolph, the jailer," Jeffers added.

Katanga frowned. "I don't think that Randolph is in the same category."

"He is the hangman and he is the jailer," Timothy said.

The doctor continued. "One hanging only — for an actual convicted criminal. Sergeant Randolph is a soldier, following orders. That is his duty. Other members of this crew have killed in the line of duty — many of you this very day." He swept his arm around the council. "Are we also all to be killed?"

Jane spoke up. "If Sergeant Randolph does not resist, we shall not harm him. If you are with me in the morning, you must agree to that." No one disagreed.

It was Margaret's turn to speak. "And I do not believe that we shall execute Governor Tarkington."

She saw Justine scowl and cross her arms.

"You mentioned that Lieutenant Governor Hooker has tried to run an honest office. Is he trustworthy?"

Those from Queenstown nodded.

"Very well," she continued, "there is a visitor in Queenstown, a Mr. Gareth Speedwell, Esquire, who will document Governor Tarkington's profound change of heart and conversion. With Mr. Hooker to back up his writing when there is a formal enquiry, Mr. Speedwell will tell of Governor Tarkington's valiant fight against the pirates and his tragic death in the final battle with Captain Stanford aboard *Jacqueline Fouck*. We may even raise a statue to the brave governor and his unlikely legacy of freedom."

After a pause to ponder Margaret's scheme, Jane turned to Justine. "Did I mention that she is a frightful deceiver? That has proven useful from time to time?"

Justine puckered her mouth. "She imagines these things so quickly. When a young girl, she must have been a handful for you."

Jane nodded. "She still is."

After all members of the council confirmed their roles in the coming day's drama, the gunner secured the captain's cabin with its trove of pistols and powder until the morning.

* * *

A full moon reflected from a glassy sea, as smooth as Jane could recall. The few remains from dinner had been consumed, the songs had gone quiet, and a sense of beautiful calm permeated both ships.

She looked up at the rigging sketching an orderly web between her and the bright lunar disk. She glanced to sea, to the south, to see a few lights from Queenstown. Jane was smiling as she walked across the double-wide gangplank that the freed carpenters had constructed in a matter of hours. She stepped down onto *Jacqueline Fouck*'s deck with ease to take one final turn about the decks. Plans were complete, the crew excited to undertake their   mission. The gangplank would be withdrawn around three in the morning, and the two ships would set sail for their pre-dawn stealth arrival in Queenstown. Mr. Graham would take command of *Lady Bridget*, and Margaret would — at least by title — take command of *Jacqueline Fouck*. The latter development caused Jane to smile again.

She saw Doctor Katanga sitting on the short deck by the sealed captain's cabin.

"Good evening, Miss Jane." His sonorous greeting floated across the deck, and his smile was bright in the moonlight. "Are you having difficulty sleeping? Tomorrow is a big day and you should rest."

She sat down beside him. "I shall rest soon, Doctor. I saw Captain Margaret to her bed and wanted to make one final check."

Katanga laughed to hear "Captain Margaret." "Did she have difficulty falling asleep?"

"No, none at all. This day fatigued her. When she was preparing for bed — when she thought me asleep — I saw her looking in her mirror, posing one way and another. She rather fancies her eye patch and the air of daring it bespeaks."

He laughed. "Good. That feeling will help in the healing process if it causes her to tolerate the patch. She is a fortunate woman in many respects. Life could have gone very badly for her today. In particular, she is fortunate to have such a 'sister' to watch over her."

Jane looked down at the deck. "While Margaret has proven herself a strong woman, especially today, she is nonetheless in many ways still a young girl with big dreams and flights of fancy. I do treasure that spark and bless the day I decided to join her on this voyage, even though it be fraught with peril."

They fell silent, savoring the silvery stillness. Presently, a lone figure crossed the deck. He strung a hammock between two stanchions. Chitter climbed in and clasped his arms about him.

"Even in the tropics, he will be frightfully cold during the night," Jane whispered.

The doctor spoke, "Alas, he has no blanket of his own. He politely rejected my offer of mine, and he is afraid of the spaces below."

Jane frowned and made her way to *Lady Bridget*, returning after a few minutes. She approached Chitter and placed a covering over him. He opened his eyes and felt the cloth she had provided. He smiled. In the moonlight, his smile was not frightening, but rather childlike.

"*M-m-merci, Miss Jane, m-m-merci beaucoup.*"

She smiled. "You are welcome, Chitter. Good night."

She returned to her seat beside Doctor Katanga. "It is a cloak that I acquired for Margaret back in England at the very start of this adventure. How appropriate that it has found such a noble home."

"Your generosity will be remembered."

"I didn't know that he spoke French," she said.

"Only the important words."

* * *

It was quite dark when bells on both ships sounded at 2:45, and the crews were at their stations in a matter of minutes. Though the carpenters couldn't complete the repairs on the mast, they had been able to untangle the lines and reposition pulleys so that *Lady Bridget* was more than able to make way for the short haul to Queenstown.

Mr. Graham and Mr. Mattson shook hands and took their places on their respective bridges. At 3:00, seeing that all was ready, Mr. Graham called out, "raise the anchor!" The crew on the capstan answered back, "Raise the anchor, aye!" and put their shoulders to the task. After about six minutes, they called, "Anchor's aweigh!" and continued until it was housed in its hawse pipe. "Anchor's home!"

Lady Bridget was first to unfurl her sails. "Cast off all lines!" Graham shouted. They drifted a hundred yards east of the *Fouck*, which then unfurled her sails and began heading toward Queenstown. Jane took the abbreviated sounding and security watch on *Lady Bridget*, while Margaret took the helm of *Jacqueline Fouck*. Timothy was too much in recovery from his wounds to steer, instead providing guidance seated in a chair next to Margaret, who had never actually taken the helm on either ship.

"'Tis a peculiar turn of fate, Captain, that you nearly killed me and we labor now side by side."

She laughed. "I fancy that we will do fine work together. I am much pleased that you are on the mend, Timothy."

Lady Bridget followed the *Fouck* about a hundred yards aft. They furled their sails a short distance from the Queenstown pier. With the moon setting to the west, *Lady Bridget* lowered a small boat with half a dozen crew, who scrambled onto the wooden planks and waited for lines, first from the *Fouck,* then from *Lady Bridget.* The experienced line handlers had both ships secured in a matter of minutes.

Two groups of the most loyal and reliable crewmembers assembled. *Lady Bridget's* gunner distributed pistols and machetes. Margaret remained aboard the *Fouck* and Mr. Graham stayed on *Lady Bridget.* Jane's group walked in silence up the hill to the west toward a modest stone building near the top of a winding path. The first hint of dawn touched the sky as Harriet led a silent crew up the main street toward the imposing white building at the far end.

* * *

Jane, with her retinue of eight, arrived at the jailhouse with the eastern sky glowing soft warm pastels in anticipation of sunrise. She turned to Jeffers and whispered, "Tell them to wait."

"*Attendez,*" he whispered in French and in several other tongues. The others nodded.

The door sounded a low creak when she opened it and entered.

Sergeant Randolph had been dozing, the back of his chair leaning against the wall. The one-room jailhouse was a model of stark emptiness. Aside from the desk, the chair, and Sergeant Randolph, the room was bare and white on three sides. His desk faced a set of iron bars enclosing four tiny cells, each with a simple wooden slab — no covering — for a bed.

Randolph straightened up with a confused look. "Yes, miss?"

"I've come for Captain Johnson." When she said this, she heard a stirring in cell Number Two. The other three cells were empty.

He frowned. "Well, you can't have 'im. Me orders are to hold 'im 'til the trial."

She smiled. "Ah, that has changed, Sergeant Randolph — there will be no trial. He is free and will come with me, now."

"Are ye daft, woman? You'll not be takin' anyone from here."

"Come, come, Sergeant. This doesn't have to be difficult. I'm merely asking you to release the captain."

"And who's going to make me?"

Jane sighed. "I had hoped to avoid this." She turned to the

doorway and shouted, "Gentlemen!"

Jacób was the first to enter, ducking his head to fit his large frame through the low door. Randolph scooted his chair back to the wall and his eyes grew wide as, one by one, the other seven entered, each brandishing a machete, a pistol, or both. Chitter was the last one to enter, and they formed a grim wall of their own in front of the only door.

Randolph was breathing hard as Jane leaned forward, resting her fists on his desk. She smiled, whispering, "They're really *not* gentlemen. That is a bit of amusement among us."

He looked up at her, terror in his eyes.

"And, so, Sergeant Randolph, you have two choices."

He raised his eyebrows.

"The first choice — you will cheerfully release Captain Johnson to me and then live a long and happy life in this tropical paradise."

He bit his lip, glanced at the human wall, and asked, "And the second?"

She frowned. "The second?" She shrugged. "You will not."

He thought only a moment, opened the desk drawer, and handed the keys to Jane. She walked to the cell and unlocked it.

"Captain Johnson." She nodded.

"Miss Moseby." He returned her nod with a smile.

The men stood away from the door as she and the captain prepared to leave. She set the keys on Randolph's desk. "Thank you, sergeant. Good choice." Jane and Robert stepped outside.

Jacób turned to leave, waving his pistol in Randolph's direction. "Good choice."

Each man, in turn, with the pleasing spice of his individual accents, repeated the greeting, each waving his particular weapons departing.

"Good choice."

"Good choice."

"Good choice."

"Good choice."

"Good choice."

"Good choice."

The last to enter, Chitter was also the last to leave. "G-g-g-g-g-good ch-ch-ch-choice."

Almost out the door, Chitter stopped and turned back to

Randolph. Chitter shook his finger at the sergeant, launching into his own West African language without a trace of stutter, "*You have been spared. If it were up to us, we would have slit your throat and fed you to the fishes. But Miss Jane demanded that we show you mercy, and for her we will do anything. Still, know that we will be watching you, and that we do not forget. Miss Jane has granted you a precious gift. Do not waste her benevolence. You will not have another chance.*" He gave a quick flick of his head and was out the door.

Aside from the two references to "Miss Jane," Randolph had not understood any of Chitter's particular words, yet understood full well Chitter's passionate lecture. Once his breathing returned to normal, the jailer rose and locked the cell. He pushed his chair in and scanned the room to confirm its tidiness.

Randolph stepped out and gazed north at towering clouds piercing the turquoise sky, their pillowed shoulders drenched in sunrise reds, oranges, and golds. A faint, moist breeze greeted him, bearing the fragrances of warm, fertile soil and flowers. He locked the door, turned from the jailhouse for the last time, and walked forward into a long and happy life in his tropical paradise.

* * *

Harriet walked up the marble steps to the palace's porch and pounded on its door. After a few minutes, a young woman opened the door and surveyed the members of the party.

She addressed Doctor Katanga, "Good morning, doctor. So good to see you again. It is quite early for house calls."

He chuckled, turning to Harriet. "She was also re-enslaved and has been treated badly. I seem to recall that Captain Margaret said that all are freed again. Is my memory correct?"

Harriet nodded. "Your memory is correct, doctor."

He turned back to the woman. "Madeline, I am pleased to tell you that you are once again free. We have —"

"Is he all right?" she interrupted.

Katanga smiled. "Yes. He is quite well and on a special mission." He turned back to Harriet. "Madeline is much in love with Chitter. Nothing is of greater importance to her than his well-being."

He continued, "Madeline, we have come for Governor Tarkington."

She nodded to Harriet and turned to the only other woman on the team and nodded. "Good morning, Madame Justine. So good of you to come." She looked over the grim team with their assorted weapons. "It would seem this is going to be a bad day for the governor. He is, of course, not awake yet. I don't recall whether he had a woman last night. Hmm, it matters not. Follow me."

They followed Madeline through a grand hallway and up the stairs to the second floor. Arriving at a bedroom, she pushed open the door and stood back. The men of the party filed in first, followed by Justine and Harriet. A young woman rose from the bed and shrieked. She ran, naked, to a rear door and disappeared into an adjoining room.

Tarkington propped himself up on an elbow. "What is the meaning of this outrage?" he demanded.

"Come with us, please, sir," Harriet said.

"I'll do nothing of the sort!"

Harriet looked to the doctor, who spoke to Justine, who relayed his instructions to the men. They dragged him from the bed.

Harriet shook her head. "As humiliating as it might be, his appearance is too revolting even for me. Let us put some covering on him."

Someone flung a robe in Tarkington's face. He slipped it on, and then made a futile attempt to run. Several men blocked his escape. They let him don his slippers, and pushed him into the hallway, down the stairs, and into the dawn.

"I need my spectacles. I can barely see."

"We shall be your guides," Harriet said.

He tried several times to wrest free of his captors, the exertion exhausting him. They arrived at the Queenstown pier as the sun peeked over the eastern horizon.

* * *

Jane, Robert, and their eight companions were enjoying a more festive stroll from the jailhouse to the pier.

Robert could see the two ships from a distance. "How did you manage to convince Captain Stanford to let you go?"

Jane smiled. "It is a long story, and we shall have plenty of time for the telling. Margaret was quite convincing with the captain."

"How are our crew?"

"Quite well. We suffered no deaths. And, we have formed a good friendship with the remaining crew of the *Fouck* and their former slaves."

"Former slaves?"

"Yes. The *Fouck*'s captain granted back their freedom. You will see. Our ship remains sound. With repairs to the mast, she should be seaworthy in a week or so."

They arrived at the base of the pier where Harriet's party dragged Governor Tarkington about a third of the way down and halted. He squinted in the early morning light at the two moored ships. A figure clad in black, save a red sash and white ostrich feather, descended the gangplank of *Jacqueline Fouck*.

"Stanford, we had a compact!" Tarkington shouted. "You shall pay for this betrayal. What is the meaning of this?"

By the time the figure had closed half the length of the *Fouck*, the governor realized the person was not Captain Stanford. Clutched by two of the strongest crew, he stood in sullen silence while Captain Margaret approached.

Still squinting, he asked, "Where is Captain Stanford?"

Margaret shrugged and waved her arm toward the expanse of open sea. "Somewhere out there. With the fishes."

He looked around the crowded pier, then back to Margaret. "And Lieutenant Jasper?"

She offered her hand again to the horizon. "With Captain Stanford … with the fishes."

"You cannot hold me. I am governor of this province. Release me now!"

She shook her head. "You will be released — we have no plans to hold you. You have built a criminal empire here. You have enslaved free people. You have promoted piracy. Why, a moment ago, you confirmed your complicity with the pirates under Captain Stanford. You have authorized murders upon murders. You have stood by while innocents from many nations were tortured, raped, and killed. Oh, you shall be released, though not as you would wish it." She drew the sword from its scabbard.

His face paled. "You are going to kill me?"

Margaret first looked down at her sword, and then gazed about at the ships, then at the crowd before returning to face Tarkington. She poked him several times with the point of her sword. "I cannot. As hideous as your crimes may be, I have not suffered directly. I cannot be justified in taking your life."

He closed his eyes and sighed.

Margaret turned the hilt in her palm and handed the sword to Justine.

"You killed my precious Annabel, my darling daughter," Justine said, "Feel now her fingernails rising from the grave, tearing your heart in two."

Tarkington wrenched away, freeing an arm for a moment, until powerful arms immobilized him again. Justine ran at him and thrust the sword through his heart with all her might.

As the blade exited his back, Tarkington's face twisted in agony.

Releasing the sword hilt, Justine stepped back as her child's murderer fell to the pier, gave one great shudder and lay still. "Justice be done," Justine said, then turned and walked away.

* * *

Margaret stood at attention, watching Justine until she cleared the dock. Margaret turned to the former governor's body, put her boot on his side and tugged on the sword until it was free. She wiped the blade on his robe until she was satisfied it was clean and returned it to the scabbard. She addressed Jacób, "*Please have his body taken to the Fouck and placed just above the powder stores.*"

"Aye, Captain." He nodded and motioned for several of the other men to help haul the body away. He told others to fetch buckets to rinse the pier of blood.

Margaret saw Jane and Robert approaching. She doffed her hat to reveal her curls tied back with a red ribbon. She bowed low. "Captain Johnson."

He returned a solemn bow. "Captain Dashwood."

She frowned. "I should think it best we stay with 'Captain Margaret.' I don't believe associating with my family name is wise."

Jane chuckled. "Perhaps 'Captain Maggie' would be even better."

Margaret nodded.

"I am bewildered by what I behold," he said. "When I was spirited away yesterday — was it only yesterday? — I despaired of ever again seeing my family and my ship." Robert continued surveying the two ships and the pier.

"I told you, Robert, that they would not take *Lady Bridget*." Jane folded her arms. "For a few hours, Captain Stanford and his men thought they prevailed, yet we had cultivated an *esprit* with those the pirates had re-enslaved before you even arrived in port."

"Speaking of Captain Stanford, did I hear that he is at sea?"

"Indeed. He tried to have his way with me, but I resisted. I grabbed his rum bottle and delivered a blow strong enough that it shattered against his head. When I drew it back, the sharp edges cut his throat through many times."

Robert's eyes grew wide. "Oh, my! And Lieutenant Jasper?"

Margaret held out her hand. "That would be for your beloved Jane to tell."

Jane shook her head and colored a bit. "Captain Stanford left a small arsenal on his table, and I pocketed several pistols when I led Margaret out of the cabin to fetch the doctor. Lieutenant Jasper was enraged and sought to kill Margaret with his bare hands. In his frenzy, he failed to notice the pistol I pointed at his head and fired at close range."

Johnson stood, dumbfounded, for a moment. "Extraordinary! And the eye patch?"

"When Captain Stanford attacked me, I resisted as best I could. Then he tried to slash me with his dagger. I was quick jumping back — almost quickly enough. By good fortune, Doctor Katanga ..." Margaret turned to Jane. "He hasn't met the doctor, has he?"

Jane shook her head.

"Yes," she continued, "Doctor Katanga is a most skilled physician. He has my eye braced and plied with medicines and a special ingredient." She turned her head one way and another for him to see. "Do you like it?"

Jane and Robert laughed.

Margaret ignored their laughter. "The good doctor said that by the law of the sea and tradition, I am captain of *Jacqueline Fouck*. Does that strike you as true?"

Johnson thought a moment. "While I am uncertain of the law, I have heard traditions that agree. I can see that you comport yourself very well. Where did you learn to command? And, what do you plan to do with your ship?"

"I had a very fine example to watch, and I observed him closely."

Jane nodded, smiling.

"As to what I shall do with *Jacqueline Fouck*, I am uncertain. From what I gather from my crew, she is not seaworthy. Captain Stanford chose not to maintain her, figuring he would simply capture another when the time came. I asked Jimmy to look her over and judge the *Fouck*'s potential. I see him coming this way now, and he looks displeased."

Jimmy stopped at the small group and gave a polite bow to Johnson. "Captain, it gives me great joy to see you returned to us."

"Thank you, Jimmy. It is a joy to be back."

Jimmy turned to Margaret and gave another polite bow. "Captain."

"What say you, Jimmy?" she asked.

He shook his head. "Alas, she is a barely floating disaster. Her planks are riddled with shipworms, her anchor capstan is nearly corroded through, her sails are rotten, the blast that followed our gunner's strike on one of your cannons put a sizable hole in the side, and rats infest every space. With a proper dry dock, it might be possible to make repairs. However, the cost would far exceed building a new vessel from the keel up."

Margaret gazed at her ship. "'Tis a pity. In truth, I never set out to be the captain of a sailing ship. What shall become of her?"

Jimmy's glum expression brightened. "That is a happier story. There is much to be salvaged from her. In particular, her mainmast is free of the worms and is close to the size of our own damaged mainmast. I spoke with our new carpenter friends. Several are master shipwrights. They tell me that we could replace *Lady Bridget*'s broken mainmast with the *Fouck*'s in a reasonable time.

"The surviving cannon can be removed. The gunner says we don't need more ourselves. Instead, we can set them up to be part of the defenses for Queenstown." He nodded to Margaret. "It would make your shipyard more secure, Captain."

Jane and Robert both stared at Margaret.

"Your shipyard?" Jane asked.

Margaret smiled. "When I return, I should like to found a shipyard here. We would not take business from Geneviève, instead coordinating our services and specializing. I have already talked with some of the carpenters. They would like to call it 'Blackbelly Shipyards.' I would be the English face of the enterprise to negotiate with traders."

Johnson raised his eyebrows. "Is that name not an insult?"

She laughed. "Precisely what I asked. They reminded me that our Christian symbol — the cross — is an executioner's tool and that we have won our liberation over those who used 'blackbelly' as a cruel affront." She turned back to Jimmy. "What more?"

"Once we salvage the sound pieces, we should take her away from here and scuttle her. We don't want her rats and rot spreading to the pier and to other ships. We can leave a few kegs of powder aboard and put the rest to good use in Queenstown's defense and for *Lady Bridget*."

Margaret grew excited. "That gives me an idea!"

"Oh dear," Jane said.

Chapter Nineteen
Brighton and Beyond

"I must say, Mary, I am inspired by your devotion to Charlotte."

In the early morning light, Elizabeth stood beside the wagon at Pemberley's entrance as servants finished placing Mary's three large trunks aboard.

Mary smiled. "It is the least I can do. Charlotte's friendship changed my life in so many ways. When I ponder my dismal prospects two years ago, my heart swells with gratitude." She ensured her luggage was secured before turning back to Elizabeth. "I shall not be idle. I have a plentiful stock of good paper, pens, and inks. My own writing will flow uninterrupted, and, not only *my* writing, but Charlotte's as well. Her stories of intrigue are well along, and they will be well received."

"Have the two of you resolved the concerns over her reception as a female author?"

Mary chuckled. "Indeed we have. Her stories will appear under the name of Charles LaCologne, pronounced 'sharles.' Constance suggested his name, and we think it most clever. His biographer says Charles hails from Toulouse, in France."

"I see. Have I read any of this biographer's work?" Elizabeth sported a mischievous smile.

"You have — he is the same biographer who wrote so well of Joseph Weatherstone and Gareth Speedwell, Esquire."

Elizabeth laughed. "Then I shall anticipate reading Monsieur LaCologne's adventure stories. Oh, Mary, I shall miss you so. Your clever humor and mature outlook have brought me such pleasure these last few years. I know for certain you will be a wonderful companion for Charlotte alongside Constance. Perhaps I shall come visit you three in Brighton when the weather warms. I should think you, Charlotte, and Constance will be needing some assistance before your stay is finished."

"Do not trouble yourself, my sister. Though it will likely be much quieter here at Pemberley without my disruptive influence, you have so very many high responsibilities to keep you occupied, particularly with the new stables." She smiled. "And, Joseph Weatherstone has provided a most generous grant, so we will be well settled. An acquaintance from the abolition movement has offered comfortable lodging in Brighton at a very reasonable rate. Charlotte and I shall write often and keep you informed of our progress. We may send you some of our evolving writing."

They hugged, and Thomas helped Mary board the wagon.

* * *

By the time Mary arrived at Hunsford Cottage, the hired coach was nearly finished loading. Their driver transferred Mary's trunks to the coach, and announced he was ready at their convenience.

Mary and William clasped hands. "Goodbye, sir. I shall miss our working together, but we shall keep busy with our many individual tasks, and we will exchange writings quite often. I look forward to our return with a new generation ready for service."

William nodded and released Mary's hands. "And, in your and Charlotte's absence, I shall endeavor to be the good shepherd you have both encouraged me to be for the parish. Take good care, one for the other, until next we meet. I pray your discomforts will be bearable," he whispered lest the coachman should hear.

Mary and Constance boarded the coach, shut the door against the chill, and settled comfortably as William and Charlotte exchanged a loving goodbye.

"It is most kind of your sister-in-law to give us lodging on the way." Constance said. "I was not looking forward to a stopover in London."

"Georgiana has been keen for me to visit with her and Lord Brougham for some time. I have a gift for Georgiana from Elizabeth and some correspondence for his lordship from Gareth Speedwell, Esquire."

"Ah, yes, Mr. Speedwell. It was most fortunate Miss Dashwood made his acquaintance." Constance chuckled. "It would have been a tragedy for her keen observations to go untold."

Mary nodded.

"Now, tell me if I am mistaken. Lady Georgiana must be six or seven months with child. Is that correct?"

"You are correct."

"Very well," Constance continued. "I have been coaching Mrs. Collins as to the complaints she should be suffering were she three months along, so she may present convincingly. By contrast, you will do well to conceal your own discomfort. While we have been able to conceal your progress from your sister, Lady Georgiana may have been through those discomforts already, and is quite likely to see through our ruse if we are not careful. In particular, it is helpful you and Mrs. Collins are both wearing loose fitting dresses and long cloaks."

"You are right, Constance. Georgiana is a sensitive and intelligent soul. I will endeavor to appear unaffected. I know Charlotte has been rehearsing her behavior as you have guided her."

Charlotte was all smiles as William assisted her into the coach after a lingering farewell. She took her seat and signaled for the driver to proceed. The three women waved goodbye as the coach departed.

"Well, ladies, are we excited for this grand adventure?" Charlotte asked. "The coachman says we may make Warwick or even Banbury by nightfall, if the roads remain dry."

Constance nodded. "Which would put us within a day of Lord and Lady Brougham. Let us also hope for good roads. Otherwise, the ride will be taxing on our 'new Charlotte.' I have brought some herbs to calm her stomach if needed, but it is better to break from time to time and walk about. Though I fancy you would like to be reading as we travel, I would advise against it for your stomach's sake."

"Forgoing my books will be a challenge," Mary said, "But I value and respect your advice."

By mid-afternoon, Mary was weary and frustrated. "Are we not concerned the jolting and jostling will jar the child loose?"

Constance laughed. "No, my dear. God has given you good design to endure this and worse. Your bones and body will take the jolts for the tiny one."

"Lovely." Mary stared out the window.

* * *

By great fortune, the roads were in good repair and remained dry, and they traveled most of the way to Banbury before stopping at an inn for the night. After a good supper, the three slept well. Mary felt little desire to get up and start again in the morning.

"Is it normal to feel so out of sorts?" Mary asked.

"Alas, yes. I would be concerned if you did not feel out of sorts. Though your tiny one seems small, he or she is busy taking over your body for his or her own ends."

Though Mary expressed little desire for breakfast, Constance was insistent. "You must trust me when I say you will feel far more discomfort in a few hours on an empty stomach. Also, this is how you are likely to feel tomorrow morning when you awaken at Lord and Lady Brougham's. Now would be a good time to practice your robust and cheerful manner."

Charlotte chuckled. "I shall attempt in the morning to mimic how you are appearing at the moment."

Constance nodded.

After breakfast and a short walk, the three boarded their coach and travelled on. As the distance to London decreased, the quality of the roads increased, and they arrived at the Brougham estate outside Reading in late afternoon. Georgiana was overjoyed to greet them.

Lady Georgiana Brougham was quick to solicit advice from Constance, and Constance pleased to provide, confirming to Georgiana the guidance she had received from her caregivers was sound and in keeping with what Constance had observed over the years. Though Georgiana was great with child, she enjoyed the highest standard of care.

Charlotte shared with Georgiana the misery of the long trip, even over the better roads. She talked of Constance's insistence on regular meals and walks. Georgiana agreed and encouraged Charlotte to follow Constance's wisdom.

As before, they slept well. Mary was a bit more inclined to move about in the morning, the fine beds of the estate having given her a better rest. Constance assisted Mary dressing.

"You are beginning to show, Mary — about on schedule, I'd say. We will continue with the looser dress today and Charlotte will do likewise to frustrate comparisons. Are you ready for breakfast?"

"I believe so. We have given a convincing show, have we not?"

Constance smiled as she shook her head. "No."

"No?"

"I've been watching Lady Georgiana. She has furtively inspected the two of you. I have little doubt she senses something is afoot. Neither of you has made any missteps, but, as you have acknowledged so often, she is bright and observant in the extreme."

"I hope you are mistaken," Mary said.

* * *

After breakfast, the coachman prepared their horses for the final leg of the journey and inspected the coach for readiness. Charlotte sat and read a book in one of the parlors.

"Oh, Mary," Georgiana said with excitement. "You have not seen my new horse! It was a gift on my birthday from his Lordship."

Mary followed Georgiana to the stables and met Boadicea, a handsome chestnut.

"She's beautiful!" Mary exclaimed.

"And gentle as well. Dy wanted me to have a well-behaved horse during these times." She watched Mary admiring Boadicea.

After a bit, Georgiana continued, "I must say you and Constance have been wonderfully attentive to Mrs. Collins. She appreciates your friendship and nurture, I am certain."

Mary nodded. "Charlotte has been a good friend to me as well. Without her support, I would never have been able to participate in the historic events of the past year."

"Well, you and Constance have served her admirably. She is looking quite well. I remember being miserable in my third month — not wanting to arise in the morning, little appetite for breakfast."

Mary and Georgiana eyed each other.

"Charlotte is strong and healthy," Mary said. "Constance says she was well prepared for these times."

"Excellent. And you? How are you feeling these days?"

Mary folded her arms. "Excellent. Thank you for asking."

Georgiana was smiling now. "I thought how fine you look. You've gained a bit of rosiness, filled out a little since last we met."

Mary nodded.

"You know, secrets between 'sisters' are special things, and I most certainly think of you as my sister. You of all people know the value of secrets — you and Joseph Weatherstone. But, even as a young girl, I learned to read the clues of my brother's demeanor. I fancy you and I might know something Elizabeth does not, hmm?"

Mary pondered for some time, stroking Boadicea's mane. "Would you tell Elizabeth?"

"Secrets between 'sisters' are special things," Georgiana repeated. "It is most clever going away to Brighton for 'Charlotte's confinement' — over half the island away from Pemberley. Given your skills in managing phantoms, I can imagine you have thought this part through. But, what comes after?"

Mary took a deep breath, closed her eyes and tilted back her head. "After, I shall continue with Constance to help Charlotte and William with their child. Our village knows of our deep friendship, and we believe they will welcome 'their' new child without question.

Do you think my expectation far-fetched?"

Georgiana motioned for them to head back to the coach. "It could work. I am more familiar with our family and, so, more sensitive. If Charlotte is seen in public with the child, as opposed to you, and gains its affections — as no doubt she will — then people will see what they wish to see. Feeding time will be a delicate matter, of course, but you've proven your ability to rise to far more trying challenges. At least you will not have to be watching over your shoulder for the villainous Mr. Douglas Marshall!"

They both laughed as they came into view of the coach, where Charlotte and Constance awaited their goodbyes.

Georgiana first hugged Constance. "Thank you for your kind confirmations of my care. I know you will continue to take exquisite care of Mrs. Collins. When next we meet, I should have a son or daughter of my own to show you.

"And blessings on you, Charlotte. You are in good company with Mary and Constance. Please come back to lodge with us when the time comes to return to Derbyshire. You are always most welcome. I hope I can arrange a visit north when it is time for the baptism."

Finally, Georgiana turned to Mary. "Oh, sister, we still have so much to catch up on. Do avail yourself of the salt air in Brighton. 'Miss Anna' tells me the salt air is one of the resources keeping old Joseph Weatherstone alive."

The four laughed and the Brighton-bound party boarded their coach. Lady Brougham caressed her belly and waved as they drove away.

After a while, Mary turned to Constance and smiled. "You were right, of course."

"I see." Constance nodded. "Would I also be correct in assuming she will keep our confidence?"

Seeing Charlotte's confused look, Mary said. "Though we gave our best efforts, Georgiana is too clever to be deceived. Five of us are now in on the secret."

"Five?" Charlotte looked about. "You, me, Constance, and Georgiana. I count four."

Mary smiled. "What about William, the child's father?"

Charlotte paused a moment. "Yes. Of course. How thoughtless of me."

* * *

The coach arrived in Brighton in late afternoon. The little cottage was snug and well built, warm and comfortable, located about four streets from the waterfront. After their long journey, Mary was happy to breathe the sea air carried on the prevailing winds.

A jolly housekeeper greeted them. In an effort to maintain their ruse, Charlotte introduced Mary as "Mrs. Collins," and Mary introduced Constance and then Charlotte as "Miss Bennet". Mrs. Dingle ushered them in and directed the coachman where to deposit the luggage. Mary paid the coachman and he was off. After giving them a tour of the cottage and an explanation of the neighboring markets and attractions, Mrs. Dingle left for her home.

Upon stowing bags and trunks, Constance set to work organizing the kitchen to her liking and began preparing a simple dinner. She smiled. "I am particularly keen to have access to excellent fresh sea fish. My friends in midwifery have observed that well-prepared fish is excellent nourishment for expectant mothers and their little ones. And I understand fresh vegetables from the continent are regular items in the markets here. Also good nourishment."

* * *

As the months passed, the three fell into comfortable routine. After arising with the sun and bathing, they would stroll to the waterfront if the weather was even remotely hospitable and then to the market. Breakfast followed — some bread or pastry acquired at one of the bakeries. Lunch was seafood from the dockside fishmongers. Constance did her best to find a different fish or sea creature every day.

Despite her initial skepticism, Mary enjoyed both the squid and the octopus as prepared by Constance. The one menu repeated more often than the rest was lobster, of which all three were very fond.

* * *

As Mary grew in size, she did her best to avoid complaining, instead pondering the changes in her body. She noted her swelling breasts. "Your description of Mary Bennet, the man-stealer with indecent breasts, is not so far off," she said to Charlotte. With a smile, she told Constance, "You said the little one was busy taking over my body for his or her ends. I fancy he or she is building a palace rather than a cottage."

Constance nodded. "You are doing well — right as we would expect."

In late May, Georgiana paid a surprise visit and stayed for two days. Mary, Constance, and Charlotte enjoyed adoring young Fitzwilliam Brougham. Georgiana advised Mary on what to expect in the final months of pregnancy and recounted her delivery experiences to an eager Constance. The young midwife was happy to hear repeated all of the markers she had come to know in her apprenticeship.

Georgiana gave Mary a note from Lord Brougham attached to a copy of Gareth Speedwell's description of the recent Battle of Queenstown and the heroic death of the noble Governor Tarkington.

"My, my. Margaret Dashwood finds herself in the most treacherous situations. I can't imagine she had bargained for all this," Mary said after reading the missive.

Georgiana agreed. "True. Given the extraordinary drama of his descriptions, the Home Office thought at first it was a piece of fiction, but independent witnesses have verified the events. We received a note from Margaret Dashwood at the same time. Their ship is awaiting repairs in the Caribbean, but she hopes to return to England for a time in the months ahead. She especially looks forward to a reunion with you to regale you with tales of her adventures. Charlotte will enjoy Margaret's reports as well.

"We will travel to Pemberley with young Fitzwilliam in June so he can meet his uncle and older aunt. I shall pass on how well you and Constance are caring for Charlotte and I will tell Elizabeth how well Charlotte is holding up."

At the end of her visit, Georgiana hugged Charlotte and Constance, and leaned in to hug Mary.

Mary, Charlotte, and Constance returned to their peaceful routines of morning strolls and afternoon writings until the morning of July seventh, when Mary's water broke.

* * *

Mary had been walking to the kitchen for tea when labor commenced. Constance took command immediately, and Charlotte assumed the supportive role they had practiced for months. Constance was skillful and remained calm throughout the labor, and around six in the evening Mary delivered a screaming, red-faced boy. The midwife placed him in Mary's arms and smiled as she commenced her post birth procedures.

Through her tears, Mary caressed the child and greeted him with the name they had all agreed on. "Good evening, sir. Welcome to the world, Joseph."

* * *

On the return trip north, Mary, Constance, Charlotte, and Joseph stopped for two days at the Brougham estate. Georgiana had been faithful in keeping their secret, even from her husband. They all watched to see if he perceived any hint of their deception. He did not.

When they returned to Hunsford Cottage, they were most pleased to see work progressing on a two-room extension of the parsonage. Constance enjoyed her new title of governess and would reside with the family once the extension was completed.

The parishioners immediately took to little Joseph, complimenting Charlotte on her new role as mother and expressing admiration of Mary for her doting support.

On the Sunday of Joseph's baptism, Lady Catherine de Bourgh hosted a grand dinner in celebration. She invited Fitzwilliam, Elizabeth, and Mary, Lord and Lady Brougham, the Bennets, and Charlotte's family with Governess Constance. In the late afternoon, after Mary returned from "assisting Charlotte," Lady Catherine invited Mary to sit with her.

"My, my, what a pretty child!" she said. "He will find great playmates in the Darcys' children."

"Yes, mum," Mary replied.

"He certainly favors his father," her ladyship continued. "His hair is dark and straight. One doesn't see any of Charlotte's wave or red."

Mary concentrated on Joseph, content in Elizabeth's arms across the room. "Those may come with age. Babies look like babies, each with their peculiar personalities and appearances."

Lady Catherine nodded. "Yes, true. I fancy someday, should you have children, they will have hair as dark and straight ... like yours."

"Perhaps. It depends on the father as well, of course."

"Of course." They eyed one another for some time. "Mary, you have become a much loved member of this family. Your friendship and encouragement of Lady Anne has endeared you to me more than I can tell."

"I am honored, your ladyship."

"You are wise beyond your years, dear Mary." Lady Catherine smiled. "Now, run along and dote on Charlotte and William's son.

Chapter Twenty
The Battle of Queenstown

"My word!" Governor Joseph Hooker looked up as he finished the final page of Gareth Speedwell's report.

Margaret sat in a comfortable chair before his grand desk, looking about his office, still amused by the peculiar one-eyed perspective resulting from her eye patch. She had toured the office with Justine shortly after Tarkington's death, and Margaret appreciated that a proper portrait of His Majesty replaced the huge portrait of the late governor. Gone was Tarkington's office sidebar with assorted liquors, his lurid second bedroom beside the office restored to its original function as an office. Governor Hooker kept his door open except for private meetings.

Madeline resumed her former position in the governor's outer office, keeping his schedule. She wore one of her elegant dresses from 'the old days,' and Justine provided her with finery as a way to showcase Justine's world-class fashions. Justine also devoted considerable attention to Margaret's uniform, and Margaret was the very picture of dignity. A handsome brown leather tri-corner replaced Stanford's black hat with its preposterous ostrich feather, and Margaret had learned how to sit with her sword without any awkwardness.

"Mr. Speedwell did a masterful job documenting the Battle of Queenstown." The Governor tilted his head as he watched Margaret. "For which I am particularly grateful, since I am having difficulty remembering that battle."

Margaret folded her hands. "Likely because it has not yet occurred. I fancy Mr. Speedwell wanted the story available before the battle so that those watching from shore will appreciate what is happening. All that is sound aboard *Jacqueline Fouck* is being salvaged at dockside so that we will not have to dive to recover anything of value."

Governor Hooker laughed. "We?"

"Right," she said, ignoring his bemusement. "The men who worked our docks before the late governor's time have come back to their old jobs. They are ready to service visiting ships and will be expanding their offerings. Together, *we* are developing a plan to build a shipyard here that will be the envy of the Caribbean. '*We*' will include a large portion of the town if '*we*' are successful. When I return, '*we*' will incorporate as Blackbelly Shipyards." She regarded him. "'*We*' hope to have the governor's enthusiastic support."

He demurred. "*Acting* governor. I have only taken possession of this office by virtue of the rules of protocol in the event of a governor's death or disability. I am certain the Home Office will choose a successor when word of Governor Tarkington's death reaches London."

Margaret continued, "Yes, I understand. I should tell you, though, that my colleagues have a high opinion of your administrative skills and integrity. I sense that you would do great works as our permanent governor."

"Thank you, Captain. I treasure your good opinion, and I will endeavor to do my best to earn it. There is much we could do together here."

"Excellent. I heard that Gareth Speedwell, Esquire, likewise looks quite favorably on your service to the crown and has sent letters to some acquaintances in England who have the ear of the Home Office."

He chuckled. "When am I to meet this Gareth Speedwell? I have so admired those reports, and I feel at times that I know … him."

Margaret frowned. "What a pity. He departed this very morning. I do not recall his destination — perhaps Trinidad … perhaps the States."

"That is a pity, Captain. I must have missed his ship's departure. I should like to think he would return one day."

"Mr. Speedwell is an irrepressible spirit. Feel free to give me any messages for him and I shall pass them on should an opportunity arise."

"That is most gracious. Now, is there anything I can do for you?"

Margaret nodded. "Yes, please, there are several items I would like to address. First is that Queenstown has no harbormaster. When *Lady Bridget* and *Jacqueline Fouck* entered Queenstown harbor, we were unchallenged — probably unobserved. Had our intentions been ill — and the late governor might have considered our intentions ill — we could have inflicted serious damage on the town in short order. If Queenstown is to become a thriving port hosting many ships, we will need a harbormaster to manage security and berthing. On paper, Queenstown has had a harbormaster for three years, yet the position has actually been vacant and our late governor diverted that harbormaster salary into his own accounts."

"An excellent recommendation. I shall begin a search right away."

"Governor Hooker, sir, if I may be so bold as to suggest young Michael Randolph."

"Sergeant Michael Randolph? The jailer?" Hooker raised his eyebrows.

"Former jailer, sir. Though his enlistment concluded almost a year ago, Lieutenant Jasper informed him — falsely — that he had been extended by conscription. Members of my crew and many of our re-liberated citizens have vouched for his energy and honesty. In particular, Dr. Katanga stands by his character. And Captain Johnson tells me that former sergeant former jailer Randolph was both professional and humane during the captain's brief incarceration."

Governor Hooker nodded. "High praise, indeed. I shall talk with young Michael today."

Margaret continued. "The second item concerns a large gathering three nights hence. By Gareth Speedwell's witness, there will be a great battle in our outer harbor. The townsfolk are planning to assemble on the dock to watch. There may be a reenactment of the battle, and *someone* may give a public reading of Gareth Speedwell's account of the battle."

He folded his arms. "And who might that *someone* be?"

"We were thinking that *someone* might be you, sir." She smiled.

He laughed. "I shall give it my serious consideration."

"Finally, on the morrow, there will be a wedding aboard *Jacqueline Fouck*. I shall be performing the ceremony —one of my more pleasant duties as captain. As we now know, the *Fouck* will be lost in the Battle of Queenstown, and I have chosen to no longer hold command after that, so this wedding will be my last act as captain. You are cordially invited as an honored guest to this joyous occasion."

He nodded. "Jolly good! About time we enjoyed a celebration. Would that be the wedding of Miss Moseby and Captain Johnson?"

"No, no," she said. "There is much to be done before that wedding, which will be in cold, gray England. For one thing, Captain Johnson has not proposed. Or Jane has not accepted — I am not sure which. She desires to wait until she is officially a gentleman's daughter by virtue of her adoption into our family. Tomorrow's wedding will be that of Madeline and Maurice."

Madeline peered, beaming, in to the office. "Perhaps you could give me away, Governor?"

"I would be honored," Hooker said, "Maurice? He is the one called 'Chitter'?"

"Not any more."

The Governor chuckled. "Excellent. Again, I would be honored. What else have you?"

Margaret rose from the chair, adjusted her sword and hat, and extended her gloved hand. "Those are my concerns. It has been a delight working with you, Governor. I only hope that '*we*' will continue to enjoy a long and fruitful cooperation for years to come."

They shook hands and she turned to leave the office.

"Captain Margaret," he called as she reached the doorway.

She turned back. "Yes, Governor Hooker?"

"Please pardon my overly familiar curiosity, but you intrigue me. You strike me as quite young to be responsible for so much."

"As are you, sir."

"Not to the same extent. Despite your youth, your sense of command exceeds many I have known thrice your age. You inspire a following and loyalty I have seldom encountered. I am curious about what accounts for that."

Margaret returned to the center of his office. "I have always been a problem child. Since I was a little girl, my imagination forever ran away with itself. My thoughts and dreams were always of adventure, of faraway places, of feats of daring, and dashing endeavors. Even as a small child, I made my way to danger, which is why my family found Jane. My surrogate — soon to be official — sister interposed herself between possible death and me. Yet, she did not attempt to crush my wanderlust. Rather, she channeled my impetuous longings into more productive directions, teaching me a love of literature, teaching me writing, teaching me geography, and explaining without judgment the harsh realities of a dangerous world. Beneath her calm exterior, there is a moral core of iron. I would be dead many times over but for her watchful protection.

"Still, my longing for adventure never dimmed. In my head, I fought pirates, commanded ships, and bested arrogant, thieving men. In this past year, as these imaginations have become real, I fell back on my dreams to inform me how to act. It seems my mental rehearsals proved trustworthy, though — again — without Jane beside me and behind me, I would be dead.

"Men will follow if led with integrity and vision. I have learned a 'sense of command,' as you put it, based on good commanders I have observed, in my reading, and from living under Captain Johnson. I saw that if I gave orders, they would be followed if they were clear and consequences well considered — a melding of confidence and forward-looking reasoning.

"These are choices that I make — choices most people are too timid to pursue. I seem to lack the necessary fear to restrain myself, and I suppose that penchant will fail me some day, when I will not have a Jane to save me. Still, until that day, I will be a captain, a supply agent, or a shipyard founder because I will so choose. And I shall continue to enjoy warm sun on my skin, the fragrance of spices in the air, and a bright sapphire sea in which to swim. I am living the dreams I dreamt as a girl."

Governor Hooker's chin rested on his folded hands. "Remarkable," he said after some time. "My office is at your service, Captain Margaret."

She bowed and emerged from the government offices into the hustle and bustle of Queenstown.

* * *

The day of the first wedding following Governor Tarkington's tenure broke bright and clear. Light southwesterly breezes set hundreds of flags and buntings aflutter. From the dock to the deck of *Jacqueline Fouck*, a solid, wide staircase now rose. Bright ribbons wrapped the railing and the carpenters had devoted their considerable skills to spacing the steps so that the bride could ascend with safety and grace. In elegant attire, *Fouck*'s crew manned her rails. Most former pirates owned no formal wear, but town's folk were generous in their loans for the occasion.

From her pinnacle, *Jacqueline Fouck* flew a grand British ensign. Following several days of salvage, few furnishings adorned her deck; her former cannons were positioned along shoreline fortifications with cannoneers standing at attention.

At ten in the morning, Maurice emerged from *Jacqueline Fouck*'s captain's cabin, flanked by Dr. Katanga and Captain Johnson. His wedding cloak dazzled in white with gold piping. All three faces bore radiant smiles.

As they made their way to wait near the top of the stairs, Margaret stepped down from the forecastle to the half deck in front of the captain's cabin and stood at attention. Justine had reworked Margaret's uniform, retaining its stark black image of authority, while adding dignified dark ruffles, broad lapels, and gold buttons. Margaret's black boots shone to a mirror finish, and her tattered sword belt had been replaced by one of a better grade of leather. Under Doctor Katanga's supervision, her simple leather eye patch yielded to one of better fit, edged in stamped gold filigree. Early in the day, Jane had sculpted Margaret's curls and tied them back with a broad red ribbon. Margaret's expression was serene seriousness.

Madeline walked down the dock between rows of cheering town's folk and *Lady Bridget's* crew. As she had requested, Governor Hooker escorted her, dressed in the handsome uniform of his office. Madeline's wedding gown of satin and lace floated over the boards as children ran up and down before her, scattering frangipani flowers, hibiscus, and oleander. Following behind her, Justine and Jane walked, dressed in simple white gowns.

They halted at the foot of the stairs and waited as *Fouck's* boatswain struck 12 bells and sounded "attention" on his boatswain's pipe. On Governor Hooker's arm, Madeline ascended to the deck. He embraced her, and then took her hand and joined it with Maurice's. The pair inched toward the spot before Margaret as the crowd made their way up the stairs to fill the open deck.

When everyone had come aboard, Margaret looked down, smiling at the couple, before addressing the gathering. "Crew of *Jacqueline Fouck*, crew of *Lady Bridget*, good people of Queenstown, we come together to witness the marriage of Madeline and Maurice. If any among you know cause that they should not be married, let them speak now or forever hold their peace." After a silence, she drew her sword and drove it into the deck beside her.

"Who will stand by this man that he should be married?"

"We will!" Dr. Katanga and Captain Johnson said.

"Who will stand by this woman that she should be married?"

"We will!" Governor Hooker, Justine, and Jane said together.

Margaret nodded. "Madeline, will you have Maurice to be your husband? Will you honor him, love him, and cherish him?"

"Oh, yes!" Madeline shouted.

Margaret chuckled. "And Maurice, will you have Madeline to be your wife? Will you honor her, love her, and cherish her?"

"Absolutely!" He shouted, his smile radiating across his face.

Margaret looked to the crowd. "Good people here assembled, by the law of the sea …" She looked about her ship's rigging. "… and laws of the British Empire, …" She nodded to Governor Hooker. "… I declare that Maurice and Madeline are husband and wife." She pulled her sword from the deck and raised it high. "What we here have joined together let no one put asunder!" She returned the blade to its scabbard. "May it be so!"

At this, Jacób shouted, "To Madeline and Maurice — hip, hip, hooray." Shouts rose, and the boatswain began a continuous peal of *Jacqueline Fouck*'s ship's bell. *Lady Bridget*'s boatswain answered with her bell. The two churches in Queenstown began tolling their bells. Cannoneers at the fortifications followed with a roaring salute of blanks that echoed through the town.

Everyone cheered, and the crowd dissolved into happy chaos. Margaret looked about and saw Jane gazing at her with an expression of unmistakable pride.

Several seamen brought out their musical instruments, and a banquet feast waited on the dock. From the stands, the air was laden with the fragrant smoke of roasting pork, chicken, and fish, each drenched in tangy sauces and savory herbs. Plantain leaf cups held diced fruits — mango, banana, guava, and coconut — and an unlimited variety of drinks were offered from the local rum and fruit juices. Festivities continued through the afternoon, evening, and night. Beneath a rising moon, a very tired Margaret made her way toward the inn, every item of comfort having been stripped from *Jacqueline Fouck*. On the main avenue, half way to her lodging, she spied Governor Hooker waiting for her.

He turned to walk alongside. "Well done, Captain. That service was polished and well executed. Did such a wedding feature in some of your young girl dreams?"

She laughed. "No, not really. I do remember bits of my sister Elinor's and my sister Marianne's weddings, and I have anticipated my sister Jane's wedding when that time comes. I suppose I put together what seemed right and proper."

They arrived at the inn. "Well, it was quite right … and proper … and joyous. Well done."

"Thank you, sir. Your words are most kind." She turned to enter the inn, but looked back for a moment. "Have you given thought to whether you shall give the public reading of Gareth Speedwell's account of the battle?"

"If the offer is still extended, I would be honored to do the reading."

She lingered on the steps of the inn. "May it be so. Thank you. Goodnight … Joseph."

He took her hand and kissed it. "Goodnight, Margaret." They gazed at one another a while longer before she entered the inn and he ambled toward the governor's residence.

* * *

The morning after Madeline and Maurice's wedding, Queenstown returned to a working seaport. Governor Hooker provided a carriage for the happy couple to honeymoon up in the Blue Mountains. The Governor showed up at the dock for most of the morning to observe the beehive of activity. For now, the major project afoot was the dismantling of *Jacqueline Fouck* and the reconstruction of *Lady Bridget*'s mainmast, which proceeded with great speed.

Margaret wove in and out of the activity, taking copious notes. She asked those supervising the ship work what might be provided in the future to aid the tasks once her shipyard was functional. She listened to Jacób's explanations of what cranes and derricks might be used to remove a ship's cannons rather than the awkward and dangerous efforts of twenty men. Jimmy accompanied her on rounds of the *Fouck*, pointing out why some items could be salvaged and others not. Both men appreciated her quick grasp of the challenges involved and her desire to respect their experiences and recommendations.

"I know that close collaboration between our skilled companions will be essential to the success of our enterprise," she said.

Governor Hooker conversed often with Captain Johnson and Jane, expressing his gratitude for all they had done to break the link between the old government and the pirates. Listening to the former pirates of *Jacqueline Fouck*, he discovered that their one ship had been responsible for the bulk of piracy in the area. He was particularly impressed that *Lady Bridget*'s crew managed to kill the most accomplished of the pirates during the battle when *Lady Bridget* was, for a time, captured. A British mail ship left Queenstown the following morning, carrying his report on the piracy to the Home Office, a report that would end the careers of the officers of *HMS Lancet* and its Marine detachment. The mail ship also carried Gareth Speedwell's account of The Battle of Queenstown, addressed to Joseph Weatherstone in care of Mary Bennet, along with his letter to Lord Brougham extoling the honesty and competence of Acting Governor Hooker, and Margaret's letter to her family detailing plans for Jane's induction into the family.

The governor invited Jane to a quiet luncheon at his open office, where he expressed keen interest in Margaret's family and her history. Jane was more than eager to regale him with stories of their many adventures since Margaret's childhood, including their improbable journey from Plymouth aboard *Lady Bridget*.

Jimmy and the seamen of *Lady Bridget* worked with the carpenters to remove the *Fouck*'s mainmast and install it on *Lady Bridget*. The transfer took an entire day, but installation only a few hours, followed by rigging the yardarms and sails.

Since construction moved at a fast pace, Margaret and Jane were free to negotiate provisioning of their ship for return to Plymouth. Though Margaret did not enjoy the same advantage of surprise fluency in the native language that she had enjoyed in Fort-de-France, she projected the same hard-nosed insistence on correct pricing and quality supplies. By mid-afternoon of the day of The Battle, Jimmy pronounced repairs complete and sound, and Margaret and Jane confirmed that re-supply was satisfactory. *Lady Bridget* would be ready to sail the very next day.

* * *

Once again, Queenstown's dock hosted a grand feast and celebration. Music, dancing, and eating were the order of the evening as the sun sank toward the western hills. The shell of the *Jacqueline Fouck* drifted in the outer harbor, where the harbor met the open sea.

Five seamen had used what remained of her rotten sails to get her in place and then had cut the sails down. They first twisted the sailcloth, placed the roped material around the lower deck, and then soaked it with gallons of naphtha. The farthest extent of the flammable structure ended in the middle of five barrels of black powder, a hundred pounds each, resting on the *Fouck*'s keel. The late Governor Tarkington's body lay in repose on the deck immediately above the explosives. Four of the seamen climbed into a rowboat tethered to *Jacqueline Fouck*. The fifth remained aboard with a flint and kindling, awaiting a signal.

As the disk of the sun first touched the western horizon, Governor Hooker began reciting a scripted excerpt of Gareth Speedwell's account of The Battle to the assembled town. He stood atop the stairs constructed for the wedding, handsome stairs that would be used henceforth to honor special visiting ships. To the side, a small stage had been built to support the re-enactment — terribly over-acted to everyone's delight. The most rotund of the former pirates, the cook, Eric, was chosen to play the part of Governor Tarkington.

Hooker read, "*In the past, Governor Tarkington cared little for the lives of the Queenstown workers who had been re-enslaved.*"

Eric turned up his nose and waved away half a dozen slave players. The crowd booed.

"*But, one day the governor fell gravely ill, and he was on the verge of death.*"

Eric lied flat on the platform and let out a loud, gurgling stage moan. The onlookers laughed.

"*He prayed to God that he might be spared, promising to do whatever God demanded. An angel appeared to him.*"

Jane stood above Eric in her white gown from the wedding. Some in the assembly shouted, "Let him die!" Others said, "No, wait!"

"*Governor Tarkington heard the angel say, 'you must free the slaves. You must renounce slavery and you must fight the pirates! Do these things, and you may live. Otherwise, you shall surely die!'*"

Jane raised her arms and looked heavenward. The audience shouted to Governor Tarkington, "Do it! Do it! Free them!"

"*The governor agreed, and kept his word. He rose and proclaimed freedom for all in the province, outlawing piracy and renouncing slavery forever. He was immediately cured.*"

Eric rose and made sweeping gestures while the slave players raised their hands in joy. Wild cheers erupted.

"*But the pirates' Captain Stanford would not stand for this and threatened to kill Governor Tarkington and burn Queenstown to the ground. Stanford's men seized the governor and took him aboard their ship, the Jacqueline Fouck.*"

Margaret appeared on stage, dressed in Sanford's uniform,

including his black hat with white ostrich feather, her face streaked with charcoal in a theatrically absurd imitation of Stanford's scraggly beard. She pointed to Eric and four pirate players grabbed him. The audience booed and booed. The sun had set, and the surroundings were dark save for torchlights.

"As Governor Tarkington was hauled away, he shouted to his artillerymen, 'Fire on the Fouck! Have no regard for my safety! Sink her!'"

Everyone jumped as two of the nearest cannons fired blanks. Hearing the cannons, the fifth seaman struck his flint onto the kindling and tossed the burning mass onto the end of the wick farthest from the powder kegs. He sped down the sea ladder into the boat and they rowed away from the *Fouck* with all their strength as the resulting flames became visible in the harbor. Within minutes, the entire ship was ablaze.

"The brave Governor Tarkington grabbed a sword and fought Captain Stanford, but the artillery had set fire to the pirates' ship. The brave governor fought to the end."

Margaret and Eric conducted their mock battle with wooden sticks, with the onlookers offering rousing encouragement to Eric. The five seamen were well away from the blazing *Fouck* when fire reached the black powder, the resulting blast pulverizing her keel and sending flaming debris arching hundreds of meters into the night sky. On stage, Margaret's Captain Stanford had delivered the "death thrust" to Tarkington, and all eyes turned to the harbor as the roar of the explosion rolled over the town. Wild cheers continued until the five seamen returned safely to the dock.

Throughout the performance, Margaret had glanced at Justine for her reactions. At first, Justine was not amused at the "rehabilitated" Governor Tarkington, but by the end could not stifle a laugh.

The shattered remains of *Jacqueline Fouck* would continue alight for another half hour and pieces would afterward ride currents throughout the Caribbean.

* * *

Jane sat on the edge of the stage, watching passersby. She greeted Michael Randolph, "Good evening, Harbormaster. Very effective placement of the cannons."

He laughed. "So you believe their positioning was a 'good choice'?"

She nodded. "A good choice, indeed. Thank you. Good night, sir."

He tipped his hat and was off toward town. Robert arrived and sat beside Jane.

"It is a beautiful night. Are you enjoying yourself?"

"I am." She nodded.

"Not celebrating?"

"I am doing what I like to do — watching people and listening. Look there." She nodded toward the foot of the dock, where a couple engaged in close conversation. Jane and Robert, cloaked in darkness, could not be seen by Governor Hooker as he spoke with Margaret.

"Thank you for your spirited reading, sir," she said.

"And thank you for establishing a tradition that will live on every year in Queenstown. I had but a small happy part — yours was the inspiration for the production. I hope that you will be back a year hence for our reprise, perhaps even one with practice."

She laughed. "That is my plan, though practice might spoil the fun."

"Will you truly be departing on the morrow?"

"Yes, but for fine reasons. When I return, 'twill be to stay." She gazed at him with a sweet smile.

He returned her smile and offered his arm for a stroll. "It gives me great joy to hear that. I know that you must be quite tired. May I accompany you to your lodging?"

Margaret nodded. "You are most kind, and I welcome your company. I do want to rest before tomorrow's tasks, though I am told I need a shave." She turned her head back and forth to show her charcoal "beard."

He laughed as they turned toward the main avenue and she took his arm. "Thank you, Joseph."

Jane smiled, serene, and turned back to Robert.

* * *

The next morning, the day of departure, Jane emerged on deck for a break after an hour of securing casks of spices in the hold. She encountered Robert as he continued his tour of the deck checking on *Lady Bridget's* sea readiness.

"Good morning, Jane. Are you excited to be heading home?"

She returned his greeting. "Good morning to you, Robert. I am excited to begin this leg of our journey, though I come more and more to regard *Lady Bridget* as my home."

"I understand. I truly do. Is Captain Margaret anticipating or dreading her voyage back to cold, gray England?"

"She is of mixed minds. She arose very early, finished her tasks here — and some of mine as well — before leaving the ship a few hours ago."

He frowned. "I hope she has not ventured too far. The weather is perfect and the tides will be right in the late afternoon. We would not leave her, of course, but it would delay us a day if she were not aboard."

Jane shook her head. "I am quite certain that I know where she went — not far. She is ready, her spaces and her bunk secured for sea. I have a few minutes more working down below and I will go to pay her a visit."

"I am still amazed at the understanding the two of you have, one for the other. I am chagrined by the memory of my doubts early in the voyage." He chuckled. "I think now I should fear more her taking over our ship — though she would likely perform admirably."

Jane laughed. "Margaret is most content to resume her role as diligent crewmember. She and I will return in good time for cast off."

* * *

Finished with her tasks, Jane walked in silence the length of the long fishing pier. She stopped before the end and gazed out on the great expanse of open ocean — calm, waves barely a ripple, with a slight, agreeable breeze. Brilliant cotton boll clouds decorated the sky all the way to the horizon.

"Good morning, Jane," Margaret said, though she could not have seen Jane, and continued to stare out on the water. She sat on the pier's edge, her shoes resting neatly by her side as she swung her bare feet on the water, propagating little circles.

"Good morning, Margaret. You have been quite industrious today. Thank you for securing the cinnamon and ginger boxes."

They watched in silence a flight of pelicans traversing the bay.

"That way is England," Margaret said, pointing to her left. "Four and a half thousand miles." She pointed to her right. "That way is Martinique, a thousand miles." She lowered her hand and held the edge of the pier in silence.

"Are you regretting leaving Queenstown?"

Margaret finally looked up. "No, not at all. I know that I will be back as soon as the winds and tides permit. But, I have many happy tasks to fulfill in the months ahead. I will return soon enough to the sun, the spices, and the colors."

"And Joseph Hooker?" Jane asked.

Margaret scowled. "The Governor and I have a strictly professional relationship."

"Of course. Is that why he stopped by *Lady Bridget* a while ago to inquire after you?"

"Strictly professional."

"Of course, Miss Dashwood."

"Now do not go causing mischief."

Jane clutched her chest, feigning disappointment. "But I thought that was one of the privileges of being a sister!"

Margaret shook her head, but smiled as she returned her attention to the sea. "Then again, Joseph is a man of integrity and great kindness, is he not?"

Serenity replaced Jane's laughter. "Yes, and rather handsome as well. I do think he is smitten with you."

"Maybe."

"And you with him?" Jane asked.

Margaret was silent, though Jane saw the slight nod.

They regarded the cerulean sea for a few minutes more.

"I wanted to have a sharp image of this place in my mind to carry me through to my return," Margaret said at last.

"Is this everything that you dreamed of?"

Margaret stood up, pondering, and slipped into her shoes. "I had not thought about it, but now that you ask, yes. Yes, it is. My wanderlust has found its destination."

They strolled back in silence to *Lady Bridget*. Both kept busy until time to cast off and then took their places on deck as line handlers with a good view of the dock. Along with Dr. Katanga, Justine and Jacób, and Harbormaster Randolph, they saw Joseph Hooker standing on the dock to see them off. He looked up to Margaret and saluted.

She returned his salute. "Do … not … say … a … word, Jane," she muttered while continuing to smile.

"Not a word, Margaret, my sister."

* * *

A world comprised only of blues and whites enveloped *Lady*

Bridget by the time Captain Johnson called out, "Let fall the mainsail! Set sail!"

Though Harriet assured Margaret that she would likely not experience seasickness again, she kept her pouch of hardtack filled as she and Jane resumed rounds of sounding and security, cooking, and mending the sailcloth.

On her second watch, Margaret approached the helm. "Timothy!" she cried. "Whatever are you doing here?"

"Heading home, Captain Margaret. Robert was happy to have another helmsman for this voyage, and so I shall be with my family again in short order."

"I am not a captain now, Timothy."

He laughed. "Perhaps not. Though you once nearly killed me I remember that you then helped me through … perhaps saved me … and I remember looking on your face as you squeezed my hand while the good doctor removed your round. Since the moment you dispatched Captain Stanford, you have always been 'Captain Margaret' to me."

"Well, then I am honored, Timothy. When we return to England, will you remain a sailor?"

"Mercy, no! I will go back to my family in Cornwall, where we farm barley and flax, and only glimpse the sea from a distance. If — God willing — my love, Jenny, has not found another, I will court her, and I will marry her. Does that sound like a good plan?"

She saluted. "That is a *splendid* plan, Timothy! May it be so."

He checked his heading and added a bit of right rudder. "You like that phrase."

"I do. It puts my mind in the future, not the past."

* * *

In contrast to their voyage from Plymouth to the Caribbean, their return leg was routine. With steady fair winds and no storms, *Lady Bridget* rode the Gulf Stream most of the journey, arriving in Plymouth mid-day in warm, bright late summer.

Jane chuckled. "Well, well, Margaret. So much for cold, gray England. Might you have a change of heart?"

"No," was the quick, firm reply.

At Robert's urging, Margaret and Jane prepared to head for Devon right away. "There are no particular tasks for you here," he said, "The port will handle our ship's needs. Despite our calamities —

I still marvel that we survived — we have returned with a full cargo, purchased well below prices of our prior journeys thanks to your brilliant negotiations. And our repairs, though major, cost us nothing, thanks to family in Fort-de-France and gratitude in Queenstown. You have many joyful endeavors at home, and I shall follow six days hence."

They hired two boys to cart their trunks to Plymouth station. One had served them at departure and he still remembered his encounter of many months past. Jane regaled the boys with tales of their adventures as they hauled the trunks. As on the day of departure, sailors along the wharfs accosted them with catcalls.

Jane shook her head. "If only they knew what peril they risk … if only they knew."

Their coach arrived in Crawley at nightfall and they stayed the night at an inn, rising early the next morning.

"You will be wearing that to greet your sister Elinor?" Jane folded her arms, watching as Margaret dressed.

"Yes."

"And need I remind you that Dr. Katanga said you no longer need the patch."

"I know."

After a good breakfast they returned to Crawley station.

"Hmm. This place looks familiar. If you need to purchase anything, we will go together, I fancy."

"You will not allow me to forget my treachery. You are making mischief, Jane."

"And enjoying it so," Jane replied.

A note at the station from Elinor and Edward informed them that the family would be waiting at Delaford for their return.

On arrival at Delaford, Colonel and Marianne Brandon's estate, the coach's clatter brought the entire family out. The horses stopped short of the entrance.

"Is it still our plan that I should alight first and alone?" Jane asked.

"Please, yes."

Jane opened the coach door and stepped out to greet Elinor. She curtsied. "Mrs. Ferrars."

Elinor shook her head and wagged her finger. "There will be none of that, Jane, our sister. We have already acted with joy on the entreaties in Margaret's last letter, and our solicitor has drawn up the necessary papers for you … when you are ready. We have plans for a wonderful adoption service and ceremony if that still is your desire." This she said while peering around Jane. "And where, pray tell, is my other sister?"

The coach door opened again. First, a polished black boot appeared, and then another. Margaret stepped down, stood tall, straightened her clothing, and strode toward the family.

Elinor clasped her hands to her mouth, her eyes wide.

Margaret's skin still retained a good bit of tropical bronze. Her black uniform, with Justine's ruffles, lapels, and buttons, was as grand as on Madeline and Maurice's wedding day. Her gloved hand gripped the hilt of her sword, and beneath a handsome tri-corner, the formal patch covered her left eye.

Margaret bowed. "Good morning, Elinor. I am so happy to see you again."

Chapter Twenty-one
Reunions

In the evening following Margaret and Jane's return, Colonel Brandon and Marianne hosted a family celebration dinner. Margaret promised a full recounting of their adventures in return for a restful afternoon.

After their rest, Margaret and Jane pondered whether or not Margaret should continue to wear her eye patch. Her brow and cheek had healed well, but the long, dark scar across her eyelid still invited a discomfort that Margaret did not desire. Jane, though, suggested her formal patch with its gold ornamentation bordered on pretention. By late afternoon, the two settled on the simple black patch that Dr. Katanga had provided from his medical bag when she first received her injury. Margaret and Jane dressed for dinner, smiling while watching themselves in the mirror wearing the flowing white dresses Geneviève had given them for their grand island welcome feast in Fort-de-France.

"We appear as foreigners in this finery," Margaret said. "It exudes tropical radiance."

Jane beamed as she adjusted her broad brimmed white hat. "We are most fortunate to have returned on such a warm and bright day. A month or so hence and we would be chilled to the bone."

All attention turned to Margaret and Jane as they arrived for dinner.

"You look dazzling," Marianne observed.

Margaret sat between Colonel Brandon and Marianne, Jane between Marianne and Elinor, and Mrs. Dashwood between Elinor and Edward. Once the first course was served, Colonel Brandon asked, "We have so many questions, but I dare say I am most curious about your injury. How did it occur?"

"The pirate captain Stanford attacked me aboard —" Margaret began, but Jane cut short the answer by clearing her throat, and everyone turned to Jane.

"You must provide our hosts with a much more detailed account of our adventures. It is, after all, not customary for a young lady to find herself captive aboard a pirate ship. You should start at the very beginning. We promised a full recounting, did we not?"

Margaret scowled. "I believe I am the one telling our story, my sister."

Jane shook her head. "And you must recall that I promised I would be reminding you, and often, of those perils we faced together. I dare say this is one of those times for me to remind you."

Elinor and Marianne chuckled.

Still scowling, Margaret continued, "In March of last year, I set out for Plymouth …"

Jane added, "… from Crawley Station, heading south, though our destination was meant to be Pemberley — which is, of course, in Derbyshire, to north."

Margaret sighed. "True. It shames me to admit that I abandoned Jane there, with little more than a note and return ticket to Barton Cottage." Jane nodded to Margaret.

"I searched Plymouth's docks for Captain Johnson's ship, *Lady Bridget*."

Colonel Brandon raised his eyebrows. "Alone? You were alone among Plymouth's docks? I have been there, and Plymouth's docks are hardly a safe place for a young woman!"

"You are correct, Colonel. Sailors there were most crude and unhelpful. But I found my way to *Lady Bridget* and presented myself for service aboard her to Captain Johnson and Harriet Dunsford."

Jane watched Elinor's face cloud. "It was most kind of you, Elinor, to prepare that letter for Captain Johnson giving permission for your sister Margaret to travel."

"Must have slipped my mind," Elinor said as she glowered at Margaret, who bowed her head.

Jane continued, "I fancy Robert will be bringing that note with him to thank you when he visits next week."

Margaret resumed. "Jane joined me that afternoon and we boarded *Lady Bridget*. I understand that she sent you a letter detailing my treachery and her promise of loving watchfulness. We departed Plymouth the following morning, and at once I fell victim to the dreaded seasickness. Jane did not, which was most fortunate, since she enjoyed much kind attention from Captain Johnson. Harriet helped me adjust to our rolling home and plied me with biscuits to keep my stomach occupied. Jane and I worked together throughout our ship, and I have to say that I grew to love *Lady Bridget* as home, grew to love the vast sea that surrounded us, and grew to love its ever-changing moods. We labored hard, day and night, which is how

I came to my current strength and bronzed skin.

"A couple of weeks out, we encountered a fierce storm that damaged our mast and sent us far off course. I suppose I would have been terrified but for Jane's calm and determination and for commonsense and experience of our shipmates. We did our part for our ship's welfare— I am most proud of that. As a result of damage and dislocation, Captain Johnson and our quartermaster altered course to Fort-de-France, on Martinique. There we met Geneviève, surely one of the most beautiful and generous woman I have ever been privileged to meet. Perhaps you know her, Colonel, as wife of senior Captain Johnson."

"I do, though only indirectly, by high praise from Robert Johnson, Senior. I understand her to be a powerful force on that island."

Jane nodded. "And, a clever mischief maker. It is no wonder that she and Margaret formed such a close bond. I am still amused that she hid her excellent English and that she coached Margaret to conceal her knowledge of French. Those skills proved quite useful, even life-saving."

"She did not hide her affection for Jane," Margaret said. "By that time in our journey, it was clear that Jane and Robert were meant for one another. Geneviève's adorable children, Jacques and Marie, have embraced Jane as one of their own. Our stay with her family was idyllic, our feasts legendary."

Marianne spoke up. "It seems as though their attachment is well along. Are we to gain a sister only to have her promptly taken from us?"

Margaret laughed. "No, I think not, no more than we have lost you or Elinor. Rather we have gained the Colonel and Edward as brothers and will welcome Robert as well. It seems our family is expanding over thousands of miles, our own empire within the Empire."

"The scar?" Marianne reminded.

"Yes, my scar. We set sail for Jamaica, stopping only for a bit of commerce in Puerto Rico. When we were less than a day out of Queenstown, we spied a pirate ship approaching."

Colonel Brandon sat back in his chair. "One reason father and son were here visiting — to plead for more protection."

Margaret nodded. "Precisely. We set a full speed course for

Queenstown, and likely could have outrun those pirates. We spotted a British man-of-war ahead of us."

He nodded. "A picket ship protecting Queenstown harbor. How fortunate."

"Alas, no," Jane said. "*HMS Lancet's* crew was in league with those pirates. The British ship fired on us and split our mainmast. Pirates from *Jacqueline Fouck* swarmed aboard to starboard and marines of *Lancet* to port."

"Treason!" Colonel Brandon exclaimed as his eyes widened.

"And so much worse," Jane continued. "Once our attackers had subdued us, Governor Tarkington emerged from *Fouck's* captain's cabin along with pirate Captain Stanford."

Brandon frowned. "I met Tarkington some years ago. He impressed me as a vile and unprincipled man."

"Your past impressions match ours," Margaret said. "I doubt he had authority to do so, but he turned our ship over to the pirates. *Jacqueline Fouck* had a large contingent of re-enslaved men and women from Queenstown, but we had severely reduced Captain Stanford's crew trying to prevent them from taking *Lady Isabel* — thank you for teaching me to shoot and Jane to reload, Colonel. I managed to kill five of their crew myself, and wounded one."

"You killed seven, Margaret. Remember two up front with the flaming pitch."

Margaret thought a moment in the dining room's stunned silence. "You are, of course, correct, Jane. I killed seven pirates and wounded one. By good fortune, the wounded one — Timothy — would recover, becoming a good ally and friend.

"Still, men of the two ships managed to overpower us. On Governor Tarkington's orders, Marines seized Robert and took him away to Queenstown, leaving a particularly cruel enforcer behind — Lieutenant Jasper. On his orders, women were separated to the *Fouck* and men to *Lady Bridget*, and set us to work clearing bodies and blood from *Jacqueline Fouck*. Mercifully, our crew family sustained no deaths."

The family followed their pattern of turning to Jane for more explanations.

"Margaret used her exquisite French and remarkable flights of fancy to form a bridge to *Jacqueline Fouck's* slaves. In particular, we came to admire the integrity and stubborn perseverance of Madame

Justine and Doctor Katanga. We were still under ostensible control of pirates and Lieutenant Jasper, though. When Captain Stanford desired to have his way with Margaret, she struggled mightily, and her struggle cost one of her captors an eye. Once in the captain's cabin, she used skills she had honed with John Chamberlain to fend him off."

Margaret took her turn. "He tired of my resistance and slashed at me with his dagger. That is how I earned my scar. I struck back with his rum bottle, which shattered, and I slit his throat. He died writhing in a pool of blood on his cabin floor."

Margaret paused to enjoy some of the elegant dessert, a light cake with delicate icing and fresh berries. The rest of her family, save Jane, stared, appetite at bay.

"I guided Margaret out of the captain's cabin to fetch Doctor Katanga — *médecin* I recall it is in French— and pocketed some of Captain Stanford's pistols as we left his cabin. When Lieutenant Jasper saw Margaret dripping blood, he knew what had happened and rushed to kill her with his bare hands. He did not notice me — or Captain Stanford's pistol — and I fired from a few inches away. He likewise lay in a pool of blood, though I fancy he was dead before he reached deck."

As servants had brought each serving to the table, they overheard the story and remained in place. At this point, most staff had gathered about the dining room's periphery while family looked to one another, except for Jane and Margaret who were savoring their desserts.

Margaret looked up. "Doctor Katanga treated my cut with exquisite skill and explained that, by the law of the sea, I had become captain of *Jacqueline Fouck*. My crew was at first skeptical, but we found that we worked well together. I restored freedom to those who had been re-enslaved — that was but one privilege of being captain. Before dawn, we brought both ships to berth in Queenstown Harbor. Jane obtained Robert's freedom from the jail there, and Governor Tarkington is said to have died in a spectacular battle after he had a change of heart.

"We then proceeded to make repairs to *Lady Bridget*, completed our commerce, and returned to this fair island. I may have omitted some details." She turned to see Jane laughing. "I am here only long enough to conclude some important tasks. Then, I shall return to live in Queenstown, where I have many big plans. I will be part of a remarkable society there, and I will enjoy for the rest of my life warm sun on my skin, bright sapphire seas in which to swim, and spice-scented air."

Margaret spied Colonel Brandon's knowing smile and appreciated Jane's silence.

* * *

The remaining time around their table was consumed with questions from their bewildered family. Jane recognized a look of unmistakable pride on Colonel Brandon's face.

After over an hour of conversation, most of the family drifted off to other parts of the house, leaving Margaret alone with her mother.

"Margaret, my dear youngest daughter, you left here as an impetuous girl. You return as a most fierce and imposing lady. You must know what deep pride fills my heart, both for you and for our newest daughter, Jane. I scarce can take in what you and Jane have been through and how you two have prevailed with such courage and dignity."

Margaret colored. "I am happy that you feel so, Mamá. Be assured, I owe my life many times over to Jane. Had she not elected — against all logic — to accompany me, I would not be here, alive, to converse with you."

Mrs. Dashwood looked about to confirm that she and her daughter were alone. "There is one matter of some curiosity. Are you familiar with a Mr. Joseph Hooker?"

Margaret started and sat up straight. "I do know of him. Has Jane been telling you something?"

"No, no. Your sister has been most discreet. No, I received a very well-written note from Mr. Hooker a few days ago and thought that I should enquire about him."

"What does he say?"

"Margaret, my dearest, he wrote that note to me, so I shan't divulge its contents. Is he a gentleman ... or a scoundrel?" her mother asked.

Margaret narrowed her eyes, but elected to confide in her mother. "We observed that he is a gentleman of the highest order, kind and possessed of great integrity. At significant risk to himself, he protected many citizens of Queenstown during Tarkington's tenure. He has kept in confidence some of the more ... complicated ... aspects of our defeat of pirates and Governor Tarkington." She bowed her head. "Yes, I can say that he is a gentleman of the highest order."

"Good," Mrs. Dashwood said as she rose from her chair. "That is comforting to know. I must go now and see what others are about." She walked toward the doorway, but paused to turn back for a moment. "But, my dear, you neglected to mention that he is governor of Queenstown province."

* * *

Two days prior to Jane and Margaret's return, an invitation arrived at Barton Cottage from Mary Bennet of Derbyshire. She, Charlotte and William Collins, and young Joseph Collins would be visiting Mary's sister-in-law in Reading, less than a day's journey from Barton Cottage. Mary longed for a reunion with Margaret, as well as a chance to meet her new sister. Mary and Margaret would be able to spend a day or so catching up with one another on profound changes wrought in less than two years since their companionship at Oxford's abolition meeting.

Margaret and Jane departed for Reading, promising to return with ample time to prepare for Jane's adoption and Robert Johnson's arrival. Departing in early morning, Margaret felt a serenity that she had not enjoyed in her previous journeys.

"I promise I have no hidden mission, no dark secrets this time. Our visit is one of joy, pure and simple," Margaret offered.

"My, my, that is a new and refreshing experience for you."

Margaret shook her head.

Upon their mid-afternoon arrival at the Brougham estate, Margaret and Jane were welcomed by Georgiana, Mary, William, and Charlotte. Charlotte introduced Joseph, who took an immediate shine to Jane. After settling into their room, the guests enjoyed tea and accompanied Georgiana to her stables to meet Boadicea. Jane took a turn riding, her first time on horse in many years. Afterward, all six sat, talking, on a low stone wall bordering the estate's large meadow while Joseph and Fitzwilliam played in the grass.

"I am in awe reading what all of you have done." Georgiana said, "Mary, my sister, you, with William, have constructed a phantom in Joseph Weatherstone who has helped change our world for better in a few short years. You have brought dreams of freedom to millions of people around our world. My husband shared that with me, though he has not met William.

"Now, Margaret, from what I understand from the writings of Gareth Speedwell, you have brought actual freedom to some of our fellow men and women in the Caribbean."

Jane chuckled at Margaret's pensive look.

Georgiana tilted her head, puzzled. "Am I missing something?"

Jane looked to Margaret. "You must tell her. We are bound to confidence by our sisterhood."

"I *am* Gareth Speedwell, Esquire," Margaret said, nodding to Jane. "We judged 'Esquire' essential. All that 'he' wrote regarding plantations of Martinique and Jamaica is accurate. All of the transition to commerce among freed peoples is true."

Georgiana folded her arms. "Remarkable. But, it makes sense. And his account of the Battle of Queenstown?"

Margaret shrugged. "He observed much of the battle from a distance. Some details may have been reasonable speculation, but accurate in spirit."

Georgiana turned to Jane. "And you?"

"I am Margaret's — and thus 'Gareth's' — sister. Nothing more."

"The sister who saved Gareth and me, so that we could let the world know these things," Margaret corrected.

Finally, Georgiana turned to Charlotte. "And you?"

"I cannot confess to any lofty accomplishments," Charlotte demurred, "I am known as Charles LaCologne. I write adventures, none anchored in reality."

Georgiana clasped her hands to her mouth for a time, and then began laughing. "Do not undervalue your contributions, Charles. When Dy returns from London, morose from insanities with which he must deal on a daily basis, he often finds escape in your delightful prose. Without your clever plots, he would go mad some days."

Georgiana arose and faced the others. "So, here on my own stone wall I have 'three' of the finest 'men' writers in our kingdom, along with their protector ... and they are all women but one. How remarkable, how very remarkable." She bit her lip as she watched them, and then looked to the sky to judge time. "This sets me to thinking. Dy should be back from Home Office in an hour or so. I think it wise that he share our confidences as well. I have an idea."

* * *

Lord Dy Brougham sat at his desk in his study. He examined papers he had drawn from his satchel, signing some, while setting others aside. A gentle knock on the study door interrupted his flow. "Enter."

Seeing Georgiana, a bright smile flooded his face.

"Your lordship," she said.

His smile faded. "Whenever you start that way, I know that chaos will ensue. Yes, your ladyship?"

"Your lordship, there are three gentlemen here to see you."

He folded his arms. "Well, do not keep them waiting."

She opened his door wide to allow Margaret, Jane, Mary, William, and Charlotte to enter and stand before his desk.

He looked them over. "It appears that with age, my eyesight and arithmetic are failing me." He rose from his chair, approached the five, and turned to Georgiana.

"This gentleman," she said, gesturing to both Mary and William, "is Joseph Weatherstone, complete."

"Ah!" He held out his hand to greet them. "I met half of you some time ago. It is a fine thing to meet the one who has caused me endless work. I hope that you will be around for a little while so that I may ask you a few questions. Well done, … Joseph."

Mary and William bowed and stepped back.

Georgiana next offered her hand to Margaret. "And this gentleman is your favorite reporter from the Caribbean. Your lordship, may I present Mr. Gareth Speedwell, Esquire?"

He laughed a hearty laugh. "Incredible! I hope you do not mind, but for every question I have for Mr. Weatherstone, I likely have ten for you."

"I am at your service, your lordship," Margaret said, and then stepped back.

Georgiana paused, looking coy.

"I tremble to guess who this may be," he said as he watched Charlotte.

Charlotte held out her hand. "Neither problem nor threat, your lordship. You know me as Charles LaCologne."

"Delightful!" he said. "No doubt Lady Brougham has informed you of your ability to calm my soul. I treasure my time lost in your creative fancy."

Charlotte stepped back, and he turned his attention to Jane. "And, you?"

"Oh, I am her … his … sister," she said, pointing to Margaret.

He laughed, "I am much relieved to meet at least one real person. For a moment, I expected you would reveal that you were Moses or Jeremiah."

"No, your lordship. Simply Jane."

Lord Brougham shook his head. "Given your association with these others, I doubt anything is simple in your life. Come to think of it, I have often wondered if some patriarch writers might not have been, in fact, matriarchs."

"We may never know, sir," Jane said.

He turned to his wife. "I presume, dearest, that this revelation stays within these walls."

"I fancy that would be best, and most useful for everyone."

He nodded. "You are as wise as you are beautiful, my love."

* * *

After dinner, Lord Brougham invited Margaret and Jane to his study to solicit their understanding of the situation in Queenstown.

"Did you have opportunities to observe the current government's workings?"

Jane and Margaret looked to one another, and then Jane addressed him. "Yes, sir. Given the rather open condition of Queenstown during our visit, I'd say we had considerable access. I myself have come to know all of the governor's office staff. We assisted in curating and preserving records and fixtures of the late governor, and it was a pleasure to work with — I recall it is 'Acting' — Governor Hooker. He was most efficient in providing contacts to facilitate our repairs and re-provisioning."

Brougham turned to Margaret. "While the Home Office has enjoyed Mr. Speedwell's reports from the scene, I must be honest that we received those narratives with considerable skepticism at first."

Margaret nodded. "Given the trials that Jane and I have been through in the last year, I can imagine that those narratives sounded like a fabrication. But we have provided records and artifacts to verify those tumultuous days."

"Yes, and those have been most valuable in our investigations. For my own part, I found it most difficult to believe that Tarkington would change his ways. We had sent undercover agents to assess his performance, and were preparing to send a force to remove and replace him. Do you still believe that he changed his character so dramatically?"

Margaret shrugged. "Such information was secondhand, I admit, but a powerful tropical fever followed by a miraculous recovery can certainly alter one's outlook."

He folded his arms and stared at Margaret for some time. Finally, he continued, "My apologies, Margaret. I was probing for inconsistencies — habit of my office. Our agent has already confirmed the essence of Gareth's report. Madeline, an assistant in the governor's office, documented the recent events and shared them with us. While she was treated badly by Tarkington, she seems to be competent and, by good fortune, quite resilient.

"She is an ardent supporter of Acting Governor Hooker, reporting that he is a man of integrity, hoping to develop the province to the benefit both of the crown and the local populace. Does that ring true?"

"Yes, sir," Jane and Margaret answered as one.

He laughed. "There were others who have reported the same. I will be sending him notice that he can dispense with the 'Acting' in his title. I understand you will be returning to Queenstown soon, Margaret. May I prevail upon you to pass on my congratulations and best wishes when next you see him?"

Margaret nodded. "I would be honored, sir." She glanced to the side to see Jane struggling to suppress a smile.

The rest of their time in his study was devoted to discussions of Margaret's plans for Black Belly Shipyards and for promotion of the Queenstown spices and fashions. Lord Brougham was keen to connect her with colleagues in the Home Office who could facilitate these ventures. She told him of her idea of a medical college in Queenstown. His initial skepticism softened a bit as she detailed Dr. Katanga's service aboard *Jacqueline Fouck* and his lucid explanations of his medical inventions.

Lord Brougham considered her proposal. "Hmm. I could imagine it appealing to a young medical apprentice to spend his time of education in a tropical paradise, as your sister describes it."

* * *

After bidding good night to Lord Brougham, Jane and Margaret departed — Jane to their room to get ready for bed, and Margaret to stroll the house and its interesting rooms.

After twenty minutes or so, she entered the library to find Mary seated, little Joseph nursing at her breast. "My apologies. I did not mean to intrude."

Mary saw Margaret's eyes fixed on Joseph and looked to the doorway. "Are you alone?"

"Yes. Most have retired for the night."

"Please, have a seat," Mary offered.

Margaret sat and put her hand to her chin. "I had observed how you are a good and doting friend to Charlotte, but I find this level of friendship quite extraordinary."

Mary chuckled softly so as not to startle Joseph. "You recall during our many discussions at the abolition meeting how you wished me great good fortune with my mysterious involvement, how I told you my personal aspirations were complicated."

Margaret nodded, remembering.

"Well, here we have the great good fortune. With William, Joseph Weatherstone is the union of our minds, but Joseph Collins is the union of our bodies."

"My mind should be awhirl in surprise, Mary, but you seem to have managed this 'complication' with the same deftness as with Joseph Weatherstone. Do I sense that Charlotte is accepting — or more — of this arrangement?"

"Quite. We will reveal the truth to Joseph when he is of age, but until then, Charlotte will be his mother to society and I her dearest, closest friend."

"Do you feel no sadness that you cannot proclaim him your son?"

"You are wise to ask, Margaret. From early on, I have examined my deepest feelings, and can say with all honesty that I harbor no meaningful regrets. One cannot go back in time and change the course of events. I cannot go back and marry William. My respect for Charlotte and William, and our close — if unconventional — relations steel my resolve to respect their marriage ... within our peculiar context. I love Joseph, but he is their child. I accept that."

Margaret rose and examined the shelves of books before turning back to Mary. "How very odd life can be," she mused. "What secrets lie beneath even the most mundane appearances? What strengths and courage course through our supposed weak bodies? I turn and look back three years or so at myself and I wonder, 'who was that girl?' I can see that you must share that wonder as well. We have emerged as very different people, people who can and have changed the worlds around us. We have gained a measure of freedom from the strictures of a society that expects our submission and meekness. Where does that fire come from? Whence comes freedom?"

Chapter Twenty-two
Ten Years On, Cold and Gray

"Then you must go to Brighton, my love." Darcy grew weary of Elizabeth's fretting over Mary and Charlotte. "Though I believe your suspicions are a result of an overworked fancy."

"So, you really think I should not go?"

"I just said that you should go. Your explanation of sisterly affection should be convincing when your concerns are allayed. And I am certain that Charlotte will enjoy your companionship as her time approaches."

Elizabeth smiled. "My, my. You have come a long way from that skeptical and cynical man I first fell in love with. I must say it suits you."

* * *

Elizabeth and her maid, Jenny, took their family coach for the three-day journey to Brighton.

"Where shall we stay, Miss Elizabeth? By their writing, that cottage scarcely has room for the three of them. And we have made no preparation for lodging in Brighton."

"Brighton hosts a large population of summer visitors, with a number of fine inns and guest houses. I am quite sure we shall find adequate accommodations in this dreary month of March."

"Do you know your way about Brighton? Have you been there before?"

"No, Jenny, but we shall make inquiry in the market. I'm certain the merchants there can direct us to their cottage."

"I could not help but overhear your conversations regarding Mary. Do you sincerely believe she is up to concealment, on the order of a secret child?"

"I do not know. I really do not. Mary was such a reserved child growing up …"

"Except for issues of justice," Jenny interrupted.

Elizabeth laughed. "True, except for issues of justice. Yet, when she was nineteen, she formed a peculiar attachment to Charlotte while supporting Charlotte's projects. And her work with Mr. Collins is legendary. Further, young Joseph seems as loving to Mary as he is to Charlotte. Then there is the matter of their seven months' seclusion in Brighton, when Joseph was born, and that he favors Mary far more than Charlotte."

"Those are interesting observations, m'lady, but the one he truly favors is William. I do not see that great a disparity."

"I am sure you are right. I hope that you are right. Nevertheless, we shall know in a few short hours. These conversation are in strictest confidence between us."

"Of course. And, …" Jenny tilted her head. "… should your suspicions prove correct, what then?"

"I do not know. I shall remain a loving sister, I suppose. Only wiser, whatever we find."

Their coach arrived in Brighton in mid-morning and drove to the marketplace edge near the seafront. Their coachman waited while Elizabeth and Jenny alighted and began walking toward a vegetable seller's stall.

"Miss Elizabeth!"

They turned to see Constance approaching, market basket in hand.

"Whatever are you doing here? We received no letter announcing your coming. We would have made preparations had we known."

"I wanted it to be a surprise. I have so missed the company of you three. I did not wish to cause a fuss." Elizabeth assured.

"Well, I was just coming to market to gather items for our noon meal. If you please, I will guide your coach to our cottage. Your arrivals will be a surprise indeed!"

Constance gave directions to the coachman and they boarded for a short trip a few streets from the seafront. They passed along the way myriad snug cottages, each with a fenced-in yard containing evergreens and the remains of last summer's gardens. While the homes were painted white, each cottage sported trim painted in vibrant colors, giving each a festive air. The streets themselves were well-travel cobblestone with sand between the stones, drifted in from the beaches. One could imagine throngs of vacationers in the summertime, but these winter streets were deserted.

Constance opened the cottage door. "Miss Mary, we have visitors."

Mary sat at table, pen in hand, working on a manuscript. As her sister and Jenny entered, her face registered shock. "Elizabeth! We were not expecting you!" She rose from her seat and hurried forward, arms outstretched.

Elizabeth looked Mary up and down, and then locked her in a tight embrace. "For these many months, I have longed for your companionship, longed to converse with you. Jenny and I have brought treats to delight your appetites and some little bits of finery to show off in this fair town. The salt air must suit you as you are looking wondrously trim. I'm sure the treats will be welcome. I even included your favorite chocolates."

Mary turned and called into the other room. "Charlotte, you will never guess who has come calling!"

Charlotte appeared in the doorway and entered slowly, hands cradling her belly. "Elizabeth! Upon my word, I could not have expected you. What is it occasions your visit?"

"Merely a desire to be with my sister, my best friend, and their superb governess. I brought some comforts to delight in your last month. We can leave behind the small trunk."

"How lovely," Constance said. "By your leave, I need to return to market to acquire our noon meal. You two will be quite impressed by such a variety of fresh foods that bless this town."

"Splendid," Elizabeth replied. "I hope to join you at market in the days ahead. If it is not an imposition, I would treasure perhaps five days here before returning north. Our journey was tiring. We should like to avail ourselves of some local accommodations, settle in, and return in time for the meal. Can you recommend a place to stay?"

Mary spoke. "Indeed, Ocean View Inn on the rise two streets north of here has a reputation as a comfortable and well-run establishment. It is owned by one of my abolition movement friends. Let them know that you are visiting us and they will give you excellent treatment and a good rate for you and the coachman. Constance, would you please give their driver directions?"

Constance returned presently, and she and Mary escorted Elizabeth and Jenny to the coach. They waved goodbye and returned inside. Once the door was closed, they began laughing.

Mary wiped a tear from her eye. "I dare say that Elizabeth was not expecting what she found. I recall her many queries in the month prior to our journey here. I know she suspects the truth about Joseph, but has been reluctant to confront me directly. Perhaps her stay here will bring her some peace of mind."

"With her stay in mind, I must away to market or we shall have a very late meal. I was going to look for some cod or sole, but perhaps we should elevate our meal to lobster in celebration of Elizabeth and Jenny's visit."

"A capital idea, Constance. Do you have enough for the grander meal?" Charlotte asked.

"I do." She picked up her basket and headed out the door.

In the stillness of the cottage, Mary looked to Charlotte. "Though we may suspect some of Elizabeth's motives for her visit, it is good to see her again."

Charlotte agreed. "Indeed it is. I am just realizing how much I have missed our regular visits."

The five women established a pleasant daily routine. Elizabeth and Jenny took their morning meal at Ocean View and met at the cottage in mid-morning to begin a stroll about the seafront. Mary and Constance joined them each day, and Charlotte as well when she was feeling up to it. In the market, Elizabeth contributed to the noon and evening meals, amazed at the variety of tasty foods so lacking from the inland markets proximate to Lambton and Pemberley, with all its grandeur.

After noon meals, they read or caught up on news from Pemberley and Brighton. Charlotte related her growing fatigue and its toll on her writing. She was careful to describe her fatigue in terms of "again" in reference to when Joseph was born. Elizabeth seemed satisfied.

Mary shared her current writing, a presentation that she and Mr. Collins would give to the final abolitionists' convocation in Oxford in late summer. Their address was billed as "A Final Commentary from Joseph Weatherstone," and Mary expected a strong reaction to their address, even among the great author's most committed followers.

Elizabeth and Jenny remained for five days before departing, happily, for home. Three weeks later, Charlotte gave birth to Hannah Marie Collins. Her fine red hair sparkled in warm spring sunlight.

* * *

Sir Thomas Fowell Buxton took the podium in Oxford's auditorium. "My fellow freedom fighters, it is my great honor to yield the floor to our esteemed colleague, Miss Mary Bennet of Derbyshire, who with her friend, Mr. William Collins, has served these many years as conduit for our great mentor, Mr. Joseph Weatherstone. We are privileged to still enjoy his insight and guidance despite his age and infirmity."

Mary took the podium, William at her side. She spoke with a strong voice without any trace of nerves. "Ten years ago, a courageous and wise woman mused with me one evening as to the source of our noble fire, our drive to bring freedom to all our fellow souls on this Earth. She was not possessed of great education, nor steeped in disciplines of theology and philosophy. But she was endowed with innate wisdom and an unshakable fire for justice. Her question to me was simple — whence comes freedom? After a decade, I have come to recognize one ultimate source.

"While the powers of the world may seek to crush the human yearning, freedom comes from within. In the end, often against great odds and cruel oppression, it is upon the individual to seize freedom. Freedom is not handed to us, but is always present. Yet freedom is only real when we choose to make it so. Whether one lives in luxury or poverty, palace or prison, freedom comes to those who grasp it.

"We have — all of us here — chosen to grasp freedom and inspire in others recognition that God has endowed each and every person with the choice of freedom. All of us have been lifted by Joseph Weatherstone's writings. His clarity of vision and his gift of practical action have united our purposes. You have followed him — despite having never laid eyes on him or inclined your ears to his voice.

"Or so it seemed. This day of our final convocation is to be a day of revelation. I am honor bound to proclaim that *we* ..." She opened her hand to William. "... *are* Joseph Weatherstone."

A loud murmur raced among those assembled.

"Mr. William Collins has honed his God-given talents for scholarship to provide the spiritual and philosophical dimension of Joseph. God granted me a talent for clarity and brevity. Separately, neither of us could have been Joseph Weatherstone. Together, we created a person who has galvanized our kingdom. Plantation owners and traders fought Joseph Weatherstone, imagining an old and feeble man sequestered in an oceanside hideaway. As a flesh-and-blood person, he could surely be silenced, and many sought to do just that. But Joseph Weatherstone was, and is, an ideal, a bright spark of free thought that cannot be extinguished. He is in us — all of us here — and he cannot be removed.

"Whence comes freedom? It comes from within, first in the individual, then in the assembly, then in the nation, and then in the world. You have fought the good fight and you are prevailing. God grant lives of freedom to every soul on earth."

The murmur in the assembly had grown to a low roar. As Mary concluded, the entire assembly erupted in cheers. She and William stepped down...

Chapter 23 Ten Years On, Jamaica

Lady Bridget drifted toward Queenstown's newly extended pier as line handlers heaved their lines to waiting pier hands. Within minutes, *Lady Bridget* was secured to the dock.

On deck, Jane held nine-year-old Timothy's hand and he held Maggie's. Eight-month-old Gina slept in her sling. Margaret could be seen on the dock, waving and jumping up and down in excitement. Jane waved and then turned to her children. "Your Aunt Margaret seems most eager to meet us. And I see your cousins with her."

The children smiled in delight. Timothy waved both hands in wild greeting while Maggie hopped in joy.

Jane appreciated the changes she could already see from deck. The ceremonial stairway constructed for the wedding had been enlarged and painted. The sea-facing side sported "Welcome to Queenstown." Most striking were the new cargo handling cranes positioned along the pier. Margaret had written about their construction and their ability to move cargo with speeds unimaginable when last they visited.

After docking activities were concluded, Jane kissed Robert and descended the stairs with their children. At Margaret's urging, they both wore the flowing white dresses and hats that Geneviève had given them many years ago. Jane noted that the scar across Margaret's eye had healed to the point that only a light line against her tropical bronzed complexion remained. They hugged as the cousins exchanged plans for their visit.

"We shall host a grand island feast this evening to officially welcome you. If you approve, our governess can take the children now. We have a large fenced-in play yard with all manner of constructions for exercising their imaginations and bodies. In the mean time, these two gentlemen wished to greet you."

Jane turned and bowed. "Doctor."

Doctor Katanga laughed the same jolly laugh that Jane recalled from their first meeting a decade prior. He appeared unchanged save a few gray hairs. "It is so good to see you again. And your family continues to grow, I see. That is most wonderful."

The second gentleman presented himself.

"Sergeant Randolph?" Jane asked.

He laughed as well. "I have not heard that title in a very long time. It is still Harbormaster Randolph. Your sister's constant expansions have aged me perhaps."

"And your beard gives you a marvelous air of authority."

"That was my wife's idea. You shall meet her and our children at the feast this evening. But I wanted to say 'thank you' as early as possible for the chance you gave me that glorious morning in the jail house. That choice set my life aright."

Jane embraced him. "What we do with our choices can change the world. I am so happy for you, Harbormaster Randolph."

The two men took their leave and Margaret gave Jane an abbreviated tour. "As you see, we've added two more piers. At the peak of shipping time, they may all be filled, with ships anchored in the harbor awaiting a berth. Randolph has a staff of over twenty during that time of year, and we can double the town's population with visiting crews. Keeping order can some days be a challenge. I am increasingly convinced that *Lady Bridget*'s model of a family ship is the way of the future."

They arrived at the end of the pier, where Margaret swept her arms toward the gap to the next pier. "And this is my pride and joy. It took far longer than I expected and still isn't much to look at, but this is the only dry dock in the Caribbean, the crown jewel of Blackbelly Shipyards. It took five years of labor by hundreds of men, but it is a fully functional double-gated dry dock. I have been visiting Geneviève at least once a year and we have worked out an efficient, mutually beneficial arrangement. Her operations in Fort-de-France are the finest in the Caribbean for top work — masts and yardarms. We work with everything below decks and the hull.

"Unfortunately, it currently takes four days and twenty men to drain the dry dock and we must man the buckets around the clock for the inevitable seepage. That is the reason for an enormous machine that should be in *Lady Bridget*'s hold. It is a pump powered by a steam engine from Soho Foundry. With that contraption in place, we will be able to drain the dock in eight hours and require only a single watch to take care of seepage. At the moment, there are only three other dry docks in the Empire, and the closest is over four thousand miles away. With the extra business, we should pay for the pump in about three years."

Jane eyed Margaret. "You amaze me, sister. All has come together as you imagined it."

Margaret lowered her head as they turned and strolled toward town. She spoke softly. "As with my time as pirate captain, my life has been a series of choices. I still lack the proper fear to hold me back from these audacious endeavors. I am blessed with a wonderful husband who is willing to back my better-studied plans, and to talk reason about some of my less realistic ones. And we have maintained a powerfully ethical working community here on the island. Did you realize that half the line handlers who met *Lady Bridget* today were once pirates aboard *Jacqueline Fouck*?"

Jane presented Margaret with a package wrapped with bright paper and red ribbon. Margaret opened the gift to reveal a handsome shawl.

"It is fine lace," Jane said, "knit by Jenny, who married Timothy, our helmsman — the one you shot and almost killed. They are farmers in Cornwall, very happy with four children. Among their crops, they raise flax, which was harvested to make the linen for this gift. The lace is a tribute of love to you from Jenny."

"I am blessed beyond measure. I shall write them my gratitude. Oh, this is a wonderful development." Margaret draped the shawl around her shoulders and examined the exquisite handiwork.

They stopped by the play yard on the way to their inn. The children were re-enacting the Battle of Queenstown aboard the play yard's miniature wooden ships. Margaret's daughter Emma played the role of pirate captain, complete with an eye patch that Doctor Katanga had given her.

* * *

The feast was a leisurely affair with all the magnificent fragrances Jane remembered from Fort-de-France. Margaret introduced Jane to a number or citizens, many from the days of their first encounter with Queenstown.

An elegantly dressed man with confident smile beneath his broad hat approached.

"And, this gentleman," Margaret intoned, "is our village apothecary, a colleague of Doctor Katanga."

Jane glanced at Margaret's attempt to conceal a grin and responded, "It is an honor to meet you, sir."

"The honor is mine, Miss Jane," came the deep reply. His smile opened up to reveal less than the normal complement of teeth.

"Chitter!" she shouted, and flung her arms around him while he laughed. "I did not recognize you. Your transformation is complete!"

"We can thank my beloved Madeline for that," he said as Madeline approached. She and Jane hugged.

He continued. "You will have an opportunity to meet my children during the evening. The boys are off somewhere having an adventure with Captain Margaret's children. But here comes my pride and joy, my darling daughter."

A young girl in crisp white dress approached. She carried a pretty purse with her gloved hands and her bearing was nothing short of regal.

Jane knelt to greet her. "Hello."

The girl smiled sweetly. "Good evening."

"What is your name?"

The girl tilted her head upward with pride. "My name is Jane."

The elder Jane covered her mouth as tears streamed down. She opened her arms and the child embraced her.

"Papá, she is crying."

"It is because she is so happy."

Jane released her embrace and wiped away some tears. "You see, my name is Jane, also. I see that I have much to live up to since we share the same name."

The dinner bell called the crowd to table. The sun was setting on the western hills, at the spot where the old jailhouse stood. Orange beams of sunset reflected off the blossoms of oleander and frangipani beneath stately palms, reflected off the silver, the glasses, and the flagons of wine. The evening stillness hung delightful with fragrances of dozens of platters of succulent pork and chicken, mangos, peppers, and spices in profusion. The guests stood beside their chosen seats around the table, a rainbow of Caribbean races.

Margaret addressed her guests. "Many years ago, we met under very different circumstances. We were then most of us captives. But we did not accept our cruel situations. We united, and we overcame our captivity to great and noble ends. We chose freedom and justice, we fought for it, and here we are. Blessings be on all of you. *Bon appétit!*"

ABOUT THE AUTHOR

Baltimore author Clark Thomas Riley has written and published
non-fiction since the 1970s in support of careers at The University
of North Carolina, Chapel Hill, the United States Navy, Graduate
Studies at The University of Chicago, biomedical research, and
information technology. He began writing fiction in 1994 and has six
novels finished to the first draft level or beyond. *Mary and Margaret
— Whence comes Freedom* is his fourth novel after *What If They Lied
(just a little)?; Dots, Cancer Sleuthing on the 21st Century Frontier;* and
Patchwork, A Pioneer's Story. Following this work will be a spy novel,
the continuation of the *Patchwork, Tales from the Voyage* — and a
commentary on building the 21st-century hobby greenhouse.

Other interests include teaching Sunday School, growing and
speaking about orchids, publishing services, teaching, and social
activism. The author can be reached at ClarkTRiley@gmail.com.
You can join a moderated discussion of *What If They Lied (just a
little)?* at http://clarkriley.com/whatif, *Dots, Cancer Sleuthing on the 21st
Century Frontier* at http://clarkriley.com/dots, and *Patchwork* at http://
starshipcourageous.space.